EDUCATION
IN
MODERN INDIA

EDUCATION
IN
MODERN INDIA

Compiled & Edited
by
Dr. R.K. Pruthi

SONALI PUBLICATIONS
NEW DELHI-110002

Edition : 2026

ISBN 81-88836-66-4

Published by

SONALI PUBLICATIONS
4228/1, Ansari Road,
New Delhi-110 002 (India)
Phone: 23266109, 23279245 • Fax: 91-11-23253475

Printed by :
Navya Digital, Delhi-110092

Preface

Education is the most important single factor in achieving rapid progress, prosperity and happiness of the nation. It helps to create social order and values of freedom, equality and justice.

Aim of this book is to make available to our readers valuable material on the growth and development of modern education in India. Effort has been to trace its history, philosophy and principles, along with perspectives of educational planning and the future of education in India.

We gratefully acknowledge the authorities on the subject. We are deeply indebted to them all.

Librarians and staff members have rendered all possible help and assistance. We thank them.

My publisher and his staff members of various levels have worked hard. They deserve my readers love and patronage.

R.K. Pruthi

Contents

1

Education in India

Introduction

Though modern education in India has its origins in the establishment of three universities Calcutta, Bombay and Madras in 1857—Indian education has a hoary past. Ancient Indian education with the *Rig Veda* and the other three *Vedas* as the basic knowledge sources was conducted in the *Ashrams* (forest abodes) of eminent sages for their own sons as well as for disciples coming from different homes in society. That education, to start with, was mostly religious and ethical. Though other mundane subjects like Mathematics, Statecraft, Ayurveda, Astronomy etc., were added later, nothing like a big centre comparable in any way to the modern college or a university existed.

It was in Buddhist times that the old Brahmanical education system was modified and great centres of religious and secular education were established on a big scale. University-type centres like Nalanda and Taxila or Nagarjunakonda and Kanchipuram developed between 300 B.C. and 5th century A.D. It was said that nearly 10,000 students stayed at Nalanda studying different subjects under hundreds of eminent scholars. Nalanda attracted students from not only other parts of India but even from far off lands. But with the revival of Bahmanism by the 5th century A.D., Buddhist centres slowly decayed and great Buddhist scholars left India for other countries.

In about 1000 A.D. Muslims from the West invaded India and established their rule. They brought with them Islamic learning and other secular arts like music, painting, architecture etc. They established thousands of centres of learning called *madrasas* in places like Delhi, Agra, Lucknow and Lahore in the north. Muslim rulers in the South—the Bahamani Kings and Adilshah of Bijapur—established well-known *madrasas* in Bihar. Gulbarga, Bijapur and Honavar. The *madrasa* established by Muhammad Gawan in the Bahamani kingdom rose to great heights becoming what could be called a University of Islamic Learning.

The advent of British rule, especially in the first half of the 19th century, really marks the beginning of modern Indian education. In the stormy controversy between the Orientalists and the Anglicists about the nature and medium of education in India, the Anglicists won the battle after Lord William Bentinck accepted the now famous Macaulay's Minute on Education in 1835. Accordingly Western Education with English as the medium of instruction became the basis of future education in India.

With the acceptance and implementation of Sir Charles Wood's Despatch of 1854 which is called the Magna Carta of Indian education, the way to the establishment of the Calcutta, Bombay and Madras Universities in 1857 was cleared. Two more universities viz Lahore and Allahabad, were added in the 1880s. Later with the support and encouragement of Lord Curzon and the recommendations of the University Commission of 1902-04 a further impetus was given to the establishment of colleges in various parts of India. All the universities till then established in India were based on the model of London University in the United Kingdom which was an affiliating university. A new line was struck by Ashutosh Mukherjee, the Vice-Chancellor of Calcutta University, who introduced the concept of teaching at the post-graduate level in the university departments and introducing the mother tongue, Bengali, as an additional medium of education. Another deviation from the affiliating model was the starting of Benares Hindu University in 1916 as a unitary, residential type of university.

In Karnataka, the first University to come up was Mysore University which became possible on account of the efforts and reputation of Sir M. Visvesvaraya, then Dewan of Mysore. Though it was intended to be a unitary type like that of Benares, subsequent events in Karnataka resulted in the Mysore University becoming only an affiliating university with teaching and research added to it later.

On the model of Benares Hindu University also came up the Aligarh Muslim University in Aligarh which was also a unitary, teaching and residential university. A different type of innovation was introduced in the Princely State of Hyderabad where a University was established in 1918 with Urdu as medium of higher education including medical and engineering education. This was a revolutionary step and was made possible by translating a large number of books from English into Urdu for various courses. On the dawn of Independence of India in 1947, there were 19 universities in India.

Attempts at Indianisation

The Western education introduced and developed by the British in India was vehemently criticised as an education preparing only loyal servants for the British Government and an educated class of people who "were Indians by birth and blood but Western and Anglicised in tastes and behaviour" The idea of Indians becoming "hewers of wood and drawers of water" for the alien masters was insulting. Secondly, the system uprooted Indian culture and was in no way compatible with the aspirations of the Indians for National development. As a matter of fact, the National Schools had been started in 1920-21 itself. But many of them could not survive. In the face of extreme odds and difficulties, a few shining examples at Indianisation of education stand out. Swami Dayananda Saraswati revived ancient learning and synthesised it with useful elements of Western education. He started a number of schools and colleges which are now run under the name of D.A.V. educational institutions. Swami Vivekananda spiritualised the concept of education by defining education as manifestation of the perfection already in man." He inspired the followers of Ramakrishna Paramahamsa, as a result of which a number of Ramakrishna Mission educational and spiritual centres were established all over India. Following Vivekananda's footsteps is the radiant example of Annie Besant who founded a number of institutions under the Theosophical Society and started the Central Hindu College at Benares and initiated the movement together with Pandit Madan Mohan Malaviya, for the setting up of the Benares Hindu University.

Sri Aurobindo, Rabindranath Tagaore and Mahatma Gandhi developed their own individual Indianised models of education. Sri

Aurobindo enunciated the preliminary ideas for a national system of education in India which he called"integral education". It laid emphasis on the psychological, logical, practical and spiritual aspects of education. The experiment was conducted in the school at Pondichery and later the International University at Auroville. It is also practised in the Mother School, Delhi and a number of schools in Orissa.

Rabindranath Tagore worked hard throughout his life not only for the establishment and development of Santiniketan where he attempted to revive the ancient system of education in what became famous as Sriniketan. Tagore's experiment remained isolated in Santiniketan now known as the International University of Vishwabharathi. The same thing is true of the Auroville International University of Sri Aurobindo. Gandhiji's scheme of craft-centred basic education developed into a fullfledged system of higher education and is still vibrant in two centres viz. Gujarat Vidyapeeth and Gandhi Gram (Tamil Nadu).

The greatest tragedy of Indian education including higher education is that the same Congress leaders who had complained bitterly against the un-Indianness of Western education did not pay any attention to developing a really Indian model based on the three great experiments referred to above or a totally new variety suited to the aspirations of India for national development. On the contrary, our leaders stuck to the Western models slavishly to such an extent that all modifications and improvements suggested by various Commissions and Committees on education after Independence, have resulted in only peripheral and cosmetic changes. Not that attempts were not made. In the very year after Independence the Dr. Radhakrishnan Commission was appointed in 1948. That Commission's emphasis on ethical and moral values as well as restructuring of the framework and the curriculum remained by and large unimplemented. As it was found that real improvements in higher education would not be possible unless secondary education was improved, the Mudaliar Commission was constituted in 1953. Two of its recommendations have been implemented viz. (i) Restructuring of the education ladder as 10+2+3 and (ii) Emphasis on vocationalisation of education. It was, however, realised that all stages of education are so interlinked that unless the entire educational system was reviewed and reformed national development will not be possible. It is on the plea that the Education Commission headed by Dr. Kothari was constituted in 1964. This Commission which suggested sweeping changes at all levels of education and in all aspects has become the basic document for all future developments of education in India. The latest in the series of Commissions and Committees was the Commission for evolving the National Policy on Education (NPE) in 1986. This policy document has been the basis for the Programme of Action (POA) document finalised in 1992. This document contains a large number of recommendations for improvements at all levels of education including higher education.

The Legacy and the Challenge

Independent India inherited a system of education which was an integral part of the colonial set-up. The development up to 1947 was not only quantitatively small and microscopic. But was also qualitatively anaemic and dysfunctional" in relation to the task of building a self-reliant and growth-oriented economy as well as an integrated progressive nation. Independent India, therefore, faced the challenge of societal transformation through education as an instrument. The vision and dreams generated by Independence resulted in:

(i) a fast upsurge in demand for more schools and colleges;

(ii) developing manpower with appropriate technical skills for a fast changing science and technological revolution; and

(iii) education as a right for those who for various reasons had remained out of the portals of university education, but who dreamed of education as a passport to comfortable white collared jobs directed towards upward mobility in social status.

As an outcome of this blend of triple thrusts an expensive expansion took place in school education. Diversification started in curriculum. This was seen in a variety of new courses especially at the post-graduate level and the admission and recruitment of a large number of persons not suitable for excellence in higher education.

Quantitative expansion can be visualised from the fact that while in 1947 the number of universities was 19, it rose to 211 (including Deemed Universities) by 1992; in the same period the number of colleges rose from 491 to about 7500; and enrolment rose from 2,29,611 to 36,81,870. This means that the universities increased by 11 times, colleges by 15 times and students by more than 16 times. This has resulted in each university managing on an average 1½ times the number of colleges in 1992 as compared to 1947. There is a comment that the unplanned development of Education has resulted in slums of non-viable educational institutions all over India. This has also resulted in a number of colleges becoming either too small and non-viable or too large and unmanageable. The first category has resulted in wastage of expenditure and the second category in gross indiscipline and malpractices in examinations.

Three Other Types of Institutions

In addition to the affiliating, teaching and examining university types, other types of institutions relating to higher education and research have come up in post-Independent India. Under the University Grants Commission Act of 1956, the institutions fit to be described as "Deemed to be Universities" could be established and recognised as per procedure laid down in the Act. Under this category a number of institutions have been recognised as Deemed Universities like the Indian Agricultural Research Institute. New Delhi; Gujarat Vidyapeeth, Ahmedabad; Jamia-Millia Islamia, New Delhi; Birla Institute of Technology and Science, Pilani; Central Institute of English, Hyderabad; Tata Institute of Social Sciences, Bombay; Gurukul Kangri, Hardwar; Indian School of Mines, Dhanbad; Indian Institute of Science. Bangalore; Indian Institutes of Management, Bangalore, Ahmedabad and Calcutta; Central Food and Technological Research Institute, Mysore; and the National Law School University, Bangalore etc.

The second category is termed as "Institutions of national importance". Under this are included the five Indian Institutes of Technology (Kharagpur, Bombay, Madras, Kanpur and Delhi) which are established under a statutory provision. The All India Institute of Medical Sciences, New Delhi, the Post-graduate Institute of

Medicine and Research, Chandigarh and the Indian Statistical Institute, Calcutta are also included. These university-level institutions are empowered to grant degrees. Similarly the degrees awarded by the other national level institutions viz. Indian Institutes of Management (Ahmedabad, Calcutta, Bangalore and Lucknow) are treated on a par with university degrees.

The third category relates to high-level research institutes outside the university orbit. Under the category are included:

(i) Indian Institute of Public Administration, New Delhi;

(ii) Centre for Policy Research, New Delhi;

(iii) Indian Institute of Education, Pune and Several others. The Indian Council of Social Science Research supports about two dozens of such institutes with funds.

In addition more than 40 research laboratories were established under the auspices of the Council of Scientific and Industrial Research (CSIR). These institutes are not oriented towards granting degrees. But they relate to research in industrial and technological development. Some of them, however, have been recognised as Centres for Doctoral work and quite a few of the scientists working there are recognised as guides for Ph.D. students of universities.

In addition, high-level research laboratories are maintained by the Ministries of Agriculture, Health, Industries and others connected with development. The Atomic Energy Commission of India has a large network of establishments all over India. So has the Ministry of Electronics and the Ministry of Space. All these are geared to application of scientific knowledge rather than creation of new knowledge. The Tata Institute of Fundamental Research at Bombay is a different kind of institution. It does more fundamental research than applied. However, a large number of its professors are recognised as guides for Ph.D. students. Similarly there are other institutes of advanced study in a number of places. In the scientific sphere, though the universities are also doing significant work, funding for the same is not well matched. Hence the National Policy on Education 1986 has strongly reiterated the need to strengthen and diversify scientific research in the universities.

Co-ordinating Bodies

For the university sector, it was necessary to have a number of coordinating bodies at various levels. The latest of them is the Association of Indian Universities established in 1925. Almost all the universities and deemed Universities and Institutes of national importance have representation on the A.I.U. The A.I.U. functions through a secretariat located at AIU House, 16 Kotla Marg, New Delhi-110002. On the recommendation of the AIU two important Co-ordianting Bodies in the university sector were established.

(i) The Indian Medical Council was created in 1934 with statutory bodies to regulate admissions, courses of study, examinations and all matters having bearing on medical education in the country.

(ii) The University Grants Commission was established in 1956 with statutory powers to determine and co-ordinate standards in higher and professional education. The University Grants Commission is required to regulate academic standards for which the Central Government provides grants to be routed through the University Grants Commission.

Like the Indian Medical Council, there are other co-ordinating bodies—All India Council of Technical Education (AICTE). Bar Council of India, the Dental Council of India, the Pharmacy Council of India, the Nursing Council of India and the National Council of Teacher Education which was created under a recent Act.—which are statutory bodies to regulate academic standards in their respective fields.

At the apex policy-making level, the Central Advisory Board of Education has been in existence for almost half a century. Ministers of Education of all the States and the Union Territories are all members of this Board (CABE). Its meetings are presided over by the Union Minister for Human Resource Development. The CABE meets once in two or three years. But after the NPE (1986), it has been meeting more frequently.

Types of Universities

The largest number belongs to the Affiliating and Teaching type. Each of them has a number of Departments dealing with post-graduate education and research. But one of its main tasks is to deal with affiliation of a large number of undergraduate colleges of which a small number may be conducting post-graduate classes also.

The second is the unitary type like Benares. Aligarh, Allahabad, Annamalai, Baroda, Patna, Lucknow etc. No colleges are affiliated to them. All teaching and research are done in the university itself. They hold their own examinations and award degrees.

The third is the Agricultural University. The first one to be established in this category was the G.B. Pant Agricultural University (1960). There are now 26 such universities of which two are in Karnataka (Bangalore and Dharwad). The Agricultural Universities have played a significant role in bringing about the Green Revolution in India in respect of self-sufficiency of food.

The fourth category is the Technical University. The oldest of this type is Roorkee. The Thompson Engineering College established in 1847 was raised to the status of a Technical University in 1949. Jawaharlal Technical University, Hyderabad and Anna University in Madras come under this category. Karnataka has no Technical University. With the largest network of Engineering Colleges, Polytechnics and ITIs, and Technical establishments, Karnataka richly deserves to have a Technical University.

The fifth type is a Medical University. Now there is only one i.e. the Andhra Pradesh University of Health Sciences. Karnataka with a large number of Medical Colleges of all types as well as colleges of Pharmacy needs to have one to regulate standards in Medical education. Recently Tamil Nadu has set up one (The M.G.R. Medical University, Madras).

There is also a category of universities known as Central University. Its management is controlled by the Union Government and funded by it. There are 12 Central Universities in India now.

Internal Management

The internal management of the university follows the old British pattern usually. The Governor is the Chancellor who on the recommendations of a Committee or Government appoints a Vice Chancellor who is the Executive Head of the University dealing with both academic and administrative matters. He functions through the Syndicate which is an Executive Council. The Senate which is a large body of 100 to 200 members is like Parliament to approve all actions. All academic proposals come up to it from the Boards of Studies through the respective Faculties and then the Academic Council. There are a few non-academic elected members on the Academic Council and the Syndicate. Deans of Faculties have an important role to play. The whole set-up has become outmoded and needs a change.

Governmental Control

Since more than 90 per cent of funding comes from the Government (States and Centre), control lies in their hands. This has led to a number of problems due to delay in the release of funds and also due to inadequate finances for improvements and research. The problem is more acutely felt in the case of affiliating universities in which State Government interference is experienced in affiliation and other aspects. Due to vast increase in the number of universities (now it is 211), the University Grants Commission is finding it difficult to manage. Decentralisation is a necessity. There are proposals to create State Councils of Higher Education. Andhra Pradesh has already one such body.

Management of Colleges

Colleges broadly fall under two categories (1) Government and (2) Private. Each of them comprises (A) Colleges of General Education (Arts. Science, Commerce), and (B) Professional Colleges (Engineering, Medical, Law, Education).

Before 1947, Government colleges, especially in Princely States, were predominant in number. It was difficult to establish and run a private college because financial assistance or grant from the Government was not adequate. After Independence, the situation changed vastly, Demand for higher education increased rapidly even in rural areas because of the link between education and the glamour of Government jobs. Secondly, for political and social leaders, it became a matter of local prestige to have a college in their own constituency. A fillip to their aspiration came when Government grants increased to more than 80 per cent of expenditure. This was further boosted in States like Karnataka and Maharashtra where the scheme of 100 per cent salary grants (equal to salaries of staff in Government colleges) was introduced in about 1970. As a result of this, power of making appointments of staff and admission of students passed into the hands of local leaders who were Presidents or Secretaries of Managements of Private Colleges. Proliferation of private colleges started. While private colleges prospered. Government colleges, which were filled with mostly poor students and first generation learners, were plagued by transfers and non-filling of posts of staff as well as the financial crunch for infrastructure. Due to vast number of colleges to be controlled and supervised, the State Directorates of Collegiate Education who have the overall administrative control over both Government and Private Colleges have not been able to see that standards are maintained. Nor have the universities which deal with courses and examinations been able to control and guide teaching standards. This dual control has led to deterioration in standards.

2

English Education in India

In the sixteenth and the seventeenth century four European nations Portuguese, French, Dutch and the English entered India for the sake of trade. In the course of time propagation of Christianity also became their aim. Their companies in their mother countries used to send chaplains in their factories in India. The function of these chaplains was to look after the morals and religious education of the people serving in the factories. Since many Indians were employed in the factories, they were brought under the influence of Christianity and many of them embraced this religion.

The Portuguese were the first to open schools in their places of settlement like Goa, Diu, Daman, Cochin, Hooghly. Not only were 3 R's taught in these schools but also the principles of Catholic religion. In such schools children were drawn from the neighbouring villages. Poor Children were supplied with books, food and clothes as well besides free education which was given to all who attended such schools. Such children were provided with some industrial and agricultural work along with formal education. Besides these elementary schools, there were Jesuit colleges for higher education and seminaries for priesthood training. One such college was built at Bandra near Bombay as early as 1575. Another was started at Chaul in Goa five years later. The former college, however, was closed in 1739.

Like the Portuguese, the French opened schools in their possessions such as Pondicherry, Mahe, Chander Nagar and Yaman. In these, Indian teachers taught through the medium of Indian languages. French was taught in the secondary school at Pondicherry, where the children of French settlers and soldiers along with the children of advanced Indians in the company's service were taught. Principles of Christiany formed an item of the curriculum. The poor and needy were supplied the material needs. With the decline, however, of the power of Portuguese Dutch and French, their educational systems vanished and only the English schools have survived till today.

Elizabeth I of England granted a character to the East India Company in 1600 and the English traders established their first factory in Surat in 1613 and the second factory in 1633 in Masaulipatnam. Like their contemporary nations in India the English company also received Protestant chaplains and in 1614 they began to recruit Indians to preach Protestant Christianity (as against Catholic Christianity of the Portuguese and the French) among the natives. In 1638, the Oxford University established professorship of Arabic in order to train future missionaries for India and in 1659 the Court of Directors of the East India Company sent missionaries to India to propagate the Gospel. These missionaries found that the best means to propagate the Gospel was to open schools where Christian religion should be taught. This was the beginning of the educational activities of the English. These activities began in the towns of their settlements and went in extending as more and more territories came under the possession of the company.

Educational Activities in the Province of Madras in the Seventeenth and the Eighteenth Centuries

Madras was founded in 1640 but in 1673 a person was appointed to teach the children of the English and the Portuguese and of Eurasian descent and a few selected Indian subordinates of the company through the medium of Portuguese. In 1687 the Court of Directors asked the Governor of Madras to form a Municipality for the town of Madras. It was suggested that the Municipality should levy a rate for opening schools for Indian children. The Municipality was formed and the rate was levied but no schools were started.

When the East India Company's charter was renewed in 1698 a very important clause was added to it. The company was asked to maintain a minister in every garrison and superior factory. This minister was enjoined to learn the native language of the region of his residence and instruct the servants and the agents of the company in Protestant religion. It was further asked that school masters should be appointed where necessary in the garrison and the factory. The objective was to make the education of the people as one of the duties of the company's chaplains. As a result of this St. Mary's charity school was founded in Madras in 1715 to provide instruction to children of English soldiers. This school was semi-official, as the company showed direct interest in it though the expenses were met partly by the company and jointly by raising subscriptions. Besides this official effort, there were certain officials of the Company who took interest in Indian education in their private capacity. Two orphan asylums—one for males and the other for females—were opened in Madras in 1787 with the financial aid from the Company and subscriptions from the military officers. These asylums were attended by the children of European and Eurasian soldiers.

In these educational efforts of the eighteenth century the Company was also helped by the Danish missions. Two Danish missionaries arrived in 1706 in Tanquebar—a Danish station in the South. They opened a teachers' training institution there. In 1717 the Danish missions established two charity schools in Madras. One of these was meant for Portuguese children and the other for Tamil children. English and principles of Christians were taught in both of them. Similarly schools were opened in Calcutta, Trichinapally and Tanjore. John Sulivan, the representative of Madras Government at Tanjore persuaded the Rajas Shiv Ganga and Ram Nath to open English Schools in these towns. Financial help to these three was given by the Company and help was promised for starting any other English school. Very soon the number of schools run by missionaries and aided by the Company rose to 17. But it so happened that the missionaries failed to teach as much about Christianity as they wanted and consequently interest in them gradually diminished.

Educational Activities in Bombay in the Eighteenth Century

Bombay was acquired by the English in 1688. When a Charity school was founded in Madras in 1715, Bombay followed suit in 1718. Through the efforts of a missionary another school was established here in 1719 to teach poor European children. Until 1807 it was run by raising subscriptions but in that year the Company took it under its own control and eight years later this school was handed over to the Bombay Educational Society. The only other school started in Bombay in the eighteenth century was the Portuguese.

Educational Activities in Bengal

In 1731 the society for promoting Christian Knowledge opened a school in Calcutta. With the efforts of Lord Clive another school was started there in 1758. To educate the Muslims through the medium of Arabic, Lord Warren Hasting started the Calcutta Madrasah in 1781. The subjects of instruction that institution were Koranic theology, law, geometry, arithmetic logic, grammar and natural philosophy. For the first two years Warren Hastings bore the expenses out of his own pocket. In 1783 the Company took it over and bore all the expenses. The course study extended over seven years. Very few boys were attracted to it and those who came, were drawn with the bait of stipends. Another step for the encouragement of Indian language, literature and arts was the foundation of the Royal Asiatic Society of Bengal in the eighteenth century. Its object was to enquire, "into the history, the antiquities, arts, sciences and literature of Asia".

To cater to the needs of Hindus, Lord Cornwalis opened a Sanskrit College at Benares in 1791. In this the study Hindu law was given prominence, although theology, medicine, basic grammar, philosophy, ethics and poetry were also taught. The college received Rs. 20,000/- per annum as grant from the Company.

Besides these two major ventures, there sprang up a number of schools in Calcutta and its suburbs by the efforts of Free School Society in Bengal or officials of the Company in their private capacity or by the retired and disabled soldiers who earned a living by teaching boys and girls. These schools besides teaching 3 R's did teach some crafts like needlework and lace making.

Educational Policy of the British from 1783-1813

Like Madras and Bombay, missionary activity would have achieved much more in the field of education in Bengal, but in 1783 British Parliament declared its policy of neutrality in the matter of religion and education. Entry into India without licence was prohibited. It was suspected that private persons, by preaching Christianity, wounded the religious susceptibilities of the Hindus and the Muslims. By that time the British suzerainty had come to stay. The Company's territorial limits began to increase. It was realised that consolidation of their possessions was possible only if they maintained cordial relations with the Hindus and the Muslims. The English, therefore, followed a policy of appeasement and sympathy with the existing social, religious and educational institutions. Impelled by such motives the Company had begun to support the Calcutta Madrasah and the Benares Sanskrit College.

While the British Parliament followed the policy of appeasement, the missionaries and their supporters started an agitation in England that the Company should encourage the propagation of Christian religion in India. The chief leader of the agitation was Mr. Charles Grant, whose "*Observations on the State of Society among the Asiatic subjects of Great Britain, particularly with respect to morals and the means of improving it*", aroused great interest. He proposed that the only remedy to raise the Indians from social and moral degradation was to introduce Protestant Christianity and to teach them arts and sciences of Europe. He suggested that the medium of teaching these subjects should be English. In Grant's words "By planning our (English) language, our knowledge our opinions and our religion in our Asiatic territories, we shall put a great work beyond the reach of contingencies. We shall probably have wedded the inhabitants of these territories to this country (England); .... at any rate we shall have done an act of strict duty to them and a lasting service to mankind."

This was the time when the Company's Charter was being renewed in 1793. It was, therefore, insisted that a clause should be added to the Charter for encouraging educational and missionary work in India. To this effect a resolution was introduced in Parliament by Wilberforce. It enjoined upon "the British Parliament to promote by all just and prudent means, the interest and happiness of the British dominions in India; and that for these ends such measures ought to be adopted as may gradually tend to their advancement in useful knowledge and to their religious and moral improvement". The resolution was rejected as the Board of Directors remained adamant and did not wish to take any definite policy of systematic programme for the education of Indians. They were of the opinion "that the Hindus had as good a system of faith and of morals as most other people and that it would be madness to attempt their conversion or give them any more leaving or any other description of learning than what "they already possessed". The British Parliament was warned that "America was lost by imparting our (English) education there, we (Britishers) need not do so in India too". It is interesting, however, to note that forty years later the Government accepted Charles Grant thesis minus his advocacy for the introduction of Protestant Christianity. If the Government had accepted his suggestions regarding education in the last decade of the eighteenth century, India would have gained fifty years in education. By accepting teaching to European arts and sciences through the medium of English in 1833. Indians lost fifty years in education.

Since the British Parliament had rejected the resolution, the missionaries, instead of working in the East India Company territories, carried on their activities at places occupied by other nations. Several of them started their work in the Danish colour of Serampore and the Dutch colony of Chinsura, both of them being near Calcutta. Marquis of Wellesley (1798-1805) however allowed them to carry on their work in the British territory. So their educational activities were seen in several towns of India. Taking unfair advantage of Lord Wellesely's broad-mindedness some missionaries, carried by the enthusiasm of propagating Christianity, issued a pamphlet in 1807, wherein they denounced the Hindu and Muslim religions. On this the Court of Directors issued a Despatch in 1808, reiterating their policy of religious naturality and non-association with the propagation of Christianity.

In 1811 Lord Minto, the then Governor-General of India lamented the progressive decay of science and literature among the Indians, in a Minute. In this he said, "the number of the learned is not only diminished, but the circle of the learned...appears to be considerably contracted...the immediate consequence of this state of things is the disuse and even actual loss of many valuable books.... Unless Government interfere with a fostering hand, the revival of letters may shortly become hopeless from want of books, or of persons capable of explaining them." They decay, according to him, was due to' "want of that encouragement which was formerly afforded to it (literature) by princes, chieftains and opulent individuals under the native Governments." He strongly advocated that fostering care should be extended to Indian literature and proposed that the existing two colleges—Calcutta Madrasah and Banares Sanskrit College—should be improved and two more sanskrit colleges and some Madrasahs should be established to preserve the Hindu and the Muslim culture.

Acceptance of Educational Responsibility by the Company in 1813

What the missionaries failed to achieve in 1793, they succeeded partially in 1813. All these years Wilberforce continued to remain vocal in the House of Commons, "on measures for the moral and religious instruction of the Indians". In the first decade of the nineteenth century there began a movement in England that the State should make some efforts for the education of the poor people in thai country. At that time the position of the Company in India had been stabilised. It had emerged as a ruler and sole heir of the decadent Mughal empire. Charles Grant, who had advocated the moral uplift of India, was a member of Parliament. He intensified his campaign of impressing upon Parliament to force the Company to undertake educational and moral uplift of the Indians. The fillip to this movement was also given by Lord Minto's Minute referred above.

At the time of the renewal of Charter in 1813, therefore, the question of education was strongly pressed. Two things were demanded—(1) freedom of missions in India, (2) defining the nature and scope of Company's educational responsibility. According to Kichter, no less than 850 petitions, advocating the freedom of missions in India, were submitted to the House of Commons. In spite of vehement opposition the missionaries carried the day. A resolution was adopted enjoining England, "to promote the interests and happiness of the native inhabitants of the British dominions in India and that measures ought to be adopted as may tend to the introduction among them of useful knowledge and moral improvement". The resolution also suggested that facilities should be afforded to the persons who wanted to go to India to further these objectives there. This was a triumph for the missionaries who got freedom to go and preach as they wished.

In order to counteract the missionary tendency, their opponents compelled the Company to accept some responsibility for the education of the Indians. And, in spite of the vigorous opposition of the Board of Directors, a clause was inserted in the Charter Act of 1813 enjoining the Company to spend "a sum of not less than one lakh of rupees each year" for "the revival and improvement of literature and encouragement of the learned natives and for the introduction and promotion of a knowledge of the sciences among the inhabitants of the British territories in India". This one lakh of rupees was subject to one proviso. It could be spent only after defraying all civil and military expenses. The objectives on which this sum could be spent were also mentioned. The Company was asked to open colleges, arrange public lectures and establish other institutions at places within the British territories.

This insertion of an educational clause in the Charter Act of 1813 has a historical and an academic interest. It is an important land-mark in the History of Indian Education. The Company accepted the responsibility of educating the people of India twenty years earlier than their Home Government did the same in England. But while the responsibility was accepted two decades earlier, the pace at which Indian education proceeded was ridiculously slow as compared with the pace of educational progress in England. A glance at the educational system of England today will show how much perfected and well organised their system is. Their education is being given according to age, ability and aptitude. Compared with them we are still at a formative stage and it will take a long time to put our plans and policies into action.

Since the education clause in the Charter Act of 1813 was inserted in spite of the apathy of the Board of Directors, their reactions for its implementation were not wholesome. In their Despatch of 1814 the Directors opposed the openings of colleges on the European models, arguing that "the natives of caste and of reputation will not submit to the subordination and discipline of a college". Instead, they suggested that "instruction at their own houses" and "cultivation of their talents" in their own way should be encouraged by conferring on them honorary marks of distinction or by pecuniary grants. The Directors, however, wanted to develop

Benares as an educational centre. Although not specifically mentioned it was implied in their Despatch that some of the tacts and treatises on useful knowledge should be reprinted in Sanskrit to stimulate Indians to learn their forgotten lore. Likewise, the Company's servants, whosoever desired, were also to be encouraged to learn Sanskrit. It was their declared policy that the allotment should be spent to improve the "intercourse of Europeans with the natives" and to "produce those reciprocal feelings of regard and respect which are essential to the permanent interest of the British Empire in India".

All this clearly shows that the Company was not anxious to do anything substantial in the matter of education. For one full of decade even the nominal sum of rupees one lakh was not wholly spent. Some portion of it, however, was spent on publishing some oriental classics—and giving some financial help to some educational institutions run by missionaries, natives and individuals.

Although the Board of Directors followed a passive policy of education, the officials of the Company urged a vigorous educational programme. Lord Hastings, the then Governor General of India suggested in 1815 that the assignment of one lakh rupees should be spent not only in improving the existing schools but also in opening new schools where none existed. He wanted the British Empire to be "the source of blessings to the immense population of India". He found "intellect neglected and sterile" and thus felt obliged "to cultivate it". He said, "the field is noble; may we till it worthily." Similar noble sentiments were expressed by Sir Charles Metcalfe, who believed that by conferring on Indians "the blessing of independence and education" was promoting their happiness. But these things did not have any effect for a decade and the years from 1813 to 1823 may be called the years of 'masterly inactivity'.

While the Government showed the spirit of inertia, missionary enterprise, however, continued to promote the educational betterment of Indians. By 1817, they were running 115 schools and according to W.H. Carey 10,000 scholars attended these institutions. Missionary activity produced a very significant result. Some of the notable Indians like Raja Ram Mohan Roy and Radha Kant Dev were convinced that Indians should have English education. This would improve the social, economic and political (though the stress then on the political aspect was not as much as in later times) conditions of people of India. Raja Ram Mohan Roy denounced the Company's policy of encouraging oriental literature. These two gentlemen—Raja Ram Mohan Roy and Radha Kant Dev—in co-operation with David Hare founded a Hindu College in 1917. In this institution Indian students were taught European sciences and English literature. In the following year the missionaries founded the Serampur College and two years later a Bishop College was founded.

In popularising the English education, the pioneers got full support from the so-called "Babu Class of India". These Babus had seen that a little knowledge of English could bring them white collared jobs in English firms and business houses, whose number was multiplying with the expansion of the British empire of India. There was a craving for having even a smattering of English. This brought into being many venture schools where students were taught to cram English vocabulary. But at the same time there came into existence better schools, where besides English other subjects were also taught through the medium of English. Calcutta School Book Society; established in 1817, provided good printed text books. A year latter Calcutta School Society was founded. In 1822 Bombay also had Bombay Native School Society. The objective of these two Societies was to open schools of the new type.

The Decade of Activity 1823-1833

In the decade from 1823 to 1833 the Company was prompted into action, partly on account of the educational efforts of the missionaries and Indians like Ram Mohan Roy and partly influenced by the spirit of reform and liberalism that was found in English due to the modification of criminal laws and removal of the disabilities of the Catholics, abolition of slavery and the passing of the first Parliamentary Reforms Act. All these factors moved the Board of Directors to write to the Governor General of India in 1924 "We wish you to be fully apprised of our zeal for the progress and improvement of education among the natives of India". With this directive or encouragement by the Board of Directors, the organisation by the local Governments of Bengal, Bombay and Madras commenced simultaneously in all these three Presidencies.

Education in Bengal 1823-1833

A General Committee of Public Instruction was set up in 1832 for Bengal. This Committee consisted of ten members. They were asked to formulate the educational policy of the Government. It so happened that the Committee contained members, majority of whom were admirers of eastern classical languages and literature. The Secretary of the Committee, Mr. H.H. Wilson was a great oriental scholar. They, therefore, formulated three principles of educational policy viz. (1) to win the confidence of educated and influential natives by encouraging their learning and literature, (2) to avoid all attempts at proselytism, (3) to utilise the available funds for the higher education of the upper classes rather than for elementary education of the masse. Consequently the Government of Bengal, advised by the Committee, began to set up institutions for the teaching of Sanskrit, Persian and Arabic at important places. Calcutta Madrasah and Benares College were improved. Oriental colleges were established at Agra and Delhi. Sanskrit and Arabic books were printed and published on a large scale. Oriental scholars were employed to translate English books of useful knowledge into the oriental languages.

When a Sanskrit College was proposed to be opened at Calcutta, there arose opposition and that also from the Hindus, led by Raja Ram Mohan Roy. He wrote a letter to the then Governor-General, urging the Government that instead of Sanskrit College. They should "promote a more liberal and enlightened system of instruction; embracing mathematics, natural philosophy, chemistry, and anatomy". A Despatch of 1824 from the Court of Directors supported the view of Raja Ram Mohan Roy. They said, "the great end should not have been to teach Hindu learning, but useful training". But the General Committee of Public Instruction satisfied the Directors with the arguments that Hindus and Mohammedans had prejudices against European learning, that oriental learning was useful for Indians, that classical language was the only medium and that there was paucity of books and teachers to impart instruction through such a medium. They, however, assured the Directors that as soon as books and teachers were available Indians would be taught European sciences. The Directors accepted the plea and the Committee continued their work of encouraging classical education. In the words of H.P. Howell, "it is one of the most unintelligible facts in the history of English education in India that at the very time when the natives themselves were crying out for instruction of European literature and science and were protesting against the continuance of the prevailing orientalism, a body of English gentlemen (General Committee of Public Instruction) appointed to initiate a system of education for the country, was found to insist upon the retention of oriental learning to the practical exclusion of European learning."

In the process of time, however, public opinion grew rapidly in favour of English education. English being the language of the rulers, it ensured better jobs. The General Committee of Public Instruction was compelled to attach English classes to the Agra College and Calcutta Madrasah by 1833. Some district English schools were also established at Delhi and Agra. In 1827 the Court of Directors advised the local Governments of all the three Presidencies that they should "keep utility in view, but not to introduce alteration more rapidly than a regard to the feelings of the natives will prescribe". They declared, "that the first objects of the improved education should be to prepare a body of individuals for discharging public duties". They expected "that the Intended course of education will not only produce a higher degree of intellectual fitness but that it will contribute to raise the moral character of those who partake of its advantages". This, in their opinion, would, "supply civil servants to whose probity", the Company could, "with increased confidence, commit offices of trust". Two years later they declared that it was "the wish and admitted policy of the British Government to render its own language (English) gradually and eventually the language of public business throughout the country." They urged upon the local Governments that every opportunity and encouragement should be given to achieve this end. They categorically wanted the Indians to be familiar, "with European literature and science" and wanted them to be "imbued with the ideas and feelings of the civilized Europe, on the general cultivation of their understanding, and specifically on their instruction in the principles of morals and general jurisprudence". As a result of this new policy, there was a split in the Committee and thus ensued a controversy—historically known as Anglicist-Classicist controversy, to which a reference will be made at the appropriate place.

Education in Bombay 1823-1833

Vigorous educational activity in the Presidency of Bombay commenced in 1818. To encourage oriental learning, a Sanskrit College was established in Poona in 1821. The Bombay Native Education Society was established in 1823 through the efforts of Mountstuart Elphinston, Governor of the presidency. In the same year Elphinston wrote his famous Minute in which he advocated, "(I) to improve the mode of teaching at the native schools and to increase the number of schools; (2) to supply them with school books; (3) to hold out some encouragement to the lower orders of the natives to avail themselves of the means of instruction thus afforded them; (4) to establish schools for teaching the European sciences and improvements in the higher branches of education; (5) to provide for the preparation and publication of books of moral and physical science in native language; (6) to establish schools for the purpose of teaching English to those disposed to pursue it as a classical language, and as a means of acquiring a knowledge of the European discoveries, (7) to hold forth encouragement to the natives in the pursuit of those higher branches of knowledge".

Some of these proposals were accepted. The Native School Book Society was given a grant of Rs. 600/- per mensem. The Government also undertook to bear the cost of compiling and printing the society's school books. An English school was opened in Bombay in 1824. The Bombay Native Education Society received financial aid from the Company. By 1840 the Society was running 140 Vernacular Secondary Schools, where western science and knowledge was taught through the mother tongue. The Society also opened the Engineering Class and the Medical Class. Instruction in both these classes was given through the medium of Indian language.

Education in Madras 1823-1833

In 1822, Sir Thomus Munro, the then Governor of Madras conducted an enquiry into the state of education in the Presidency. His intention was to help the existing institutions with funds needed. The enquiry, completed in 1826, showed that there were 12498 schools; having 188,650 students in a population of 12,8150,941. This low state of education was attributed to the poverty of people. There was, therefore, a necessity that the schools should be endowed by Government. He wanted better teachers superior in knowledge and diligence". His first proposal, therefore, was to support the Teachers Training School, which was being proposed by the Madras School Book Society. His next proposal was that the Government should establish in each Collectorate, two principal schools, one for Hindus and the other for Mohammedans and he also wanted one school for each Tehsil. For the control of these schools he suggested the establishment of a Committee of Public Instruction, which was appointed in 1826. In a couple of years about 70 schools were established in the tehsils. But in 1830 the Directors instructed the Government of Madras to concentrate on the spread of English education—rather than on mass education. Mass education in that province thus got a set-back for a considerable period of time.

Missionary Activity 1823-33

Side by side with the educational efforts of the Government, Missionary activity was going on extensively in all the three Presidencies although no statistics of their educational activities are available. The Church Missionary Society, which had three chief centres—Calcutta, Bombay and Madras—was running 107 schools by 1835 in the province of Madras alone. Two major contributions of the Missionaries cannot be overlooked. One was the development of Indian languages and the other was the pioneering work in the matter of education of women. In the domain of education of women they opened girls schools, established orphan homes and even undertook domestic instruction among the families of middle and higher classes, whose females observed Purdah and did not like to attend public schools.

❋

3

The Necessity of English Education

(Macaulay (1800-59) became President of the Committee of Public Instruction in 1834. His Minute on English education for India swung the authorities in favour of the decision to educate their conquered peoples in the English tongue. The decision was taken on March 7, 1835 by the Governor-General of India, Lord Bentinck, and was a turning-point in Indian history.)

A sum is set apart "for the revival and promotion of literature and the encouragement of the learned natives of India, and for the introduction and promotion of a knowledge of the sciences among the inhabitants of the British territories." It is argued, or rather taken for granted, that by literature the Parliament can have meant only Arabic and Sanskrit literature . . . .

I hold this lakh of rupees to be quite at the disposal of the Governor-General in Council, for the purpose of promoting learning in India, in any way which may be thought most advisable. I hold his Lordship to be quite as free to direct that it shall no longer be employed in encouraging Arabic and Sanskrit, as he is to direct that the reward for killing tigers in Mysore shall be diminished, or that no more public money shall be expended on the chanting at the cathedral. We now come to the gist of the matter. We have a fund to be employed as Government shall direct for the intellectual improvement of the people of this country. The simple question is, what is the most useful way of employing it? All parties seem to be agreed on one point, that the dialects commonly spoken among the natives of this part of India contain neither literary or scientific information, and are, moreover, so poor and rude that, until they are enriched from some other quarter, it will not be easy to translate any valuable work into them. It seems to be admitted on all sides, that the intellectual improvement of those classes of the people who have the means of pursuing higher studies can at present be effected only by means of some language not vernacular amongst them.

What, then, shall that language be? One-half of the Committee maintain that it should be the English. The other half strongly recommend the Arabic and Sanskrit. The whole question seems to me to be, which language is the best worth knowing? I have no knowledge of either Sanskrit or Arabic. But I have done what I could to form a correct estimate of their value. I have read translations of the most celebrated Arabic and Sanskrit works. I have conversed both here and at home with men distinguished by their proficiency in the Eastern tongues, I am quite ready to take the Oriental learning at the value of the Orientalists themselves. I have never found one among them who could deny that a single shelf of a good European library was worth the whole native literature of India and Arabia. The intrinsic superiority of the Western literature is, indeed, fully admitted by those members of the Committee who support the Oriental plan of education....

How, then, stands the case? We have to educate a people who cannot at present be educated by means of their mother tongue. We must teach them some foreign language. The claims of our own language it is hardly necessary to recapitulate. It stands pre-eminent even among the languages of the West. It abounds with works of imagination not inferior to the noblest which Greece has bequeathed to us; with models of every species of eloquence; with historical compositions, which, considered merely as narratives, have seldom been surpassed, and which, considered as vehicles of ethical and political instruction, have never been equalled; with just and livery representations of human life and human nature, morals, government jurisprudence and trade; with full and correct information respecting every experimental science which tends to preserve the health, to increase the comfort, or to expand the intellect of man. Whoever knows that language has ready access to all the vast intellectual wealth which all the wisest nations of the earth have created and hoarded in the course of ninety generations. It may safely be said that the literature now extant in that language is of far greater value than all the literature which, three hundred years ago, was extant in all the languages of the world together. Nor is this all. In India English is the language spoken by the ruling class. It is spoken by the higher class of natives at the seats of Government. It is likely to become the language of commerce throughout the seas of the East. It is the language of two great European communities which are rising, the one in the south of Africa, the other in Australasia; communities which are every year becoming more important, and more closely connected with our Indian Empire. Whether we look at the intrinsic value of our literature, or at the particular situation of this country, we shall see the strongest reason to think that, of all foreign tongues the English tongue is that which would be the most useful to our native subjects. The question now before us is simply whether, when it is in our power to teach this language, we shall teach languages in which, by universal confession, there are no books on any subject which deserve to be compared to our own; whether, when we can teach European science, we shall teach systems which by universal confession, whenever they differ from those of Europe, differ for the worse, and whether, when we can patronize sound Philosophy and true History we shall countenance, at public expense, medical doctrines, which would disgrace an English farrier; Astronomy, which would move laughter in girls at an English boarding school; History, abounding with Kings thirty feet high, and reigns thirty thousand years long; and Geography, made up of seas of treacle and seas of butter....

To sum up what I have said, I think it clear that we are not fettered by the Act of Parliament of 1813; that we are not fettered by any pledge, expressed or implied; that we are free to employ our funds as we choose, that we ought to employ them in teaching what is best worth knowing, that English is better worth knowing than Sanskrit or Arabic; that the natives are desirous to be taught English, and are not desirous to be taught Sanskrit or Arabic; that neither as the languages of law, nor as the languages of religion, have Sanskrit and Arabic any peculiar claim to our engagement; that it is possible to make the natives of this country thoroughly good English scholars, and that to this end our efforts ought to be directed.

In one point I fully agree with the gentlemen to whose general views I am opposed. I feel with them, that it is impossible for us, with our limited means, to attempt to educate the body of the people. We must at present do our best to form a class who may be interpreters between us and the millions whom we govern—a class of persons, Indian in blood and colour, but English in taste, in opinions, in morals and in intellect.

The Government of India Act, 1858[1]

This Act was an outcome of the Indian Mutiny of 1857. After the Mutiny the Government of India was taken out of the hands of the East India Company and placed directly in the hands of the Crown. This led to the creation of a Secretary of State for India, responsible to Parliament, and a Council of India to act as a check.

Government of India Act, 1858 (21 and 22 Vict, c. 106)

I. The Government of the territories now in the possession or under the Government of the East India Company, and all powers in relation to Government vested in or exercised by the said Company in trust for Her Majesty, shall cease to be vested in and exercised by the said Company; and all territories in the possession or under the government of the said Company, and all rights vested in or which if this Act had not been passed might have been exercised by the said Company in relation to any territories, shall become vested in Her Majesty, and be exercised in her name, and for the purposes of this Act India shall mean the territories vested in Her Majesty as aforesaid, and all territories which may become vested in Her Majesty by virtue of any such rights as aforesaid.

II. India shall be governed by and in the name of Her Majesty, and all rights in relation to any territories which might have been exercised by the said Company if this Act had not been passed shall and may be exercised by and in the name of Her Majesty as rights incidental to the Government of India; and all the territorial and other revenues of or arising in India, and all tributes and other payments in respect of any territories which would have been receivable by or in the name of the said Company if this Act had not been passed, shall be received for and in the name of Her Majesty, and shall be applied and disposed of for the purposes of the Government of India alone, subject to the provisions of this Act....

Queen Victoria's Proclamation to the Princess, Chiefs and Peoples of India, November 1, 1858[2]

This Proclamation marks the transition from Company to Crown Government. The Queen appointed Lord Canning, Viceroy of India and promised to respect all treaties and engagements made by the East India Company. She also promised religious toleration, the admission of Indians to government service and the maintenance of the 'ancient rights, usages and customs of India'.

Victoria, by the Grace of God of the United Kingdom of Great Britain and Ireland, and of the Colonies and Dependencies thereof in Europe, Asia, Africa, America, and Australia, Queen, Defender of the Faith.

Whereas, for divers weighty reason, we have resolved, by and with the advice and consent of the Lords Spiritual and Temporal, and Commons, in Parliament assembled, to take upon ourselves the government of the territories in India, heretofore administered in trust for us by the Honourable East India Company.

Now, therefore, we do by these presents notify and declare that by the advice and consent aforesaid, we have taken upon ourselves the said government; and we hereby call upon all our subjects within the said territories to be faithful, and to bear true allegiance to us, our heirs and successors, and to submit themselves to the authority of those whom we may hereafter, from time to time, see fit to appoint to administer the government of our said territories, in our name and on our behalf.

And we, reposing especial trust and confidence in the loyalty, ability and judgement of our right trusty and well-beloved cousin Charles John, Viscount Canning, do hereby constitute and point him, the said Viscount Canning, to be our first Viceroy and Governor-General in and over our said territories, and to administer the Government thereof in our name, and generally to act in our name and on our behalf, subject to such orders and regulations as he shall, from time to time, receive through one of our Principal Secretaries of State.

And we do hereby confirm in their several offices civil and military, all persons now employed in the service of the Honourable

East India Company, subject to our future pleasure, and to such laws and regulations as may hereafter be enacted.

We hereby announce to the native princes of India, that all treaties and engagements made with the, by or under the authority of the East India Company are by us accepted, and will be scrupulously maintained, and we look for the like observance on their part.

We desire no extension of our present territorial possessions; and, while we will permit no aggression upon our dominions or our rights to be attempted with impunity, we shall sanction no encroachment on those of others.

We shall respect the rights, dignity, and honour of native princes as our own; and we desire that they, as well as our own subjects, should enjoy that prosperity and that social advancement which can only be secured by internal peace and good government.

We hold ourselves bound to the natives of our Indian territories by the same obligations of duty which bind us to all our other subjects, and those obligations, by the blessing of Almighty God, we shall faithfully and conscientiously fill.

Firmly relying ourselves on the truth of Christianity, and acknowledging with gratitude the solace of religion, we disclaim alike the right and the desire to impose our conviction on any of our subjects. We declare it to be our royal will and pleasure that none be in any wise favoured, none molested or disquieted, by reason of their religious faith or observances, but that all shall alike enjoy the equal and impartial protection of the law; and we do strictly charge and enjoin all those who may be in authority under us that they abstain from all interference with the religious belief or worship of any of our subjects on pain of our highest displeasure.

And it is our further will that, so far as may be our subjects, of whatever race or creed, be freely and impartially admitted to office in our service, the duties of which they may be qualified by their education, ability, and integrity duly to discharge.

We know, and respect, the feelings of attachment with which the natives of India regard the lands inherited by them from their ancestors, and we desire to protect them in all rights connected therewith, subject to the equitable demands of the State; and we will that generally, in framing and administering the law, due regard to paid to the ancient rights, usages, and customs of India.

We deeply lament the evils and misery which have been brought upon India by the acts of ambitious men, who have deceived their countrymen by false reports, and led them into open rebellion. Our power has been shown by the suppression of that rebellion in the field; we desire to show our mercy by pardoning the offences of those who have been misled, but who desire to return to the path of duty....

When, by the blessing of Providence, internal tranquillity shall be restored, it is our earnest desire to stimulate the peaceful industry of India, to promote works of public utility and improvement, and to administer the government for the benefit of all our subjects resident therein. In their prosperity will be our strength, in their contentment our security, and in their gratitude our best reward. And may the God of all power grant to us, and to those in authority under us, strength to carry out these our wishes for the good of our people.

The Indian Councils Act, August 1, 1861[3]

The British realized that one of the reasons for the Mutiny was their lack of knowledge of Indian opinion. They therefore reorganized the Legislative Council at the centre and in the provinces to include Indian non-official representatives. Although these Indians generally consisted of the old aristocracy, the 1861 Indian Councils Act did mark the beginning of the association of Indians with the work of government.

III. There shall be five ordinary members of the said Council of the Governor-General, three of whom shall from time to time be appointed by the Secretary of State for India in Council, with the concurrence of a majority of members present at a meeting, from among such persons as shall have been, at the time of such appointment, in the service in India of the Crown, or of the Company and the Crown, for at least ten years; and if the person so appointed shall be in the military service of the Crown he shall not, during his continuance in office as a Member of

Council, hold any military command, or be employed in actual military duties, and the remaining two, one of whom shall be a barrister or a member of the Faculty of Advocates in Scotland of not less than five years standing, shall be appointed from time to time by Her Majesty by Warrant under Her Royal Sign Manual; and it shall be lawful for the Secretary of State in Council to appoint the Commander-in-Chief of Her Majesty's Forces in India to be an extraordinary member of the said Council, and such extraordinary member of Council shall have rank and precedence at the Council Board next after the Governor-General.

VIII. It shall be lawful for the Governor-General from time to time to make rules and orders for the more convenient transaction of business in the said Council; and any order made or act done in accordance with such rules and orders (except as hereafter provided respecting laws and regulations) shall be deemed to be the order or act of the Governor-General in Council.

IX. The said Council shall from time to time assemble at such place or places as shall be appointed by the Governor-General in Council within the territories of India; and as often as the said Council shall assemble within either of the Presidencies of Fort Saint George or Bombay, the Governor of such Presidency shall act as an extraordinary member of Council; and as often as the said Council shall assemble within any other division, province, or territory having a Lieutenant-Governor, such Lieutenant-General shall act as an additional Councilor at meetings of the Council, for the purpose of making laws and regulations only, in manner hereinafter provided.

X. For the better exercise of the power of making laws and regulations vested in the Governor-General in Council, the Governor-General shall nominate, in addition to the ordinary and extraordinary members above mentioned, and to such Lieutenant-Governor in the case aforesaid, such persons, not less than six nor more than twelve in number, as to him may seem expedient, to be members of Council for the purpose of making laws and regulations only, and such persons shall not be entitled to sit or vote at any meeting of Council, except at meetings held for such purpose: provided that not less than one half of the persons so nominated shall be non-official persons, that is, persons who, at the date of such nomination, shall not be in the civil or military service of the Crown in India, and that the seat in Council of any non-official member accepting office under the Crown in India shall be vacated on such acceptance.

XI. Every additional member of Council so nominated shall be summoned to all meetings held for the purpose of making laws and regulations, for the term of two years from the date of such nomination.

XIX. No business shall be transacted at any meeting for the purpose of making laws and regulations, except as last hereinbefore provided, other than the consideration and enactment of measures introduced into the Council for the purpose of such enactment; and it shall not be lawful for any member or additional member to make or for the Council to entertain any motion, unless such motion be for leave to introduce some measure as aforesaid into Council, or have reference to some measure actually introduced there into: Provided always, that it shall not be lawful for any member or additional member to introduce, without the previous sanction of the Governor-General, any measure affecting:

(i) The Public Debt or Public Revenues of India, or by which any charge would be imposed on such Revenues;

(ii) The religion or religious rites and usages of any class of Her Majesty's subjects in India;

(iii) The discipline or maintenance of any part of Her Majesty's Military or Naval Forces;

(iv) The relations of the Government with foreign Princes or States.

XX. When any law or regulation has been made by the Council at a meeting for the purpose of making laws and regulations as aforesaid, it shall be lawful for the Governor-General, whether he shall or shall not have been present in Council at the making thereof, to declare that he assents to the same, or that he withholds his assent from the same, or that the reserves the same for the signification of the pleasure of Her majesty thereon; and no such law or regulation shall have validity until the Governor-General shall have declared his assent to the same, or until (in the case of a law or regulation so reserved as aforesaid) Her Majesty shall have signified her assent to the same to the Governor-General, through the Secretary of State for India in Council, and such assent shall have been duly proclaimed by the said Governor General.

XXI. Whenever any such law or regulation has been assented to by the Governor-General, he shall transmit to the Secretary of State for India an authentic copy thereof; and it shall be lawful for Her Majesty to signify, through the Secretary of State for India in Council, her disallowance of such law; and such disallowance shall make void and annual such law from or after the day on which the Governor-General shall make known, by proclamation or by signification to his Council, that he has received the notification of such disallowance by Her Majesty.

Jawaharlal Nehru: The Early Fruits of English Education[4]

English education first appealed to those members of the Hindu Higher castes who had been literate under previous regimes. There were few openings for educated Indians under the British, and whilst the majority became lower government servants a few struck out into independent professions such as the law. The English-educated were active in social reform movements, and later in political associations aimed at wringing concessions from the British.

English education brought a widening of the Indian horizon, an admiration for English literature and institutions, a revolt against some customs and aspects of Indian life, and a growing demand for political reform. The new professional classes took the lead in political agitation, which consisted chiefly in sending representatives to government. English educated people in the professions and the services formed in effect a new class, which was to grow all over India, a class influenced by Western thought and ways and rather cut off from the mass of the population. In 1852 the British Indian Association was started in Calcutta. This was one of the forerunners of the Indian National Congress and yet a whole generation was to pass before the Congress was started in 1885. This gap represents the period of the revolt of 1857-58, its suppression, and its consequences. The great difference between the state of Bengal and that of northern and central India in the middle of the century is brought out by the fact that while in Bengal the new intelligentsia (chiefly Hindu) had been influenced by English thought and literature and looked to England for political, constitutional reform, the other areas were seething with the spirit of revolt.

In Bengal one can see more clearly than elsewhere the early effects of British rule and Western influence. The breakup of the agrarian economy was complete, and the old feudal classes had almost been eliminated. In their place had come new landowners whose organic and traditional contacts with the land were far less, and who had few of the virtues and most of the failings of the old feudal landlords. The peasantry suffered famine and spoliation in many ways and were reduced to extreme poverty. The artisan class was almost wiped out. Over these disjointed and broken-up foundations rose new groups and classes, the products of British rule and connected with it in many ways. There were the merchants who were really middlemen of British trade and industry, profiting by the leavings of that industry. There were also the English-educated classes in the subordinate services and the learned professions, both looking to the British power for advancement and both influenced in varying degrees by Western thought. Among these grew up a spirit of revolt against the rigid conventions and social framework of Hindu society. They looked to English liberalism and institutions for inspiration.

This was the effect on the upper fringe of the Hindus of Bengal. The mass of the Hindus there were not directly affected, and even the Hindu leaders probably seldom thought of these masses. The Moslems were not affected at all, some individuals apart, and they kept deliberately aloof from the new education. They previously had been backward economically, and they became even more so.

Debendranath Tagore: The Meaning of Brahmoism[5]

One of the first fruits of exposure to English ideas was the Brahmo Samaj, founded in Calcutta by Ram Mohan Roy (1772-1833) in 1828. The Samaj was a theistic society strongly influenced by Christianity; and it denounced idolatry, infanticide, polygamy and other evils of Hindu society. After Ram Mohan's death the Samaj was led by Debendranath Tagore (1817-1905) until a split occurred over the society's interpretation of Christianity. Debendranath produced the following manifesto on "gradualism" in social reform matters.

We are worshippers of Brahma, the Supreme Being. In this we are at one with Orthodox Hinduism, for all our shastras declare with one voice the supremacy of the worship of Brahma, enjoining image worship for the help of those who are incapable of grasping the highest Truth.

Our first point of distinction is in the positive aspect of our creed wherein worship is defined as consisting in "Loving Him and doing the works He loveth"—this at once differentiates us from all religions and creeds which postulate a special or verbal revelation, or wherein definite forms, rites or ceremonials are deemed essential one way or the other.

The negative aspect of our creed which prohibits the worship of any created being or thing as the Creator further distinguishes us from all who are addicted to the worship of avatars or incarnations or who believe in the necessity of mediators, symbols, or idols of any description.

We base our faith on the fundamental truths of religion, attested by reason and conscience and refuse to permit man, book, image to stand in the way of the direct communication of our soul with the Supreme Spirit.

This message of the Brahmo Samaj in the abstract does not materially differ from the doctrines of the pure theistic bodies all the world over. Viewed historically and socially, however, the Brahmo Samaj has the further distinction of being the bearer of this message to the Hindu people. This was the idea of its founder Ram Mohun Roy, this points to the duty incumbent upon all Brahmos of today, and will serve as the guiding principle in the selection of texts, forms and ceremonials as aids to the religious life.

We are in and of the great Hindu community and it devolves upon us by example and precept to holkd up as a beacon the highest truths of the Hindu shastras. In their light we must purify our heritage of customs, usages, rites, and ceremonies and adapt them to the needs of our conscience and our community. But we must beware of proceeding too fast in matters of social change, lest we be separated from the greater body which we would guide and uplift.

While we should on no account allow any consideration of country, caste, or kinship to prevent our actions being consistent with our faith, we must make every allowance for, and abstain from, persecuting or alienating those who think differently from us. Why should we needlessly wound the feelings of our parents and elders by desecrating an image which they regard with the highest reverence, when all that our conscience can demand of us is to refrain from its adoration?

The steering of this middle course is by no means an easy task, but during my long experience I have been led greatly to hope for a brighter future by the sympathetic response of our orthodox brethren to the ideal held up before them. The amount of conformity expected nowadays by even the most orthodox, demands so little of us that a little tact and common sense will in most cases be sufficient to obviate all friction.

Nevertheless, great as are the claims of our land and our people, we must never forget that we are Brahmos first, and Indians or Hindus afterwards. We must on no account depart from our vow of renouncing the worship of images and incarnations, which is of the essence of our religion. It is a sound policy on our part to sink our minor differences, but on matters of principle no compromise is possible. Our Motherland is dear to us, but Religion is dearer, Brahma is dearest of all, dearer than son, dearer than riches, supreme over everything else.

Swami Vivekananda: The Spiritual Force of Hinduism[6]

Vivekananda (Narendranath Datta) (1863-1902) was a disciple of the great Bengali mystic Ramakrishna. Vivekananda represented Hinduism on the offensive. He believed that although India was poor and backward, she had inestimable spiritual treasurers with which she could once again endow the world. To the traditional gospel of contemplation he now added the gospel of action, and founded a social service society entitled the Ramakrishna Mission. He also attempted to proselytize for Hinduism in the West, and attended the World Parliament of Religions in Chicago in 1893. The following is an address he gave in England:

People who are capable of seeing only the gross external aspect of things, can perceive in the Indian nation only a conquered and suffering people, a race of dreamers and philosophers. They seem to be incapable of perceiving that in the spiritual realm India conquers the world. No doubt it is true that just as the too active Western mind would profit by an admixture of Eastern introspection and the meditative habit, so the Eastern would benefit by a somewhat greater activity and energy. Still we must ask, what may be that Force which causes that afflicted and suffering people, the Hindu, and the Jewish too (the two races from which have originated all the great religions of the world), to survive, when other nations perish? The cause can only be their Spiritual Force. The Hindus are still living though silent, the Jews are more numerous today than when they lived in Palestine. The philosophy of India percolates throughout the whole civilized world, modifying and permeating as it goes. So also in ancient times, her trade reached the shores of Africa before Europe was known, and opened communication with the rest of the world, thus disproving the belief that Indians never went outside of their own country.

It is remarkable also that the possession of India by a foreign power has always been a turning point in the history of that power, bringing to it wealth, prosperity, dominion and spiritual ideas. While the Western man tries to measure how much it is possible for him to possess and enjoy, the Eastern seems to take the opposite course, and to measure how little of material possessions he can do with. In the Vedas we trace the endeavour of that ancient people to find God. In their search for him they came upon different strata; beginning with ancestor worship, they passed on to the worship of agni, the fire-god, of Indra, the god of thunder, and of Vanina, the God of gods. We find the growth of this idea of God, from many gods to one God, in all religions, its real meaning is that He is the chief of the tribal gods, who creates the world, rules it and sees into every heart; the stages of growth lead up from a multiplicity of gods to monotheism. This anthropomorphic conception, however, did not satisfy the Hindus, it was too human for them who were seeking the Divine. Therefore they finally gave up searching for God in the outer world of sense and matter, and turned their attention to the inner world. Is there an inner world? And what is it? It is Atman. It is the Self, it is the only thing an Indian can be sure of. If he knows himself, he can know the universe, and not otherwise. The same question was asked in the beginning of time, even in the Rig-Veda, in another form: "Who or what existed from the beginning?" That question was gradually solved by the Vedanta philosophy. The Atman existed. That is to say, what we call the Absolute, the Universal Soul, the self, is the Force by which from the beginning all things have been and are and will be manifested.

While the Vedanta philosophers solved that questions, they at the same time discovered the basis of ethics. Though all religions have taught ethical precepts, such as, "Do not kill, do not injure, love your neighbour as yourself", etc., yet none of these has given the reason. Why should I not injure my neighbour? To this question there was no satisfactory and conclusive answer forthcoming, until it was evolved by the metaphysical speculations of the Hindus who could not rest satisfied with mere dogmas. So the Hindus say, that this Atman is absolute and all-pervading, therefore infinite. There cannot be two infinities for they would limit each other and would become finite. Also each individual soul is part and parcel of that Universal Soul, which is infinite. Therefore in injuring his neighbour, the neighbour actually injures himself. This is the basic metaphysical truth underlying all ethical codes.

Surendranath Banerjea: The Indian Association[7]

In addition to social reform associations, Indians very early established political associations to make their wishes heard by the British. In Bengal the British Indian Association was founded in 1851, and in Bombay, the Bombay Association was established the following year. Both these associations were heavily dominated by the traditional elite, the landlords in Bengal and the great merchants in Bombay, and they were very cautious in approaching government. The English-educated wanted their own associations to deal more actively with their demands, and this led to the founding of the Indian Association by Surendranath Banerjea (1848-1925) in 1876, and the Bombay Branch of the East India Association by Dadabhai Naoroji (1825-1917) in 1869.

After my return from England in June, 1875, and along with the work of organizing the students and infusing into them a new life and spirit, I began seriously to consider the advisability of forming an Association to represent the views of the educated middle-class community and inspire them with a living interest in public affairs. There was indeed the British Indian Association, which, under the guidance of the great Kristo Dal Pal, who was then secretary, valiantly upheld the popular interests when necessary; but it was essentially and by its creed an Association of land-holders. Nor did an active political agitation, or the creation of public opinion by direct appeals to the people, form part of its recognized programme. There was thus the clear need for another political Association on a more democratic basis, and the fact was indeed recognized by the leaders of the British Indian Association....

After a year's preparation, the Indian Association was established on July 26, 1876. The name was the subject of anxious consideration among our friends. Pundit Iswar Chunder Vidyasagar and Mr. Justice Dwarakanath Mitter, while still a member of the Bar, had formed the idea of organizing a similar Association which was to be the voice and organ of the middle classes. The idea had to be given up as it did not at the time meet with much support; but the name they had chosen for their proposed organization was the Bengal Association. We thought that such a name, or anything like it, would restrict the scope of our work. For the idea that was working in our minds was that the Association was to be the centre of an all-India movement. For even then, the conception of a united India, derived from the inspiration of Mazzini, or, at any rate, of bringing all India upon the same common political platform, had taken firm possession of the minds of the Indian leaders in Bengal. We accordingly resolved to call the new political body the Indian Association....

I kept myself in the background, but I worked zealously for the Association, knowing no higher pleasure or duty, and bent upon realizing through this institution the great ideals which even at that early period had taken definite possession of my mind. They may be set forth as follows: (1) The creation of a strong body of public opinion in the country; (2) the unification of the Indian races and peoples upon the basis of common political interests and aspirations; (3) the promotion of friendly feeling between Hindus and Mahomedans; and, lastly, the inclusion of the masses in the great public movements of the day....

Upon my mind the writings of Mazzini had created a profound impression. The purity of his patriotism, the loftiness of his ideals, and his all-embracing love for humanity, expressed with the true eloquence of the heart, moved me as I have never before been moved. I discarded his revolutionary teachings as unsuited to the circumstances of India and as fatal to its normal development, along the lines of peaceful and orderly progress; but I inculcated, with all the emphasis that I could command, the enduring lessons of his noble life, lived for the sake of others, his lofty patriotism, his self-abnegation, and his heroic devotion to the interests of humanity. It was Mazzini, the incarnation of the highest moral forces in the political arena—Mazzini, the apostle of Italian unity, the friend of the human race, that I presented to the youth of Bengal. Mazzini had taught Italian unity. We wanted Indian unity. Mazzini had worked through the young. I wanted the young men of Bengal to realize their potentialities and to qualify themselves to work for the salvation of their country, but upon lines instinct with the spirit of constitutionalism.

Lord Ripon and Local Self-government, 1882[8]

In 1880 Lord Ripon was sent as Viceroy of India by the Gladstone government. The previous Viceroy, Lord Lytton, had followed a reactionary policy where educated Indians were concerned. The liberal Ripon saw that educated India stood at the crossroads, and that if the English-educated were not taken into some sort of partnership by the government, they would become inalienably hostile to the British Raj. Ripon began by repealing the Vernacular Press Act, by which Lytton had put Indian newspapers under certain disabilities. He then turned to local government as a way of associating educated Indians more closely with their rulers and giving them some elementary political training.

Memorandum to the Secretary of State, December 25, 1882

No one who watches the signs of the times in this country with even moderate care can doubt that we have entered upon a period of change: the spread of education, the existing and increasing influence of a free Press, the substitution of legal for discretionary administration, the progress of railways, telegraphs, etc., the easier communication with Europe, and the more ready influx of European ideas, are now beginning to produce a marked effect upon the people; new ideas are springing up; new aspirations are being called forth; the power of public opinion is growing and strengthening from day to day; and a movement has begun which will advance with greater rapidity and force every year. Such a condition of affairs is one in which the task of Government, and especially practically despotic Government, is beset with difficulties of no light kind; to move too fast is dangerous, but to lag behind is more dangerous still; and the problem is how to deal with this new-born spirit of progress, raw and superficial as in many respects it is, so as to direct it into a right course, and to derive from it all the benefits which its development is capable of ultimately conferring upon the country, and at the same time to prevent it from becoming, through blind indifference or stupid repression, a source of serious political danger. Considerations such as these give great importance to measures which, though small in themselves, are calculated to provide a legitimate outlet for the ambitions and aspirations which we have ourselves created by the education, civilization, and material progress which we have been the means of introducing into the country such measures will not only have the immediate effect in promoting gradually and safely the political education of the people, which is in itself a great object of public policy, but will also pave the way for further advances in the same direction, as that education becomes fuller and more widespread. It is only what ought to be expected by every thoughtful man that after 50 years of a free Press and 30 years of expanding education, with European ideas flowing into the country on every side, and old, indigenous customs, habits, and prejudices breaking down all around, as caste is breaking down through the instrumentality of railways and other similar influences, changes should be taking place in the thoughts, the desires, and the aims of the intelligent and educated men of the country which no wise and cautious Government can afford to disregard, and to which they must gradually adapt their system of administration if they do not wish to see it broken to pieces by forces which they have themselves called into being, but which they have failed to guide and to control. And even if there were no such necessity as the present circumstances of the country create for meeting the needs and providing for the aspirations of a time of change and progress, it would always be an aim worthy of the English Government in India to train the people over whom it rules more and more as times goes on to take an intelligent share in the administration of their own affairs. Among the political objects attainable in India, I see at present none higher. The credit of having set that object before the Government of India belongs to a Conservative, not a Liberal statesman; but it surely behoves the friends of liberal principles in the wide, not in any narrow party sense of the words, not to let Lord Mayo's policy become unfruitful in their hands, nor to allow it to be stifled beneath the stolid indifference or the covert hostility of men who can not understand its meaning or appreciate its wisdom. There are, of course, always two policies lying before the choice of the Government of India. The one is the policy of those who have established a free Press, who have promoted education, who have admitted natives more and more largely to the public service in various forms, and who have favoured the extension of self-government; the other is, that of those who hate the freedom of the Press, who dread the progress of education, and who watch with jealousy and alarm everything which tends, in however limited a degree, to give the Natives of India a larger share in the management of their own affairs. Between these two policies we must choose; the one means progress, the other means repression. Lord Lytton chose the latter. I have chosen the former, and I am content to rest my vindication upon a comparison of the results.

The Ilbert Bill, 1883[9]

Ripon continued his liberal policy by a Bill which made the simple administrative change of empowering Indian magistrates to try up-country Europeans. The Bill caused uproar among Indian-domiciled Europeans, and ultimately it was changed in their favour. The European outcry and its excellent organization strongly affected politically minded Indians and led to the calling of the first National Conference in December 1883, the forerunner of Congress.

The Ilbert Bill controversy helped to intensify the growing feeling of unity among the Indian people. The Anglo-Indian community had formed their Defence Association with its branches in different parts of the country. They had raised over a lakh and fifty thousand rupees to protect what they conceived to be their own interests, and to assert their special privileges. Their organization and their resources had secured success to their cause. The educated community all over India watched the struggle with interest. There was the Ilbert Bill agitation with all its developments taking place before their eyes. They could not remain insensible to the lesson that it taught, of combination and organization, a lesson which in this case was enforced amid conditions that left a rankling sense of humiliation in the mind of educated India. It was, however, fruitful of results. It strengthened the forces that were speeding up the birth of the Congress movement; and...before the year was out the first National Conference was held in Calcutta....It was the reply of educated India to the Ilbert Bill agitation, a reasonant blast on their golden trumpet. The Conference met for three days from December 28 to 30.

The questions that even now substantially from the chief planks in the Congress platform were taken up for discussion. They were Representative Councils or Self-government, Education, general and technical, the separation of Judicial from Executive functions in the administration of Criminal Justice, and, lastly, the wider employment of our countrymen in the public service.

The Aims and Objects of the Indian National Congress, December, 1885[10]

In December 1885 the first Indian National Congress was held in Bombay, with seventy-two delegates attending the session. Support came from the English-educated, mainly lawyers, with a few Bombay businessmen and Bengali landlords. Congress began by being a meeting place for this class, and it was also joined by a number of interested Englishmen. It was exceedingly deferential to the British connection. Its first demands were centered on the need for more Indians in the Civil Service, and more India representation on the Legislative Councils. The following is taken from the presidential address of the Bengali lawyer, W.C. Bonnerji (1844-1906):

And now it seemed a fitting occasion for answering a question that had continually been asked in the world outside during the past few weeks, viz., what the objects and aims of this great National Congress really were. He would not pretend to reply to this question exhaustively. The ensuing proceedings would, he believed, do this more effectively than any single speaker could hope to do; but he might say briefly, that the objects of the Congress could for the most part be classed under the following heads:

(a) The promotion of personal intimacy and friendship amongst all the more earnest workers in our country's cause in the different parts of the Empire;

(b) The eradication, by direct friendly personal intercourse, of all possible race, creed, or provincial prejudices amongst all lovers of our country, and the fuller development and consolidation of those sentiments of national unity that had their origin in their beloved Lord Ripon's ever memorable reign;

(c) The authoritative record, after this has been carefully elicited, by the fullest discussion of the matured opinions of the educated classes in India on some of the more important and pressing of the social questions of the day;

(d) The determination of the lines upon, and methods by which, during the next twelve months, it is desirable for native politicians to labour in the public interests.

Lord Dufferin: The Aspirations of the Congress, November 30, 1888[11]

Lord Dufferin, Ripon's successor, was originally favourable to Congress. However, he gradually began to dislike Congress's criticism of Government acts and policy and its making of demands on Government. He then came to belittle Congress achievements, as in this speech at the St. Andrew's Day dinner in Calcutta, where he referred to the Congress members as "a microscopic minority".

But if no native statesmen of weight or importance, capable of appreciating the true interests of England and of India, is found to defend this programme, who are those who do? Who and what are the persons who seek to assume such great powers—to tempt the fate of Phaeton, and to sit in the chariot of the Sun? Well, they are gentlemen of whom I desire to speak with the greatest courtesy and kindness, for they are, most of them, the product of the system of education which we ourselves have carried on during the last thirty years. But thirty years is a very short time in which to educate a self-governing nation from its primordial elements. At all events, let us measure the extent of educated assistance upon which we could call at this moment; let us examine the degree of proficiency which the educated classes of India have attained, and the relation of their numbers to the rest of the population. Out of the whole population of British India, which may be put at 200 millions in round numbers, not more than five or six per cent. can read and write, while less than one per cent has any knowledge of English. Thus, the overwhelming mass of the people, perhaps one hundred and ninety out of the two hundred millions, are still steeped in ignorance, and of the ten or twelve millions who have acquired education, three-fourths have attained to merely the most elementary knowledge. In our recent review of the progress of education, it was pointed out that ninety-four and a half per cent of those attending our schools and colleges were in the primary stage, while the progress made in English education can be measured by the fact that the number of students who have graduated at the universities since their establishment in 1857—that is, during the course of the last thirty-one years—is under eight thousand. During the last twenty-five years probably not more than half a million students have passed out of our schools with a good knowledge of English, and perhaps a million more with a smattering of it. Consequently, it may be said that, out of a population of 200 millions, there are only a very few thousands who may be considered to possess adequate qualifications, so far as education and an acquaintance with Western ideas or even Eastern learning are concerned, for taking an intelligent view of those intricate and complicated economic and political questions affecting the destinies of so many millions of men which are almost daily being presented for the consideration of the Government of India. I would ask, then, how any reasonable man could imagine that the British Government would be content to allow this microscopic minority to control their administration of that majestic and multiform empire for whose safety and welfare they are responsible in the eyes of God and before the face of civilization? It has been stated that this minority represents a large and growing class, and I feel very sure that, as time goes on, it is not only the class that will grow, but also the information and experience of its members. As present, however, it appears to me a groundless contention that it represents the people of India. It they had been really representatives of the people of India—that is to say, of the voiceless millions—instead of seeking to circumscribe the incidence of the income tax, as they desired to do, they would probably have received a mandate to decuple it. Indeed, is it not evident that large sections of the community are already becoming alarmed at the thought of such self-constituted bodies interposing between themselves and the august impartiality of English rule? These persons ought to know that in the present condition of India there can be no real or effective representation of the people, with their tessellated nationalities. They ought to see that all the strength, power, and intelligence of the British Government are applied to the prevention of one race, of one interest, of one class, of one religion, dominating another; and they ought to feel that in their peculiar position there can be no greater blessing to the country than the existence of an external, dispassionate, and immutable authority, whose watchword is Justice, and who alone possess both the power and the will to weld the rights and status of each separate element of the empire into a peaceful, coordinated and harmonious unity.

Syed Ahmad Khan: Muslims and Congress[12]

Congress consisted of those who had received English education by the end of the nineteenth century, and for this reason it was chiefly a Hindu body. One quarter of India's population was Muslim, and most Muslims had held aloof from English education as objectionable to their beliefs and customs. Syed Ahmad Khan (1817-98) was the first to point out that Muslims were falling behind their Hindu compatriots. But while urging English education for them, he argued that Muslims should make peace with the British rather than be led into opposition by the Congress. Syed Ahmad declared that the ultimate aim of Congress was majority rule, and majority rule in India meant Hindu rule. Any step in this direction would be disastrous for Muslims.

Long before the idea of founding the Indian National Congress was mooted, I had given thought to the matter whether representative government is suited to the conditions of India. I studied John Stuart Mill's views in support of representative government. He has dealt with this matter exceedingly well in great detail. I reached the conclusion that the first requisite of a representative government is that the voters should possess the highest degree of homogeneity. In a form of government which depends for its functioning upon majorities, it is necessary that the people should have no differences in the matter of nationality, religion, ways of living, customs, mores, culture and historical traditions. These things should be common among a people to enable them to run a representative government properly. Only when such homogeneity is present can representative government work or prove beneficial. It should not even be thought of when these conditions do not exist.

In a country like India where homogeneity does not exist in any one of these fields, the introduction of representative government cannot produce any beneficial results; it can only result in interfering with the peace and prosperity of the land. I sincerely hope that whichever party comes into power in Great Britain—be they the Conservatives, the Liberals, the Unionists, or the Radicals—they will remember that India is a continent, it is not a small and homogeneous country like England, Scotland, Wales or Ireland. India is inhabited by different peoples, each one of whom is numerically large and different from the others in its culture, its moral code, its social organization, its political outlook, its religion, its physique, and its historical associations. These peoples have never been united since the downfall of the Muslim empire. Instead of being able to organize some other form of government they have just indulged in fighting and internecine wars. . . .

The aims and objects of the Indian National Congress are based upon an ignorance of history and present day realities; they do not take into consideration that India is inhabited by different nationalities; they presuppose that the Muslims, the Marathas, the Brahmins, the Kshatriyas, the Banias, the Sudras, the Sikhs, the Bengalis, the Madrasis, and the Peshawaris can all the treated alike and all of them belong to the same nation. The Congress thinks that they profess the same religion, that they speak the same language, that their way of life and customs are the same, that their attitude to History is similar and based upon the same historical traditions....I consider the experiment which the Indian National Congress wants to make fraught with dangers and suffering for all the nationalities of India, special for the Muslims. The Muslims are in a minority, but they are a highly united minority. At least traditionally they are prone to take the sword in hand when the majority oppresses them....The Congress cannot rationally prove its claim to represent the opinions, ideals, and aspirations of the Muslims.

Lord Dufferin: The 1892 Reforms[13]

As a result of Congress pressure a minor reform of the Legislaive Councils was carried out in 1892. However, this only introduced an elected minority, and it was made perfectly plain that no progress towards a Parliamentary system was intended.

Our scheme may be briefly described as a plan for the enlargement of our provincial councils, for the enhancement of their status, the multiplication of their functions, the partical introduction into them of the elective principle, and the liberalization of their general character as political institutions. From this it might be concluded that we were contemplating approach, at all events, as far as the provinces are concerned, to English parliamentary government and an English constitutional system. Such a conclusion would be very wide of the mark; and it would be wrong to leave either the India Office or the Indian public under so erroneous an impression. India is an integral portion, and it may be said one of the most important portions, of the mighty British Empire. Its destinies have been confided to the guidance of an alien race, whose function it is to arbitrate between a multitude of conflicting or antagonistic interests, and its Government is conducted in the name of a monarch whose throne is in England. The executive that represents her imperium in India is an executive directly responsible not to any local authority, but to the Sovereign and to the British Parliament. Nor could its members divest themselves of this responsibility as long as Great Britain remains the paramount administrative power in India. But it is of the essence of constitutional government as Englishmen understand the term, that no administration should remain at the head of affairs which does not posses the necessary powers to carry out whatever measures or policy it may consider to be "for the public interest." The moment these powers are withheld, either by the Sovereign or Parliament, a constitutional executive resigns its functions and gives way to those whose superior influence with the constituencies has enabled them to overrule its decisions, and who consequently become answerable for whatever line of procedure may be adopted in lieu of that recommended by their predecessors. In India this shifting of responsibility from one set of persons to another is under existing circumstances impossible, for if any measure introduced into a legislative council is vetoed by an adverse majority, the Governor cannot call upon the dissentients to take the place of his own official advisers, who are nominated by the Queen-Empress on the advice of the Secretary of State. Consequently the vote of the opposition in an Indian council would not be given under the heavy sense of responsibility which attaches to the vote of a dissenting majority in an constitutional country; while no responsible executive could be required to carry on the government unless free to inaugurate whatever measures it considers necessary for the good and safely of the State, It is, therefore, obvious, for this and many other reasons, that no matter to what degree the liberalization of the councils may now take place, it will be necessary to leave in the hands of each provincial Government the ultimate decision upon all important questions, and the paramount control of its own policy. It is in this view that we have arranged that the nominated members in the councils should outnumber the elected members, at the same time that the Governor had been empowered to overrule his council whenever he feels himself called upon by circumstances to do so.

The Indian Councils Act, June 20, 1892[14]

The following is an extract from the 1892 Act. It will be seen that the Councils could only discuss bills submitted to them, but not initiate legislation.

Be it enacted…, as follows:

I. (1) The number of additional members of Council nominated by the Governor General under the provisions of Section Ten of the Indian Councils Act, 1861, shall be such as to him may seem from time to time expedient, but shall not be less than ten nor more than sixteen; and the number of additional members of Council nominated by the governors of the presidencies of Fort St. George and Bombay respectively under the provisions of Section Twenty-nine of the Indian Councils Act, 1861, shall (besides the Advocate General of the presidency or officer acting in that capacity) be such as to the said governors respectively may seem from time to time expedient, but shall not be less than eight nor more than twenty.

(2) It shall be lawful for the Governor General in Council by proclamation from time to time to increase the number of councilors whom the lieutenant governors of the Bengal Division of the presidency of Fort William and of the North-Western Provinces and Oudh respectively may nominate for their assistance in making laws and regulations: Provided always, that not more than twenty shall be nominated for the Bengal Division, and not more than fifteen for the North-Western Provinces and Oudh.

(4) The Governor General in Council may from time to time, with the approval of the Secretary of State in Council, make regulations as to the conditions under which such nominations, or any of them, shall be made by the Governor General, Governors, and Lieutenant Governors respectively, and prescribe the manner in which such regulations shall be carried into effect.

II. Notwithstanding any provision in the Indian Councils Act, 1861, the Governor General of India in Council may from time to time make rules authorising at any meeting of the Governor General's Council for the purpose of making laws and regulations the discussion of the annual financial statement of the Governor General in Council and the asking of questions, but under such conditions and restrictions as to subject or otherwise as shall be in the said rules prescribed or declared: And notwithstanding any provisions in the Indian Councils Act, 1861, the Governors in Council of Fort St. George and Bombay respectively, and the lieutenant governor of any province to which the provisions of the Indian Councils Act, 1861, touching the making of laws and regulations, have been or are hereafter extended or made applicable, may from time to time make rules for authorising at any meeting of their respective councils for the purpose of making laws and regulations the discussion of the annual financial statement of their respective local governments, and the asking of questions, but under such conditions and restrictions, as to subject or otherwise, as shall in the said rules applicable to such councils respectively be prescribed or declared. But no member at any such meeting of any council shall have power to submit or propose any resolution or to divide the council in respect of any such financial discussion, or the answer to any question asked under the authority of this Act, or the rules made under this act: Provided that any rule made under this Act by a governor in council, or by a lieutenant governor, shall be submitted for and shall be subject to the sanction of the Governor General in Council, and any rule made under this Act by the Governor General in Council shall be submitted for and shall be subject to the sanction of the Secretary of State in Council: Provided also that rules made under this Act shall not be subject to alteration or amendment at meetings for the purpose of making laws and regulations.

VII. Nothing in this Act shall detract from or diminish the powers of the Governor General in Council at meetings for the purpose of making laws and regulations.

T.B. Macaulay, February 2, 1835

REFERENCES

1. A.B. Keith, *Speeches and Documents on Indian Policy, 1750-1921* (Oxford, 1923), I, 370-371.
2. A.B. Keith, *Speeches and Documents on Indian Policy, 1750-1921* (Oxford, 1923), I, 382-386.
3. 24 and 25 Vict., c. 67.
4. Jawaharlal Nehru, *The Discovery of India* (New York, 1959), 231. Copyright © 1946 by The John Day Company. Inc.
5. Debendranath Tagore, *The Autobiography of Maharshi Devendranath Tagore* (Calcutta, 1909), 610-611.
6. *The Complete Works of Swami Vivekananda* (Mayavati, 1946). I. 382-384.
7. Surendranath Banerjea, *A Nation in Making. Being the Reminiscences of Fifty Years of Public Life* (Calcutta, 1963), 37-40.
8. A.C. Banerjee, *Indian Constitutional Documents, 1757-1939* (2nd edn., Calcutta, 1948), II, *1858-1917*, 79-82.
9. Surendranath Banerjea, *A Nation in Making. Being the Reminiscences of Fifty Years of Public Life* (Calcutta, 1963), 79-80.
10. *Congress Presidential Addresses, 1885-1916* (Madras, N.D.), 2. The report is in indirect speech.

11. A.C. Banerjee, *Indian Constitutional Documents, 1757-1939* (2nd edn, Calcutta, 1948), II. *1858-1917,* 91-95.

12. Syed Ahmad Khan, *Akhari Madamin, Compiled by Muhammad Imam-ud-din Gujerat and Maulvi Ahmad Baba Makhdumi* (3rd edn., Lahore, N.D.), 46-50.

13. *The Report of the Indian Statutory Commission* (London, 1930), 117, para 134.

14. 55 and 56 Vict., c. 14.

4

Indian Educational Policy Being a Resolution Issued by the Governor General in Council on the 11 March 1904

History up to 1854

Education in India, in the modern sense of the word, may be said to date from the year 1854, when the Court of Directors, in a memorable despatch, definitely accepted the systematic promotion of general education as one of the duties of the State, and emphatically declared that the type of education which they desired to see extended in India was that which had for its object the diffusion of the arts, science, philosophy, and literature of Europe; in short, of European knowledge.

The acceptance of this duty was an important departure in policy. The advent of British rule found in India systems of education of great antiquity existing among both Hindus and Muhammadans, in each case closely bound up with their religious institutions. To give and to receive instruction was enjoined by the sacred books of the Brahmans, and one of the commentaries on the Rig Veda lays down in minute detail the routine to be followed in committing a text-book to memory. Schools of learning were formed in centers containing considerable high caste populations, where Pandits gave instruction in Sanskrit Grammar, logic, Philosophy, and law. For the lower classes, village schools were scattered over the country, in which a rudimentary education was given to the children of traders, petty landholders, and well-to-do cultivators. The higher education of Muhammadans was in the hands of men of learning, who devoted themselves to the instruction of youth. Schools were attached to mosques and shrines and supported by State grants in cash or land, or by private liberality. The course of study in a Muhammadan place of learning included grammar, rhetoric, logic, literature, jurisprudence, and science. Both systems, the Muhammadan no less than the Hindu, assigned a disproportionate importance to the training of the memory, and sought to develop the critical faculties of the mind, mainly by exercising their pupils in metaphysical refinements and in fine-spun commentaries on the meaning of the texts which they had learnt by heart.

The First instinct of British rulers was to leave the traditional modes of instruction undisturbed and to continue the support which they had been accustomed to receive from Indian rulers. The Calcutta Madrasa for Muhammadans was founded by Warren Hastings in 1782, and the Benares College for Hindus was established in 1791. Provision was made for giving regular assistance to education from public funds by a clause in the Charter Act of 1813, which empowered the Governor General in council to direct that one lakh of rupees in each year should be "set apart and applied to the revival and improvement of literature and the encouragement of the learned natives of a knowledge of the sciences among the inhabitants of the British territories in India."

This grant was at first applied to the encouragement of Oriental methods of instruction by paying stipends to students. But the presence of the British in India brought about profound changes in the social and administrative conditions of the country; and these in their turn reacted on the educational policy of Government. The impulse towards reform came from two sources, the need for public servants with a knowledge of the English language, and the influence in favour both of English and of Vernacular education which was exercised by the missionaries in the early years of the nineteenth century. The well known Minute written by Lord Macaulay (at that time Legal Member of Council and Chairman of the Committee of Public Instruction) in 1835 marks the point at which official recognition was given to the necessity of public support for Western education. Then followed a period of attempts, differing in different Provinces, to extend English education by the establishment of Government schools and colleges, and by strengthening the indigenous schools; while missionary effort continued to play an important part in promoting educational progress.

Despatch of 1854

In their despatch of 1854, the Court of Directors announced their decision that the Government should actively assist in the more extended and systematic promotion of general education in India. They regarded it as a sacred duty to confer upon the natives of India those vast moral and material blessings which flow from the general diffusion of useful knowledge. They hoped by means of education to extend the influence which the Government was exerting for the suppression of demoralizing practices, by enlisting in its favour the general sympathy of the native mind. They also sought to create a supply of public servants to whose probity offices of trust might with increased confidence be committed, and to promote the material interests of the country by stimulating its inhabitants to develop its vast resources. The measures which were prescribed for carrying out this policy were: (1) the constitution of a Department of Public instruction; (2) the foundation of Universities at the Presidency towns; (3) the establishment of training schools for teachers; (4) the maintenance of the existing Government colleges and schools of a high order, and the increase of their number when necessary; (5) increased attention to all forms of vernacular schools; and finally (6) the introduction of a system of grants-in-aid which should foster a spirit of reliance upon local exertions, and should in course of time render it possible to close or transfer to the management of local bodies many of the existing institutions.

History since 1854

The policy laid down in 1854 was re-affirmed in 1859 when the administration had been transferred to the Crown. The Universities of Calcutta, Madras, and Bombay were incorporated in 1857 and those of the Punjab and Allahabad in 1882 and 1887, respectively. The growth of schools and colleges proceeded most rapidly between 1871 and 1882, and was further augmented by the development of the municipal system, and by the Acts, which were passed from 1865 onwards providing for the imposition of local cesses which might be applied to the establishment of schools. By the year 1882 there were more than two million and a quarter of pupils under instruction in public institutions. The Commission of 1882-83 furnished a most copious and valuable report upon the state of education as then existing, made a careful inquiry into the measures which had been taken in pursuance of the despatch of 1854, and submitted further detailed proposals for carrying out the principal of that despatch. The advised increased reliance upon and systematic encouragement of private effort, and their recommendations were approved by the Government of India. Shortly afterwards a considerable devolution of the management of Government schools upon Municipalities and district Boards was affected, in accordance with the principles of local self-government then brought into operation.

Extent of the Present System

As a result of these continuous efforts we find in existence today a system of public instruction, the influence of which extends in varying degrees to every part of India, and is upon the whole powerful for good. The system includes five Universities, those of Calcutta, Bombay, Madras, the Punjab, and Allahabad, which prescribe courses of study and examine the students of affiliated colleges. These colleges are widely scattered throughout the country and number in all 191 (exclusive of some colleges outside British India, which are not incorporated in the Provincial statistics), with 23,009 students on the rolls. In them provision is made for studies in Arts and Oriental learning, and for professional courses of Law, Medicine, Engineering, Teaching, and Agriculture. Below the colleges are secondary schools, to the number of 5,493, with an attendance of 5,58,378 scholars, and primary schools numbering 98,538, with 32,68,726 pupils including special schools, technical and industrial schools of art, normal schools for teachers, the total number of colleges and schools for public instruction amounts to 1,05,306, with 38,87,493 pupils; and if to these are added the "private institutions" with do not conform with departmental standards, the total number of scholars known by the Education Department to be under instruction reaches about 4½ millions. The gross annual cost of maintaining these institutions exceeds 400 lakhs, of which 127 lakhs are derived from fees, and 83 lakhs from endowments, subscriptions, and other private sources, while the expenditure from public funds aggregates 191 lakhs, of which 104 lakhs are derived from Provincial and Imperial revenues, 74 lakhs from local and Municipal sources and 13 lakhs from the revenues of Native States.

It is a striking feature of the system, and one which must constantly be borne in mind when dwelling upon its imperfections, that its total cost the public funds, provincial and local together, falls short of £13,00,000 annually. The wider extension of education in India is chiefly a matter of increased expenditure; and any material improvement of its quality is largely dependent upon the same condition.

Its Merits and Defects

It is almost universally admitted that substantial benefits have been conferred upon the people themselves by the advance which has been made in Indian Education within the last fifty years; that knowledge has been spread abroad to an extent formerly undreamed of; that new avenues of employment have been opened in many directions; and that there has been a marked improvement in the character of the public servants now chosen from the ranks of educated natives, as compared with those of the days before schools and Universities had commenced to exercise their elevating influence. But it is also impossible to ignore the fact that criticisms from many quarters are directed at some of the features and results of the system as it exists at present, and that these criticisms proceed especially from friends and well-wishers of the cause of education. Its shortcomings in point of quantity need no demonstration. Four villages out of five are without a school; three boys out of four grow up without education, and only one girl in forty attends any kind of school, In point of quality the main charges brought against the system are to the general effect (i) that the higher education is pursued with too exclusive a view to entering Government service, that its scope is thus unduly narrowed, and that those who fail to obtain employment under Government are ill fitted for other pursuits; (2) that excessive prominence is given to examinations; (3) that the courses of study are too purely literary in character; (4) that the schools and colleges train the intelligence of the students too little, and their memory too much, so that mechanical repetition takes the place of sound learning; (5) that in the pursuit of English education the cultivation of the vernaculars is neglected, with the result that the hope expressed in the Despatch of 1854 that they would become the vehicle for diffusing Western knowledge among the masses is as far as ever from realization.

The Governor General in Council having closely considered the subject, and having come to the conclusion that the existing methods of instruction stand in need of substantial reform, has consulted the Local Governments and Administrations upon the measures necessary to this end, and believes that he has their hearty concurrence in the general lines of the policy which he desires to prescribe. He therefore invites all who are interested in raising the general level of education in India, and in spreading its benefits more widely, to co-operate in giving effect to the principles laid down in this Resolution. With this object in view, an attempt is made in the following paragraphs to review to whole subject in its various aspects, to point out the defects that require correction in each of its branches and to indicate the remedies which in the opinion of the Government of India ought now to be applied.

Education and Government Service

A variety of causes, some historical and some social, have combined to bring about the result that in India, far more than in England, the majority of students who frequent the higher schools and the Universities are there for the purpose of qualifying themselves to earn an independent livelihood; that Government service is regarded by the educated classes as the most assured, the most dignified, and most attractive of all careers, and that the desire on the part of most students to realize these manifold advantages as soon and as cheaply as possible tends to prevent both schools and colleges from filling their proper position as places of liberal education. On these grounds it has often been urged that the higher interests of education in India are injuriously affected by the prevailing system of basing selection for Government service on the school and University attainments of those who come forward as candidates for employment. Some indeed have gone so far as to suggest that educational standards would be indefinitely raised if it were possible to break off these material relations with the State, and to institute separate examinations for the State, and to institute separate examinations for the public service under the control of a special board organized on the model of the English Civil Service Commission.

The Government of India cannot accept this opinion. It appears to them that such examinations, if established admittedly as a substitute for, and not merely as supplementary to, the University course, would necessarily be held in subjects differing from those prescribed by the University; and that two distinct courses of study would thus exist side by side, only one of them leading to Government service. If students attempted to compete in both lines, in strain of excessive examination, already the subject of complaint, would be greatly intensified; while, on the other hand, if the bulk of them were attracted by the prospect of obtaining Government appointments, the result would be the sacrifice of such intellectual improvement as is achieved under the existing system. Success in the Government examination would become the sole standard of culture, the influence of the Universities would decline, the value of their degrees would be depreciated, and the main stream of educational effort would be diverted into a narrow and sordid channel. Such a degradation of the educational ideals of the country could hardly fail to react upon the character of the public service itself. The improved tone of the native officials of the present day dates from, and is reasonably attributed to, the more extended employment of men who have received a liberal education in the Universities, and have imbibed through the influence of their teachers some of the traditions of English public life, nor is there any there any reason to believe that by introducing its own examinations the Government would raise the standard of fitness, or secure better men for the public service than it obtains under the present system. There is a general consensus of opinion among all the authorities consulted that no examining board would do better than the Universities. If a separate examination did no more than confirm the finding of the Universities, it would be obviously superfluous; if it conflicted with that finding, it would be mischievous.

The Government is in the last resort the sole judge as to the best method of securing the type of officers which it requires for it service. It alone possesses the requisite knowledge and experience: and by these tests must its decision be guided. The principle of competition for Government appointments was unknown in India until a few years ago; it does not spring from the traditions of the people, and it is without the safeguards by which its operation is controlled in England. It sets aside, moreover, consideration which cannot be disregarded by a government whose duty it is to reconcile the conflicting claims of diverse recess, rival religions, and varying degrees of intellectual and administrative aptitude and adaptability. For the higher grades of Government service there is no need to have recourse to the system since it is possible in most cases for the Government to accept the various University degrees and distinctions as indicating that their holders possess the amount of knowledge requisite to enable them to fill particular appointments; while in the case of the more technical departments, a scrutiny of subjects taken up by the candidate, and of the degree of success attained in each, will sufficiently indicate how far he possesses the particular knowledge and bent of mind that his duties will demand. The Government of India are of opinion, therefore, that special competitions should, as a general rule, be dispensed with; and that the requisite acquaintance with the laws, rules and regulations of departments may best be attained during probationary service, and tested after a period of such service. In short, the Government of India hold that the multiplication of competitive tests for Government service neither result in advantage to Government nor is consistent with the highest interests of a liberal education. In fixing the educational standards which qualify for appointments, the natural division of primary secondary, and University education should be followed; school and college certificates of proficiency should, so far as possible, be accepted as full evidence of educational qualifications, regard being paid, within the limits of each standard, to their comparative value; and due weight should be attached to the recorded opinions of collegiate and school authorities regarding the proficiency and conduct of candidates during their period of tuition.

The Abuse of Fxaminations

Examinations, as now understood, are believed to have been unknown as an instrument of general education in ancient India, nor do they figure prominently in the Despatch of 1854. In recent years they have grown to extravagant dimensions, and their influence has been allowed to dominate the whole system of education in India, with the result that instruction is confined within the rigid framework of prescribed courses, that all forms of training which do not admit of being tested by written examinations are liable to be neglected, and that both teachers and pupils are tempted to concentrate their energies not so much upon genuine study as upon the questions likely to be set by the examiners. These demoralizing tendencies have been encouraged by the practice of assessing grants to aided schools upon the results shown by examination. This system, adopted in the strength of English precedents, has now been finally condemned in England, while experience in India has proved that, to whatever grade of schools it is applied, it is disastrous in its influence on education and uncertain in its financial effects. It will now be replaced by more equitable tests of efficiency, depending on the number of scholars in attendance, the buildings provided for their accommodation, the circumstances of the locality, the qualifications of the teachers, the nature of the instruction given, and the outlay from other sources, such as fees and private endowments or subscriptions. The Educational Codes of the various Provinces are being revised so as to embody these important reforms, and to relieve the schools and scholars from the heavy burden of recurring mechanical tests. In future there will be only two examinations preceding the University course. The first of these, the primary examination, will mark the completion of the lowest stage of instruction, and will test the degree of proficiency attained in the highest classes of primary schools. But it will no longer be a public examination held at centers to which a number of schools are summoned; it will be conducted by the inspecting officer in the school itself. The second examination will take place at the close of the secondary, usually an Anglo-Vernacular course, and will record the educational attainments of all boys who have completed this course. In both stages of instruction special provision will be made for the award of scholarships.

In giving effect to this change of system, it will be necessary to guard against the danger that the subordinate inspecting agency may misuse the increased discretion entrusted to them. The principles upon which the grant to an aided school is to be assessed must therefore be laid down by each Local Government in terms sufficiently clear to guide the insecting officer in his recommendations; precautions must be taken against the abuse of authority, or the perfunctory performance of the duties of inspection; and those provinces where the application of standards of efficiency other than those afforded by written examinations is a novelty, it will incumbent upon the Education Department, by conferences of inspecting officers and by other means, to secure a reasonable degree of uniformity in the standards imposed. The Governor General in Council does not doubt that the discipline and ability of the educational services will prove equal to maintaining, under the altered conditions, a system of independent and efficient inspection.

Government Control and Private Enterprise

From the earliest days of British rule in India private enterprise has played a great part in the promotion of both English and Vernacular education, and every agency that could be induced to help in the work of imparting sound instruction has always been welcomed by the State. The system of grants-in-aid was intended to elicit support from local resources, and to foster a spirit of initiative and combination for local ends. It is supplemented by the direct action of Government which, speaking generally, sets the standard, and undertakes work to which private effort is not equal, or for which it is not forthcoming. Thus the educational machinery now at work in India comprises not only institutions managed by Government, by District and Municipal Boards, and by Native States, but also institutions under private management, whether aided by Government or by local authorities, or unaided. All of these which comply with certain conditions are classed as public institutions. They number, as already stated, 1,05,306 in all; and over 82,500 are under private management.

The progressive devolution of primary, secondary, and collegiate education upon private enterprise, and the continuous withdrawal of Government from competition therewith was recommended by the Education Commission in 1883, and the advice has been generally acted upon. But while accepting this policy, the Government of India at the same time recognize the extreme importance of the principle that in each branch of education government should maintain a limited number of institutions both as models for private enterprise to follow and in order to uphold a high standard of education. In withdrawing from direct management, it is further essential that Government should retain a general control, by means of efficient inspection, over all public educational institutions.

Primary Education

Primary education is the instruction of the masses, through the vernacular, in such subjects as will best stimulate their intelligence and fit them for their position in life. It was found in 1854 that the consideration of measures to this end had been too much neglected and a considerable increase of expenditure on primary education was then contemplated. The Education Commission recommended in 1883 that "the elementary education of the masses, its provision, extension, and improvement should be that part of the educational system to which the strenuous efforts of the State should be directed in a still larger measure than before." The Government of India fully accept the proposition that the active extension of primary education is one the most important duties of the State. They undertake this responsibility, not merely on general grounds, but because, as Lord Lawrence observed in 1868, "among all the sources of difficulty in our administration and of possible danger to the stability of our Government, there are few so serious as the ignorance of the people." To the people themselves, moreover, the lack of education is now a more serious disadvantage than it was in more primitive days. By the extension of railways the economic side of agriculture in India has been greatly developed, and the cultivator has been brought into contact with the commercial world, and has been involved in transactions in which an illiterate man is at a great disadvantage. The material benefits attaching to education have at the same time increased with the development of schemes for introducing improved agricultural methods, for opening agricultural banks, for strengthening the legal position of the cultivator, and for generally improving the conditions of rural life. Such schemes depend largely for their success upon the influence of education permeating the masses and rendering them accessible to ideas other then those sanctioned by tradition.

Its Extent

How, then do matters stand in respect of the extension among the massess of primary education? The population of British India is over two hundred and forty millions. It is commonly reckoned that fifteen per cent of the population are of school-going age. According to this standard there are more than eighteen millions of boys who ought now to be at school, but of these only a little more than one-sixth are actually receiving primary education. If the statistics are arranged by provinces, it appears that out of a hundred boys of an age to go to school, the number attending primary schools of some kind ranges from between eight and nine in the Punjab and the United Provinces, to twenty-two and twenty-three in Bombay and Bengal. In the census of 1901 it was found that only one in ten of the male population, and only seven in a thousand of the female population were literate. These figures exhibit the vast dimension of the problem, and show how much remains to be done before the proportion of the population receiving elementary instruction can approach the standard recognized as indispensable in more advanced countries.

Its Progress

While the need for education growns with the growth of population, the progress towards supplying, the progress towards supplying it is not now so rapid as it was in former years. In 1870-71 there were 16,473 schools with 607,320 scholars; in 1881-82 there were 82,916 with 2,061,541 scholars. But by 1891-92 these had only increased to 97,109 schools with 28,37,607 scholars, and the figures of 1901-02 (98,538 schools with 32,68,726 scholars) suggest that the initial force of expansion is somewhat on the decline; indeed the last year of the century showed a slight decrease as compared with the previous year. For purposes of exact comparison some allowances have to be made for differences in the basis of the statistics, but their broad effect is not altered by these modifications. Nor has the rate of growth of primary schools has not kept pace with that of secondary schools, in which the number of scholars has considerably more than doubled during the last twenty years. It may be said indeed that the expansion of primary schools has received a check in recent years from the calamities of famine and plague; and it is further impeded by the indifference of the more advanced and ambitious classes to the spread of primary education. These however are minor obstacles, which would soon be swept away if the main difficulty of finding the requisite funds for expending primary education could be overcome.

Its Cost

The expenditure upon primary education does not admit of exact statement, since the cost of the instruction given in the lower classes of secondary schools is not separately shown, nor is the expenditure on the administration and inspection of primary schools capable of separate calculation. But the direct outlay from public funds upon primary schools stands as follows:

	1886-87	*1891-92*	*1901-02*
	R	R	R
From Provincial funds	16,00,239	13,43,343	16,92,514
From Local and Municipal funds	26,07,624	35,86,208	46,10,387
Total	42,07,863	49,29,551	63,02,901

Its Claims

On a general view of the question of Government of India cannot avoid the conclusion that primary education has hitherto received insufficient attention and an inadequate share of the public funds. They consider that it possesses a strong claim upon the sympathy both the Supreme Government and of the Local Governments, and should be make a leading charge upon Provincial revenues; and that in those provinces where it is in a backward condition, its encouragement should be a primary obligation. The Government of India believe that Local Governments are cordially in agreement with them in desiring this extension, and will carry it out to the limits allowed by the financial conditions of each province.

Functions of Local Authorities

In so far as District or Municipal Boards are required to devote their funds to education, primary education should have a predominant claim upon their expenditure. The administration of primary schools by local bodies is already everywhere subject to the general supervision of the Education Department as regards tuitorial matters; but the degree of control differs in different provinces, and where it is most complete, primary education is most advanced. It is impossible to extend that control to financial matters, as there are other objects besides education which have legitimate claims upon local funds. But it is essential, in order to ensure that the claims of primary education receive due attention, that the educational authorities should be heard when resources are being allotted, and that they should have the opportunity of carrying their representations to higher authority in the event of their being disregarded. In future, therefore, so much of the budget estimated of District or Municipal Boards as relates to educational charges will be submitted through the Inspector to the Director of Public Instruction before sanction.

Courses in Primary Schools

The course of instruction in primary schools naturally consists mainly of reading and writing (in the vernacular) and arithmetic. Progress has been made in several parts of India during recent years in the introduction of Kindergarten methods and object lessons. Where these methods have been applied with discretion by competent teachers, who have discarded elaborate forms and foreign appliances, and have used for the purpose of instruction objects familiar to the children in their every-day life, they have been productive of much benefit by imparting grater life and reality to the teaching, and by training the children's faculties and powers of observation. The experience which has been gained of Kindergarten teaching in Madras and Bombay has enabled those provinces to effect steady advances in the system; a complete scheme has been drawn up for Bengal, for the introduction of which teachers are being trained; and a manual of the subject is being prepared in the Punjab, where well designed courses of object lessons are already given, The Government of India look with favour upon the extension of such teaching, where competent teachers are available, as calculated to correct some of the inherent defects of the memory, and to develop a capacity for reasoning from observed facts. Physical exercises also find a place in the primary schools, and should as far as possible be made universal. A series of native exercises, systematizes for the use of schools has been adopted in the Central Provinces, and has been commended to the attention of the other Local Governments.

Rural Primary Schools

The instruction of the masses in much subjects as will best fit them for their position in life involves some differentiation in the courses for rural schools, especially in connection with the attempts which are being made to connect primary teaching with familiar objects. In Bombay a separate course of instruction with standards of its own, is prescribed. In the Central Provinces a system of half-time schools has been successfully established, providing simple courses of instruction in the mornings for the children of agriculturists, who work in the fields during the rest of the day. This system seems worthy of imitation elsewhere; at present a similar experiment made in the Punjab has met with less success. The aim of the rural schools should be, not to impart definite agricultural teaching, but to give to the children a preliminary training which will make them intelligent cultivators, will train them to be observers, thinkers, and experimenters in however humble a manner, and will protect them in their business transactions with the landlords to whom they pay rent and the grain dealers to whom they dispose of their crops. The reading books prescribed should be written in simple language, not in unfamiliar literary style, and should deal with topics associated with rural life. The grammar taught should be elementary, and only native system of arithmetic should be used. The village map should be thoroughly understood; and a most useful course of instruction may be given in the accountant's papers enabling every boy before leaving school to master the intricacies of the village accounts and to understand the demands that may be made upon the cultivator. The Government of India regard it as a matter of the greatest importance to provide a simple, suitable, and useful type of school for the agriculturist, and to foster the demand for it among the population. This and other reforms in primary schools will involve some revision of the pay of primary teachers which varies greatly, and in some provinces is too small to attract or to retain a satisfactory class of men. Thus in Bengal the rates fall as low as 5 per month, while the average pay in the Bombay Presidency rises to 17 and 18. The matter has been under consideration, the improvements will be made where they are most needed.

Secondary Education

The growth of secondly instruction is one of the most striking features in the history of education of India. The number of secondary schools has risen in the last twenty years from 3,916 to 5,493 and that of their pupils from 2,14,077 to 558,378. In all provinces there is considerable eagerness among parents to afford their sons an English education, and the provision and maintenance of a high school are common objects of liberality among all sections of the community. Whether these schools are managed by public authority or by private persons, and whether they receive aid from public funds or not, the Government is bound in the interest of the community to see that the education provided in them in sound. It must, for example, satisfy itself in each case that a secondary school is actually wanted; that its financial stability is assured; that its managing body, where there is one, is properly constituted; that it teaches the proper subjects up to a proper standard; that due provision has been made for the instruction, health, recreation, and discipline of the pupils; that the teachers are suitable as regards character, number and qualifications; and that the fees to be paid will not involve such competition with any existing school as will be unfair and injurious to the interests of education. Such are the conditions upon which alone schools should be eligible to receive grants-in-aid or to send up pupils to compete for or receive pupils in enjoyment of Government scholarships; and schools complying with them will be ranked as "recognized" schools. But this is not sufficient. It is further essential that no institution which fails to conform to the elementary principles of sound education should be permitted to present pupils for the University examinations; and in future admission to the Universities should be restricted to *bona fide* private candidates and to candidates from recognized schools. In this way the schools which enjoy the valuable privilege of recognition will in return give guarantees of efficiency in its wider sense; and the public will be assisted in their choice of schools for their children by knowing that a school which is "recognized" is one which complies with certain definite conditions.

It is frequently urged that the courses of study in secondary schools are too literary in their character. The same complaint is otherwise expressed by saying that the high school courses are almost exclusively preparatory to the University Entrance Examination and take insufficient account of the fact that most of the scholars do not proceed to the University, and require some different course of instruction. Attempts have therefore been made, in pursuance of the recommendation of the Education Commission, to introduce alternative courses, analogous to what is known in England as a "modern side" in order to meet the needs of those boys who are destined for industrial or commercial pursuits. These attempts have not hitherto met with success. The purely literary course, qualifying as it does both for the University and for Government employ, continues to attract the great majority of pupils, and more practical studies are at present but little in request. The Government of India, however, will not abandon their aim. In the present stage of social and industrial development it appears to them essential to promote diversified types of secondary education, corresponding with the varying needs of practical life. Their efforts in this direction will be seconded by that large body of influential opinion which has supported the recommendation of the Universities Commission that the Entrance Examination should no longer be accepted as a qualifying test for Government service.

School Final Examination

But the question what subjects should be taught and by what means proficiency in them should be tested forms only a part of the larger problem of the true object of secondary education. Whatever courses a school may adopt it should aim at teaching them well and intelligently, and at producing pupils who have fully assimilated the knowledge which they have acquired and are capable of more sustained effort than is involved in merely passing an examination. Some test of course there must be; and the Government of India are disposed to think that the best solution of the difficulty will probably be found in adapting to India conditions the system of leaving examinations, held at the conclusion of the secondary course, which has been tried with success in other countries. Such examinations would not dominate the courses of study, but would be adapted to them, and would form the natural culminating point of secondary education: a point not to be reached by sudden and spasmodic effort, by the orderly development of all the faculties of the mind under good and trained teaching. They would be of a more searching character than the present Entrance test, and the certificate given at their close would be evidence that the holder had received, a sound education in a recognized school, that he had borne a good character, and that he had really learnt what the school professed to have taught him. It would thus possess a definite value, and would deserve recognition not only by Government and the universities but also by the large body of private employers who are in want of well-trained assistants in their various lines of activity.

Ethics of Education

The remark has often been made that the extension in India of an education modelled upon European principles, and, so far as Government institutions are concerned, purely secular in its character, has stimulated tendencies unfavourable to discipline, and encouraged the growth of a spirit of irreverence in the rising generation. If any schools for colleges produce this result, they fail to realize the object with which they are established—of promoting the moral no less than the intellectual and physical well-being of their students. It is the settled policy of Government to abstain from interfering with the religious instruction given in aided schools. Many of these maintained by native managers or by missionary bodies of various parts of the Empire, supply religious and ethical instruction to complete the educational training of their scholars. In Government institutions the instruction is, and must continue to be, exclusively secular. In such cases of remedy for the evil tendencies noticed above is to be sought, not so much in any formal methods of teaching conduct by means of moral text-books or primers of personal ethics, as in the influence of carefully selected and trained teachers, the maintenance of a high standard of discipline, the institutions of well-managed hostels, the proper selection of text-books, such as biographies, which teach by example, and above all in the association of teachers and pupils in the common interests of their daily life. Experience has further shown that discipline and conduct are sure to decline when the competition between schools in carried so far as to allow scholars to migrate from one school to another without inquiry being made as to their conduct at their previous school and their reasons for leaving it. Rules have accordingly been framed regulating the admission of scholars to Government and aided schools to another so as to secure that a record of their conduct shall be maintained and the irregularities and breaches of discipline shall not pass unnoticed. These rules will now be extended to all unaided schools which desire to enjoy the benefits of recognition.

Languages in Schools

Except in certain of the larger towns of Madras, where, like Urdu in Northern India, it serves to some extent the purpose of a *lingua franca*, English has no place, and should have no place, the scheme of primary education. It has never been part of the policy of Government to substitute the English language of for the vernacular dialects of the country. It is true that the commercial value which a knowledge of English commands, and the fact that the final examinations of the high schools are conducted in English, cause the secondary schools to be subjected to a certain pressure to introduce prematurely both teaching of English as a language and its use as the medium of instruction; while for the same reasons the study of the vernacular in these schools is liable to be thrust into the background. This tendency however requires to be corrected in the interested of sound education. As a general rule a child should not be allowed to learn English as a language until he has made some progress in the primary stages of instruction and has received a thorough grounding in his mother tongue. It is equally important that when the teaching of English has begun, it should not be prematurely employed as the medium of instruction in other subjects. Much of the practice, too prevalent in Indian schools of committing to memory ill-understood phrases and extracts from text-books or notes, may be traced to the scholars having received instruction through the medium of English before their knowledge of the language was sufficient to enable them to understand what they were taught. The line of division between the use of the vernacular and of English as medium of instruction should, broadly speaking, be drawn at a minimum age of 13. No scholar in a secondary school should, even then, be allowed to abandon the study of his vernacular, which should be kept up until the end of the school course. It the educated classes neglect the cultivation of their own languages, these will assuredly sink to the level of mere colloquial dialects possessing no literature worthy of the name, and no progress will be possible in giving effect to the principle, affirmed in giving effect to the principle, affirmed in the Despatch of 1854, that European knowledge should gradually be brought, by means of the Indian vernaculars, within the reach of all classes of the people.

Female Education

In their efforts to promote female education the Government have always encountered peculiar difficulties arising from the social customs of the people; but they have acted on the view that through female education a "far greater proportional impulse in imparted to the educational and moral tone of the people than by the education of men," and have accordingly treated this branch of education liberally in respect on scholarships and fees. Nevertheless though some advance has been made, female education as a whole is still in a very backward condition. The number of female scholars in public schools in the year 1901-02 was 4,44,470, or less than a ninth of the number of male scholars. The percentage of girls in public schools to the total female population of school-going age has risen from 1.58 in the year 1886-87 to 2.49 in 1901-02. This rate of progress is slow. The Education Commission made recommendations for the extension of female education, and the Government of India hope that with the increase of the funds assigned in aid of education their proposals may be more fully carried out. The measures which are now being taken for further advance include the establishment in important centres of model primary girls' schools, an increase in the number of training schools, with more liberal assistance to those already in existence, and a strengthening of the staff of inspectresses. The direct action of Government will be exerted in cases where that of the municipalities and local boards does not suffice. Nearly one half of the girls in public schools are in mixed boy's-girls' schools. Their attendance along with boys is often beneficial to them, especially in village schools, and nothing in the report of the Commission of 1882 need be taken as indicating that such attendance ought to be discouraged. Great assistance is rendered to the cause of female education generally by missionary effort, and in the higher grades especially by zenana teaching. The Government of India desire that such teaching shall be encouraged by grants-in-aid.

University Education

In founding the Universities of Calcutta, Bombay, and Madras, the Government of India of that day took as their model the type of institution then believed to be best suited of the educational conditions of India, that is to say, the examining University of London. Since then the best educational thought of Europe has shown an increasing tendency to realize the inevitable shortcomings of a purely examining University, and the London University itself has taken steps to enlarge the scope of its operations by assuming tuitional functions. The model, in fact, has parted with its most characteristic features, and has set an example of expansion which cannot fail to react upon the corresponding institutions in India. Meanwhile the Indian experience of the last fifty years has proved that a system which provides merely for examining students in those subjects to which their aptitudes direct them, and does not at the same time compel them to study those subjects systematically under first-rate instruction, tends inevitably to accentuate certain characteristic defects of the Indian intellect : the development of the memory out of all proportion to the other faculties of the mind, the incapacity to observe and appreciate facts, and taste for metaphysical and technical distinctions. Holding it to be the duty of a Government which has made itself responsible for education in India to do everything in its power to correct these shortcomings, the Governor General in Council two years ago appointed a Commission, who the Hon'ble Mr. T. Raleigh as President, to report upon the constitution and working of the Universities, and to recommend measures for elevating the standard of University teaching and promoting the advancement of learning. After full consideration of the report of this Commission, and of the criticisms which it called forth, the Government of India have come to the conclusion that certain reforms in the constitution and management of the Universities are necessary. They propose that the Senates, which from various causes have grown to an unwieldy size, should be reconstituted on a working basis should be defined and regulated, Opportunity will be taken to give a statutory recognition to the privilege of electing members of the Senate which, since 1891, has been conceded by way of experiment to the graduates of the three older Universities. A limit will be placed upon the number of *ex-officio* fellows; and a reduction will be made in the maximum numbers of the Senates so as to restrict nominations to those bodies to be persons well qualified to discharge their responsible duties. Powers will be conferred upon all the Universities to make suitable provision for University teaching. The teaching given in colleges will, instead of being tested mainly or wholly by external examinations, be liable to systematic inspection under the authority of the Syndicate; and the duty of the University not only to demand a high educational standard from any new college that desires to be recommended to Government for affiliation, but also gradually to enforce a similar standard in colleges already affiliated, will be carefully defined. A college applying for affiliation will be required to satisfy the University and the Government that it is under management of a regularly constituted governing body; that its teaching staff is adequate for a courses of instruction undertaken; that the buildings and equipment are suitable, and that due provision is made for the residence and supervision of the students; that, so far as circumstances permit, due provision is made for the residence of some of the teaching staff; that the financial resources of the college are sufficient; that its affiliation, having regard to the provision for students made by neighbouring colleges, will not be injurious to the interests of education or discipline; and that the fees to be paid by the students will not involve competition injurious to the interests of education with any existing college in the same neighbourhood. Colleges already affiliated will be inspected regularly and will be required to show that they continue to comply with the conditions on which the privilege of affiliation is granted. The necessary improvements in the Universities and their affiliated colleges cannot be carried out without financial aid. This the Government of India are prepared to give; and they trust that it will be possible to afford liberal recognition and assistance to genuine effort on the part of the colleges to adapt themselves to the new conditions. They also hope that this increase of expenditure from the public funds may be accompanied by an increase in the aid given to colleges and Universities by private liberality, so that the policy of progressive development which was adopted in 1854 may be consistently followed, and that the influence of the improved Universities may be felt throughout the educational system of the country.

Education of Europeans and Eurasians in India

The problem of the education of European and Eurasian children in India has been anxiously considered by the Government of India on many occasions. As long ago as 1860 Lord Canning wrote that if measures for educating this class were not promptly and vigorously taken in hand, it would grow into a profitless and unmanageable community, a source of danger rather than of strength to the State. Since then repeated efforts have been made both by the Government and by private agency to place the question on a satisfactory basis by establishing schools of various grades, both in the plains and in the hills, by giving liberal grants-in-aid, and by framing a code of regulations applicable to all forms of instruction that the circumstances require. As a result of this action there are now more than 400 schools and colleges for Europeans in India, with nearly 30,000 scholars, costing annually 42½ lakhs, of which 8½ lakhs are contributed by public funds. Notwithstanding the expenditure incurred, recent enquiries have shown that a large proportion of these schools are both financially and educationally in an unsatisfactory condition. Munificent endowments still support flourishing schools in certain places; but in some cases these endowments have been reduced by mismanagement; and too many of the schools are unable to support themselves in efficiency upon the fees of the scholars and the grants made by Government on the scale hitherto in force. Their most conspicuous want is well qualified teachers, especially in schools for boys; and this cannot be met so long as their financial position precludes them from offering to the members of their staff fair salaries, security of tenure, and reasonable prospects of advancement. The Government in its turn is interested in maintaining a sufficient supply of well educated Europeans to fill some of the posts for which officers are recruited in India; while without efficient schools the domiciled community must degenerate rapidly in this country. The Government of India are taking steps to ascertain and to supply the chief defects in the system. A single Inspector in each of the provinces in being charged especially with the duty of inspecting European schools; a Training College for teachers in these schools is to be established at Allahabad, and stipends are to be provided for the students; a register of teachers will be formed and, in future, no one will be employed without proper tuitional qualifications. The systems, both of grants-in-aid and of scholarships, are being revised on a more liberal basis; and more intelligent methods of testing efficiency are to be substituted for the rigid system of departmental examinations which has hitherto prevailed. Measures will also be taken to secure the proper administration of endowments and to enforce sound methods of financial control in those schools which depend upon Government for assistance.

Chiefs' Colleges

During the last thirty years the idea that the changed conditions of Indian life demand a change in the traditional modes of education, has found acceptance amongst the ruling Chiefs of Native States. Chiefs' Colleges have been established, of which the most important are those at Ajmer, Rajkot, and Lahore, where some of the features of the English public school system have been reproduced, with the object of fitting young Chiefs and Nobles physically, morally, and intellectually for the responsibilities that lie before them. Convinced of the great importance of promoting this object, His Excellency the Veceroy has closely examined the organization and conduct of these colleges, which appeared to admit of improvement and has placed before the ruling Chiefs proposals of a comprehensive character for their reform. An increase will be made in the number of teachers of high qualifications to be engaged upon the staff; and in regulating the studies and discipline of the colleges, the aim kept in view throughout will be the preparation of the sons of ruling Chiefs for the duties which await them, on lines which will combine that advantages of Western knowledge with loyalty to the traditions and usages of their families or States. The proposals have been received by the Chiefs with satisfaction; the interest of the aristocratic classes has been universally aroused in the scheme; and the institution of the Imperial Cadet Corps, which will in the main be recruited from these colleges, will assist to keep this interest alive. The Governor General in Council confidently hopes that the reforms now in course of execution will result in giving a great impetus to the causes of education among the Indian nobility.

Technical Education

Technical education in India has hitherto been mainly directed to the higher forms of instruction required to train men for Government service as engineers, mechanicians, electricians, overseers, surveyors, revenue officers or teachers in schools, and for employment in railway workshops, cotton-mills, and mines. The institutions which have been established for these purposes, such as the Engineering Colleges at Rurki, Sibpur, and Madras, the Colleges of Science at Poona, the Technical Institute at Bombay, and the Engineering School at Jabulpur, have done and are doing valuable work, and their maintenance and further development are matters of great importance. The first call for fresh effort is now towards the development of Indian industries, and especially of those in which native capital may be invested. Technical instruction directed to this object must rest upon the basis of a preliminary general education of simple and practical kind, which should be clearly distinguished from the special teaching that is to be based upon it, and should as a rule be imparted in schools of the ordinary type. In fixing the aim of the technical schools, the supply or expansion of the existing Indian markets in of superior importance to the creation of new export trades, and a clear line should be drawn between educational effort and commercial enterprise. As a step towards providing men qualified to take a leading part in the improvement of Indian industries, the Government of India have determined to give assistance in the form of scholarships to selected students to enable them to pursue a course of technical education under supervision in Europe or America. The hope that the technical schools of India may in time produce a regular supply of young men qualified to take advantage of such facilities, and that the goodwill and interest of the commercial community may be enlisted in the selection of industries to be studied, in finding the most suitable students for foreign training, and in turning their attainments to practical account upon their return to this country. The experience which has been gained in Japan and Siam of the results of sending young men abroad for study justifies the belief that the system will also be beneficial to Indian trade.

Schools of Art

There are four Schools of Art in British India,—at Madras, Bombay, Calcutta, and Lahore, The aims to be pursued in them, and the methods proper to those aims, have been the subject of much discussion during recent years. The Government of India are of opinion that the true function of Indian Schools of Art is the encouragement of Indian Art and Art industries; and that in so far as they fail to promote these arts or industries, or provide a training that is dissociated from their future practice, or are utilized as commercial venture, they are conducted upon erroneous principles. Their first object should be to teach such arts or art industries as the pupil intends to pursue when he has left the school. Examples of the arts which may thus be taught to those who will practise them professionally in future, or to drawing masters are : designing (with special reference to Indian arts and industries), drawing, painting, illumination, modelling, photography, and engraving. The Art industries taught in Schools of Art should be such as are capable of being carried on in the locality, and in which improvement can be effected by instructing pupils or workmen by means of superior appliances, methods, or designs. Instruction in these arts or art industries should be directed to their expansion through the improvement of the skill and capacity of the pupil or workman, but it should not be pushed to the point of competing with local industries, of doing within the school what can equally well be done outside or of usurping the sphere of private enterprise. The schools should not be converted into shops, nor should the officers of the Education Department be responsible for extensive commercial transactions; but samples of the wares produced may legitimately be kept, for sale or for orders, and may be exhibited in public museums. A register of the workmen or pupils trained in school should be kept, with the object of enabling orders which may be received to be placed with advantage. The teaching should be in the hands of experts, trained as a rule in Indian colleges or in Art Schools. The specialization of a limited number of arts and art industries in the several schools should be preferred to the simultaneous teaching of a large number. Free admission and scholarships should, as a general rule, be discouraged, and should gradually be replaced by payment of fees; but this is compatible with giving necessary assistance to promising pupils, and with the payment of wages to students as soon as their work becomes of value.

Industrial Schools

Industrial schools are intended to train intelligent artisans of foremen, and to further or develop those local industries which are capable of expansion by the application of improved methods or implements. Schools of this type are not numerous, nor have they at present succeeded in doing much to promote the growth of industries. A recent enumeration gives their total number as 123, with 8,405 pupils in attendance, and the number of different trades taught as 48. Some are conducted by Government, either as separate institutions, or attached to Schools of Art, while others are managed by local authorities or by private persons under a system of grants-in-aid. Their shortcomings are obvious and admitted. A large proportion of the pupils who attend them have no intention of practising the trade they learn, but pass into clerical and other employments, using the industrial schools merely in order to obtain that general education which they could acquire in ordinary schools at less cost to the State, but at greater cost to themselves. Even for those who do intend to follow the trades taught in the industrial schools, it is feared that in some cases the teaching given does not provide a training of a sufficiently high standard to enable them to hold their own with artizans who have learnt their craft in the bazaar. The industries selected are frequently not those which are locally of most importance, and there is an undue predominance of carpentry and blacksmiths' work amongst them.

An attempt will now be made to remedy these defects. The Government of India do not expect a large immediate increase in the number of industrial schools, and they desire rather to encourage experiment than to prescribe fixed types for this form of education. Admission will be confined to those boys who are known by their caste or occupation to be likely to practise in after-life the handicrafts taught in the schools, and the courses of study will be so ordered as not to lend themselves to the manufacture of clerks, but to bear exclusively upon carefully selected industries. A distinction will be drawn between those types of school which will be suitable for the large centres of industry, where capital is invested on a great scale and the need of trained artisans is already recognized by the employers, and those adapted to places where hand industries prevail and where the belief in the value of technical training has yet to make its way. In the former the prospects are favourable for the establishment of completely equipped trade schools, such as are found in other countries; in the latter, search has still to be made for the kind of institution which will take root in Indian soil. Suggestions for experiment based upon observation of the habits and tendencies of Indian artisans have been placed before the Local Governments. They will be pursued further under the advice of skilled experts in particular industries.

Commercial Education

A system of education intended to impart "useful and practical knowledge, suitable to every station in life," cannot be considered complete without ampler provision than exists at present in India for school training definitely adapted to commercial life. There is at present no University course of training of a specialized description for business men; in the field of secondary education the establishment of examinations and the inclusion of commercial subjects in the optional lists of subjects for examination have outstripped the progress made in the organization of courses of instruction. The beginnings which have been made at Bombay, Lucknow, Calicut, Amritsar, and elsewhere, show that the attempt to provide suitable courses meets with encouraging response; and increased attention will now be given to the extension of such teaching in large centres of commerce and population. The proper development of the teaching demands that it should be adapted to Indian needs, and should not be based merely upon English text-books. The London Chamber of Commerce examinations supply a convenient test for those pupils (especially Europeans) who are likely to proceed to England. Commercial courses, leading up to this or other examinations, are now being placed upon an equality with purely literary courses as a qualification for Government service. But their chief aim will be to supply practical training for those who are to enter business houses either in a superior or subordinate capacity. Registers will be kept of the pupils who have been so trained, and endeavours will be made to find employment for them by communication with Chambers of Commerce and mercantile firms. The Government of India trust that they may look for the co-operation of the mercantile community in framing suitable courses of instruction, and in giving preference in selecting employees to those who have qualified themselves by directing their studies towards those subjects which will be useful in commercial life.

Agricultural Education

For a country where two-thirds of the population are dependent for their livelihood on the produce of the soil, it must be admitted that the provision for agricultural education in India is at present meagre and stands in serious need of expansion and reorganization. At Poona in Bombay and Saidapet in Madras there are Colleges teaching a three years' course, which is fairly satisfactory at Poona, though the staff is hardly strong enough, while at Saidapet the training is somewhat defective on the practical side. In the United Provinces the school at Cawnpore has a two years' course, especially intended for the training of subordinate revenue officials in which direction it has done and is doing very good work, but the teaching staff is weak and the equipment inadequate. At Nagpur a school with a two years' course gives good practical education, and special arrangements are made for a vernacular class for sons of landowners and others, Bengal has added to the Engineering College at Sibpur, near Calcutta, classes which give a two years' agricultural training to students who have taken their B.A. degree at the University or have passed the F.E. standard in the in the college; but the conditions are not such as to admit of a thoroughly satisfactory course. In the Punjab and Burma no attempt has as yet been made to teach agriculture. In all these institutions instruction is given almost entirely in English, and until advanced text-books have been compiled in the vernacular this must continue to be the case in all but the most elementary classes.

At present, therefore, while the necessity for developing the agricultural resources of the country is generally recognized, India possesses no institution capable of imparting a complete agricultural education. The existing schools and colleges have not wholly succeeded, either in theory or in practice. They have neither produced scientific experts, nor succeeded in attractive members of the land-holding classes to qualify themselves as practical agriculturists. Both of these defects must be supplied before any real progress can be looked for. In the first place an organization must be created by which men qualified to carry on the work of research, and to raise the standard of teaching, can be trained in India itself. Before agriculture can be adequately taught in the vernacular, suitable text-books must be produced, and this can only be done by men who have learnt the subject in English. The Government of India have therefore under their consideration a scheme for the establishment of an Imperial Agricultural College in connection with an Experimental Farm and Research Laboratory, to be carried on under the general direction of the Inspector General of Agriculture, at which it is intended to provide a thorough training in all branches of agricultural science combined with constant practice in farming work and estate management. In addition to shorter courses for those students who are intended for lower posts, there will be courses of instruction extending to five years which will qualify men to fill posts in the Department of Agriculture itself, such as those of Assistant Directors, Research Experts, Superintendents of Farms, Professors, Teachers, and Managers of Court of Wards of Encumbered Estates.

It is hoped that a demand may arise among the landowning classes for men with agricultural attainments and that the proposed institution may succeed in meeting that demand. Arrangements will also be made to admit to the higher courses those who have undergone preliminary training at the Provincial colleges and thereby to exercise upon those colleges an influence tending gradually to raise their standard of efficiency.

Training Colleges

If the teaching in secondary schools is to be raised to a higher level,—if the pupils are to be cured of their tendency to rely upon learning notes and text-books by heart, if, in a word, European knowledge is to be diffused by the methods proper to it,—then it is most necessary that the teachers should themselves be trained in the art of teaching. Even in England divided counsels have till recent times prevented due progress from being made with this most essential condition of the reform of secondary education. The Indian Education Commission referred to the conflict of opinion upon this fundamental principle, and to the diversity of practice which prevailed; and while hesitating to lay down a general rule requiring secondary teachers to be trained, recommended "as an inadequate, but the only practicable alternative," that an examination in the principles and practice of teaching should be instituted, success in which should hereafter be made a condition of permanent employment as a teacher in any secondary school. Other and larger views of the subject are now in the ascendant, and the Government of India are glad to know that the principle of providing training institutions for secondary teachers meets with universal acceptance among the Local Governments and Administrations. There already exist at Madras, Kurseong, Allahabad, Lahore, and Jubbulpore, institutions in which students are trained for service as teachers in the highest classes of secondary schools, Such students have either passed the Entrance or the Intermediate Examination of the University or are graduates. These institutions have done good work, and the time has come to extend the system to the provinces where it does not exist, notably Bombay, and to endeavour to create a supply of trained teachers which shall be adequate to the needs of the secondary schools throughout the country. Not only must the supply be increased, but the quality of the training given must be improved.

The details of the measures taken with the object are already engaging the attention of the various Local Governments. But the general principles upon which the Government of India desire to see to training institutions developed are these. An adequate staff of well-trained members of the Indian Educational Service is required, and for this purpose it will be necessary to enlist more men of ability and experience in the work of the agricultural practice of peasantry by agency of village school masters imbued with a smattering of scientific theory. They serve the more limited and practical purpose of supplying the village schools with teachers whose stock-in-trade is not mere book learning, and whose interests have been aroused in the study of rural things, so that they may be able to connect their teaching with the objects which are familiar to the children in the country schools. Various plans are being tried, such as drafting the teachers from the normal school to a Government farm and training them there for six months, or giving a continuous course at the normal school itself by means of lectures combined with practice in cultivating plots of ground or school gardens. Experience will show which methods work best in different provinces, and it is not necessary to pronounce in favour of one plan to the exclusion of others.

Hostels

Great importance is attached by the Government of India to the provision of hostels or boarding-houses, under proper supervision, in connection with colleges and secondary schools. These institutions protect the students who live in them from the moral dangers of life in large towns; they provide common interests and create a spirit of healthy companionship; and they are in accord not only with the usage of English public schools and colleges but also with the ancient Indian tradition that the pupil should live in the charge of his teacher. Missionary bodies have joined with alacrity in the extension of this movement. The credit for the hostel established in India is claimed by the Madras Christian College, which still continues to add others; and a striking example of the success of the residential system is to be found in the Muhammadan Anglo-Oriental College at Aligarh. The Local Governments have been active both in founding hostels for Government colleges and schools and in aiding their provision. In Madras at the present time a large hostel, the result of private munificence aided by Government, is nearing completion; in

Bombay, Calcutta, Allahabad, and Lahore signs are to be seen of the growth of similar institutions. The returns for the year 1901-02 showed that there were then 1,415 hostels, with 47,302 boarders; while the extent to which they derive their funds from sources independent of Government is made clear by the fact that more than two-fifths of boarders were in unaided hostels, and that of the total expenditure upon all hostels, ten lakhs were derived from subscriptions and endowments, as compared with two lakhs sixty-three thousand rupees from public funds. The Government of India believe that the system of hostels, if extended with due regard for its essential principles, which include direct supervision by resident teachers, is destined to exercise a profound influence on student life in India and to correct many of the shortcomings which now attend our educational methods.

Inspecting Staff

The reduction in the number of examinations which is being carried out, and the general raising of educational standards which is contemplated, demand an increased stringency in inspection and a substantial strengthening of the inspecting staff. In the Despatch of 1854, it was enjoined that inspectors should "conduct, or assist at, the examination of the scholars... and generally, by their advice, aid the managers and schoolmasters in conducting colleges and schools of every description throughout the country." The latter function is no less important than the former, and calls for wider educational knowledge, greater initiative, and the exercise of a wise discertion in adapting means to ends. It is task which will provide worthy occupation for men who are imbued with the best traditions in the matter of school management, and it is through the influence of such men alone that there is any real prospect of its accomplishment. Their assistance can only be enlisted by increasing the cadre of the Indian Educational Service. Some additions in the lower branches of the inspectorate are also needed in order to provide for a complete system of inspection *in situ* instead of collective examinations. The Government of India do not require that inspectors should be precluded from having recourse to examination as a means of inspection; but they desire that inspectors should be much more than mere examiners. They should not only judge the results of teaching, but should guide and advise as to its methods; and it is essential that they should be familiar with the schools in their ordinary working conditions. The work of schools be defined with reference rather to the courses of instruction followed than to the examinations that have to be passed, and rigid uniformity either in the arrangement of subjects or in the classification of the scholars should be avoided, free play being given to the proper adaptation of the working of the schools to their local circumstances.

Administration

The more active and progressive policy that is now being adopted in educational matters will throw a constantly increasing burden of work and responsibility upon the Directors of Public Instruction. The wider the influence that these officers exercise, the more essential is it that they should not be prevented by the growth of their routine duties from making frequent tours of inspection and thus acquiring a direct and intimate knowledge of the educational conditions of their provinces and the circumstances of the numerous schools under their control. Four officers are therefore to be added to the Indian Educational Service, in order to provide the Directors of Public Instruction in Madras, Bombay, Bengal, and the United Provinces with assistants upon whom part of their duties may be devolved. Arrangements will also be made for periodical meetings of the Directors in Conference in order that they may compare their experience of the results of different methods of work, and may discuss matters of common interest.

Educational Services

The Education Department is divided into the superior and the subordinate services. The superior service consists of two branches, called respectively the Indian and the provincial Educational Services, of which the former is recruited in England and the latter in India. The opportunities and responsibilities which work in the Department brings to an officer of this service give scope for a wide range of intellectual activity. Such an officer takes an active part in the profoundly interesting experiment of introducing an Eastern people to Western knowledge and modern methods of research; he comes into contact with the remains of an earlier civilization and the traditions of ancient learning; he can choose between the career of the professor and that of an educational administrator; and in either capacity he has great opportunity of exercising personal influence and promoting the best interests of genuine education. In order that members of the Indian Educational Service may keep themselves abreast of the advances which are now being made in other countries in the science of education, facilities are given to them while on furlough of study the theory and practice of the branches of education both in England and in other parts of the world. The part, already considerable, that is taken by natives of India in the advancement of their countrymen in modern methods of intellectual training will, it is hoped, assume an even greater importance in the future. If the reforms now contemplated in the whole system of instruction are successfully carried out, it may be expected that the Educational Service will offer steadily increasing attractions to the best educational talent. Where the problems to be solved are so complex, and the interests at stake so momentous, India is entitled to ask for the highest intellect and culture that either English or Indian seats of learning can furnish for her needs.

Conclusion

The Governor General in Council has now passed in review the history and progress of Western education under British rule in India, the objects which it seeks to accomplish, and the means which it employs. It has been shown how indigenous methods of instruction were tried and found wanting; how in 1854 the broad outlines of a comprehensive scheme of national education were for the first time, determined; how the principles then accepted have been consistently followed ever since; how they were affirmed by the Education Commission of 1882, and how they are now being further extended and developed, in response to the growing needs of the combined efforts of the Government of India and the provincial Governments. The system of education thus extended makes provision in varying degrees for all forms of intellectual activity that appeal to a civilized community. It seeks to satisfy the aspirations of students in the domains of learning and research; it supplies the Government with a succession of upright and intelligent public servants; it trains workers in every branch of commercial enterprise that has made good its footing in India; it attempts to develop the resources of the country and to stimulate and improve indigenous arts and industries; it offers to all classes of society a training suited to their position in life; and for these ends it is organized on lines which admit of indefinite expansion as the demand for education grows and public funds or private liberality afford a larger measure of support. It rests with the people themselves to make a wise use of the opportunities that are offered to them and to realise that education in the true sense means something more than the acquisition of so much positive knowledge, something higher than the mere passing of examinations, that it aims at the progressive and orderly development of the faculties of the mind, that it should form character and teach right conduct—that it is, in fact, a preparation for the business of life. If this essential truth is overlooked or imperfectly appreciated, the labours of the Government of India to elevate the standard of education in this country and to inspire it with higher ideals will assuredly fail to produce substantial and enduring results. Those labours have been undertaken in the hope they will command the hearty support of the leaders of native thought and of the great body of workers in the field of Indian Education. On them the Governor General in council relies to carry on and complete a task which the Government can do no more than begin.

5

The Swadeshi Movement and Growth of Education (1905-1920)

A. The Swadeshi Movement

Effect of the Swadeshi Movement

The educational policy of Lord Curzon had displeased the national leaders. His educational reforms were not wholly immune from certain ulterior political motives. Hence it was natural on the part of national leaders not to have overlooked it. The sequel of the warfare between Russia and Japan had evidently proved that Asiatic civilisation too held a unique position in the world. I gave much inspiration to the national sentiments of the Indian people. The natural result of it was that a keen curiosity was engendered in the hearts of the Indians to make a close study of the Japanese system of education. A Government report on Japanese system of education was published and many Indian scholars went to Japan for the sake of education. Besides this Report, another periodical Report "The Education System of Japan', was also published from Calcutta in the year 1906. The literature of these reports inspired the Indian youth with revolutionary sentiments and they agitated to bring about educational reforms in the country. India, during this period was much influenced by the events occurring in other parts of the Continent. In 1905, the Constitutional monarchy had been established in Persia. The movements for representative government were gradually heading towards success in Turkey and China. Some time prior to that, the Anti-Partition Movement had been rampant in Bengal. All these movements broke out in the form of the 'Swadeshi Movement' in the country. The Bengal province pioneered the Movement in 1905 and eventually the entire country came under its influence.

The fundamental principle underlying the Movement was the complete boycott of foreign goods. The consumption of the country made goods in place of foreign goods diverted the attention of the people towards industrial education and consequently the high-ranking leaders of the country began to imagine and form plans for the propagation of national education. This Movement led to the establishment of body known as 'The National Council of Education'. The prominent leaders of this Movement were Sir Gurudas Banerjee, Rash Behari Ghosh and Dr. Rabindra Nath Tagore. The Council chalked out a detailed scheme for national education ranging from primary to University education. The Council also founded a National College at Calcutta the first principal where of was Sri Aurobindo. A subscription of lakhs of rupees was raised within a short space of time. Besides, a technical Institute, ultimately developing itself into the Jadabpur College of Engineering and Technology, was founded at Calcutta, Soon there spread a network of innumerable national schools throughout Bengal. In these schools, education in useful subjects was imparted through the medium of the vernacular language. In other parts of the country too, several schools were started. Again, some *Gurukulas* too were established for the sake of regenerating and reviving ancient Indian culture and civilization.

As a matter of fact, it was the first movement of its kind directed to bring about reforms in the educational system of the country. But dullness crept into the movement for national education with the slackness in the Swadeshi Movement. The National College was closed down and with it other institutions too were wiped out of existence gradually. Only the Jadabpur Technical College survived as a souvenir of the glorious Movement. Its existence is an eloquent proof of the fact that there was an extreme demand of industrial education in the country at that time. In reality, this movement itself was politico-economic in nature. A strong rising tide of educational reform had, as it were, overwhelmed the entire country. The Vedic hymns chanted by the pupils in the Gurukulas at Vrindaban and Haridwar sent forth the massage of ancient glory of Indian while the Brahmacharis of Shanti Niketan were learning at the feet of the supreme poet-philosopher Ravindra Nath Tagore Oriental philosophy—one of the most famous philosophic systems of the world. G.K Gokhale's famous speeches in the Imperial Legislative Council were voicing the opinion of Indian masses.

Another important event of the period in the establishment of the Muslim League in 1906. It was founded by certain wealthy and educated Mohammedans with a view to safeguarding their political and economic interests. Lord Minto succeeded to Lord Curzon as Viceroy of India. He engendered communal feelings amongst the two important races of the country—Hindus and Muslims. The promulgation of Minto-Morely Reforms in 1909, besides bringing about constitutional changes in the political and social conditions, also influenced the contemporary educational system of the country. The policy of communalism found a great patron in the British Government. Consequently, the Muslim leaders raised an agitation for the sake of the establishment of separate schools, university and reservation of seats for Muslim teachers in Government institutions. Thus it is evident that educational atmosphere was vitiated by communalism proving an execrable curse later on.

Gokhale's Bill

Owing to the educational policy adopted by the Government in 1904, primary education made considerable progress in the country; but the demand for it was increasing from day to day with the growing population of India. The Swadeshi Movement and the resultant political awakening had drawn the attention of the country to an important issue *i.e.* the Education of the general masses, and made the people keenly interested in it. At that time the average literacy in the country was 6 per cent, a very low average indeed—and out of all the children of school-going age only 23.8 per cent male children and 2.7 female children attended schools. Under these circumstances Sri Gopal Krishna Gokhale invited the attention of the Government and public towards this direction and put forth the demand of free and compulsory primary education before the Government. He had warned the countrymen that illiterate and uneducated countries could never keep pace with other enlightened ones in the race of civilisation and culture. Therefore, it was of paramount necessity that the general masses should be educated compulsorily. His Highness of Baroda had made primary education compulsory in his own state in 1906. This revolutionary step inspired people in other parts of the country. On march 19th, 1910, Sri Gokhale moved the following Resolution in the Imperial Legislative Council:

"That this Council recommends that a beginning should be made in the direction of making elementary education free and compulsory throughout the country, and that a mixed commission of officials and non-officials be appointed at an early date to frame definite proposals".

According to the contents of the Bill, it was suggested that free and compulsory education be introduced for the boys between the age of 6 and 10 especially in those areas where 33 per cent male children had already been receiving education. Sri Gokhale had drawn a very elaborate picture of the educational condition of that time and put forth concrete suggestions for its reform. As regards expenditure of the schools, he suggested that it should be shared between the local bodies and the Government in the proportion of 1:2. He put the demand for the appointment of a separate Secretary for education along with the suggestion that a statement describing the progress of education should be included in the Budget Statement.

The resolution was, however, withdrawn by Gokhale on as assurance vouchsafed by the Government about a careful examination of the problem. Still after that, expected progress in primary education was not made. A Department of Education was created under the Government of India in 1910; but education remained entirely in the hands of Provincial Governments. Prior to 1910, education was under Home Department of the Government of India. The Department of Land and Health were also subjoined to Education Department.

Seeing the slow progress in the expansion of elementary education, Gokhale again introduced his private Bill of historic importance an March 16th, 1911. The Bill was purely private in nature, simple and humble. The object of the Bill was "to provide for the gradual introduction of principle of compulsion into the elementary educational system of the country." In the first place, the Act was to be applied to the areas of those local Boards where boys and girls were already attending the schools in certain specific percentage. This percentage was to be determined by the Governor-General-in-Council. Further the Local Boards were fully empowered to enforce the Act only subject to the previous approval of the Government concerned. The Local Boards were permitted to levy educational cess. It was made incumbent on the guardians of the boys between 6 and 10 years of age to place their wards in schools. This rule was later on to be applied to girls as well. The provision was made for the punishment of the guardians if they failed to comply with the attendance rules with regard to their wards. The bill also referred to the grants-in-aid to be sanctioned by the Provincial Governments to the Local Boards for the expenditure on the maintenance of the schools. In fact, the economic aspect of the Bill was to be held responsible for its acceptance or rejection by the Government. Therefore, Gokhale tried to clear it in the prefatory part of the Bill the following words:

"It is obvious that whole working of this Bill must depend, in the first instance, upon the share, which the Government is prepared to bear of the cost of compulsory education, wherever it is introduced. I find that in England, the Parliamentary grants cover about two-thirds of the total expenditure on elementary schools. In Scotland, it amounts to more than that proportion whereas in Ireland it meets practically the whole cost. I think that we are entitled to ask that, in India, at least two-third of the total expenditure should be borne by the State."[1]

The Bill having been prepared, it was cultivated among the local governments, universities and some private bodies with a view to inviting opinions on it. At the conclusion on a fierce debate on the Bill for two days in the Council, it was ultimately turned down by 38 votes to 13. The opposition came from the directions of the government officials and some landlords who in order to prove their allegiance to their white masters, dealt a severe blow to the educational progress of the country. it is a deplorable thing that Government did not design to accept even such an humble Bill. The arguments directed against the Bill were really quite meaningless and preposterous. For instance it was argued by the opposition that the step was unnecessary and immature. It was also urged that public opinion was running counter to the Principle of compulsion in education and that it was against educational principles as well. Further, provincial governments were quoted as being against compulsory education. Ultimately on the pretexts that the educated class was against it, that local Boards would not levy further cess for the purpose and that the system involved many a difficulty from the viewpoint of organisation and administration, the Government turned the Bill down outright. Sri Gokhale who was, however determined not to give in, wanted it to be submitted to a Select Committee of 15 members, but all in vain. Sir Harcourt Butler, a Government spokesman, was the chief antagonist of the Bill. He argued that the country was not prepared for that reform. Gokhale put forth his incontrovertible arguments through his fluent oratory but he had to meet disappointment, yet it was a glorious defeat.

There is, however, no doubt about the fact that in spite of the rejection of the Bill, government followed practically the principles embodied in the Bill the Gokhale. Most of the educated people of India began to realize the necessity of free and compulsory education. A Department a Education was created under the Central Government. The movement for elementary education advanced rapidly in the country. In N.W. Frontier Province, the elementary education was made free in 1912. In United Provinces, the Punjab, Assam and Central Province too it was introduced widely at a nominal rate of fees.

Educational Policy of Government of India in 1913

The demand for education growing popular from day to day, Government felt it necessary to revise their educational policy. Having rejected the Bill promulgated by Sri Gokhale, the Government considered it imperative to announce their own policy. Again, following the Delhi Durbar on December 12, 1911, certain important administrative changes took place in the country. The annulment of partition of Bengal was announced by the King himself. Therefore, in order to make comprehensive survey and study in the field of education, the Government of India passed the Resolution of Educational Policy on February 21st, 1913.

The following are the recommendations of the Resolution:

(i) There should be sufficient expansion of lower primary schools, where along with education in the three R's, children should be taught drawing, knowledge of the village map, nature study and physical exercise.

(ii) Simultaneously upper primary schools should be opened at the proper places and if need be, the lower primary schools should be raised to the status of upper primary schools.

(iii) The local Boards schools should be established in place of private aided schools and that the Maktabs and Pathshalas should adequately be subsidised. The inspection and management of private schools should be made more efficient.

(iv) In most of the parts of India, it is not practicable that separate curricula for rural and urban schools can be prescribed, but in the urban schools there is sufficient scope for teaching Geography and school excursion etc.

(v) The teachers may well be drawn from the same class to which students belong. They should have passed vernacular middle examination and received one years's training. Provision should be made for repetition and improvement courses for the teachers of primary education during vacations.

(vi) A trained teacher should get a salary not less than Rs.12 per month. Again there should be provision for his increment in salary, pension and provident fund.

(vii) No teacher should be required to teach more than 50 students. The number of students under one teacher should generally range between 30 and 40.

(viii) Improvement should be made in the condition of Middle or Secondary Vernacular Schools and their number should be increased.

(ix) Schools should be housed in sanitary, spacious but inexpensive buildings.

(x) Besides elementary education, emphasis was laid on the education of women too. Suggestions were put forth concerning special curriculum of practical utility for girls. It was clearly stated in the Resolution that too much importance should not be attached to examinations in the education of girls. Number of women teachers and inspectors should also be increased.

(xi) Complete withdrawal of the State from the sphere of secondary education was criticised in the Resolution. Besides further establishment of state institutions was proposed to be stopped. Existing institution should continue to serve as models and proper grants-in-aid should be sanctioned to private institutions. An improvement in the mode of examination and curriculum also recommended.

(xii) The Resolution provided for the expansion in university education. the existence of 5 universities and 185 colleges was considered to be insufficient in view of the vast need and demands of the country. Besides this, owing to certain defects having crept into the regulation in force since 1904 whereby universities had been empowered to grant recognition to high schools, the Resolution suggested that universities and high schools should be assigned distinct spheres of activities. Hence the universities should be relieved of the responsibility of granting recognition to high schools and they should be kept under provincial governments. The establishment of teaching universities was suggested by emphasising the separation of the two functions of the universities—teaching and examining. Again recommendations were made concerning the inclusion of subjects of industrial importance in the curriculum and provision of facilities to the students desirous of prosecuting research work. Further the Resolution put forth certain valuable suggestions pertaining to the character formation of students and hostel-life.

Criticism

When we consider the above-mentioned suggestions and recommendations, it becomes quite evident that the controversy pertaining to quality and quantity which had heretofore confined itself to secondary and collegiate education had entered now the sphere of primary education too. It is however, a truism that whereas the Government desired improvement in the quality of education, it was also mindful, as is clear from the suggestions of the resolution, of its expansion.

These suggestions are significant enough in the fields of secondary and university education. The credit of all-round development in education between the years 1913 and 1921, can legitimately be claimed by the Resolution. It is true that outbreak of World War 1st in 1914 and India's participation in it forced the suggestion of the Resolution 1913 to achieve only a partial success. At the close of war in 1917, the Government of India appointed a Commission to inquire into the educational conditions of the Calcutta University. This Commission holds a very important place in the history of Indian education.

B. The Calcutta University Commission (1917)

Appointment

Prior to the outbreak of the World War I, the Government of India had proposed to appoint University Commission under the presidentship of Lord Haldane, but on account of the War and reluctance of Lord Haldane to accept presidentship, it could not be materialized. At the conclusion of War in 1917, the Government appointed a small but powerful Commission. The object of the Commission was "to inquire into the condition and prospects of the University of Calcutta and to consider the question of a constructive policy in relation to the question it presents."

On September 14, 1917, the Government of India, through a Resolution appointed the Calcutta University Commission, Dr. Michael Sadler, the Vice-chancellor of the Leeds University, was appointed its Chairman. This is why it goes by the name of 'Sadler Commission' in the history. Among other members of the Commission, were Dr. Gregory, Prof. Ramsay Muir, Sir Hartog, Mr.Hornell, Dr. Zia-Uddin Ahmed and Sir Asutosh Mookerjee. Though the Commission had been appointed to inquire into the educational condition of the Calcutta University, yet it was provided that it could examine the working of other Universities as well for the sake of obtaining comparative knowledge of the Universities. That is why the Commission possesses in India-wide significance and application. After a labour of well-nigh 17 months the Commission submitted its report in the year 1919. The report consists of 13parts and presents a very comprehensive, significant and constructive account of Secondary, Collegiate and university education in India. It, however, does not touch primary education at all; but secondary education which forms the base of University education has thoroughly been surveyed and examined.

Recommendations

In the opinion of the Commission, there was a necessity of fundamental changes in the secondary education for the sake of improving University education. Hence the Commission put forth following suggestions in this respect:

(i) Intermediate classes should be separated from Universities and curriculum spreading over three years should be prescribed for the degree of B.A. The state of admission to the University was to be Intermediate and not Matriculation examination.

(ii) Intermediate colleges should be established for the sake of achieving at first end. These college's should conduct teaching in Arts, Science, Medicine, Engineering Education, Agriculture and Commerce.

(iii) A separate High School and Intermediate Board should be formed in every province, consisting of representatives of the Government, Universities, High Schools and Intermediate colleges, for the sake of managing Secondary Education. As regards the Secondary Education, recommendations were made to free the Board from the control of the Department of Education.

Thus the principal aim of the Commission in forming the Board was to free the Universities from the responsibilities of secondary education so that they might devote themselves wholly to higher education and the wide gulf existing between the Universities on the one hand and the Department of Education of the other might be bridged over. The Commission further recommended the use of the mother tongue as medium of instruction in Intermediate colleges.

After that the Commission thoroughly examined the problems of the Calcutta University and reached the conclusion that the size of the University had become abnormally large and that the number of students of colleges affiliated to it had too much increased to be efficiently dealt with under a single University. The commission put forth three suggestions in this respect:

(i) There should be established a teaching and residential university at Decca;

(ii) The teaching resources should be organised in Calcutta in such a way as to create a real teaching university; and

(iii) The development of moffusil colleges should be in such a way as to ensure the encouragement of gradual rise of University centres at a few places by concentrating all possible resources for higher education on them.

The Commission expressed their general views also upon the internal administration and organisation of the Universities as follows:

(i) The teachers of the Universities should be given more powers concerning Universities with a view to removing unnecessary State control over them;

(ii) Regulations governing the working of Universities should be rendered less rigid;

(iii) Provision should be made for the institution of Honours courses, as distinct from pass courses for the sake of abler students; the duration of degree course should be three years after Intermediate Stage;

(iv) As regards the internal administration of the University, a representative Court in place of Senate and a small Executive Council in place of syndicate should be set up;

(v) Appointments to Professorships and Readerships should be made by special Selection Committee including external experts;

(vi) Their should be set up an Academic Council and Board of studies to settle academic questions pertaining to courses of study, examinations, degrees and research work etc;

(vii) Different Faculties should be created;

(viii) A full-time and salaried Vice-chancellor should be appointed;

(ix) The Muslims should be provided all educational facilities in view of their backward state in this field;

(x) A Director of Physical Training should also be appointed to pay attention to the health and physical welfare of the students.

Besides these major recommendations, the Commission made other recommendations in connection with the training of women teachers, vocational education, and proper education in science and technology. It suggested the establishment of the Department of Education in the Universities and inclusion of Education as a subject for the B.A. (pass) and Intermediate course. It also provided for organising *'Purdah Schools'* for girls upto the age of 15 or 16 years. It empowered the Calcutta University to institute a 'Special Board of women's Education' and set up special curriculum according to the educational needs of women. It also recommended the establishment of an Iner-university Board for co-ordanating the activities of various Indian Universities.

Criticism

These were the main recommendations made by the Commission in connection with the improvement of the Calcutta University. They are in fact significant and applicable to the education of the entire country. The Indian Universities proceeded on the way to porgresss in the light of the recommendations made by the Commissions and a new life was infused into the educational system of the country. These suggestions not only envisaged the coming form of future Universities but shaped the existing ones also on new lines. It threw a new light on University education in India and brought it nearer to practical aspects of life. Indian languages were given due recognition and much encouragement was given to research work. The internal administration and organisation of the Universities became much more efficient. As a matter of fact, the Report of the Commission holds good even today with respect to University education. Having thoroughly examined all the aspects of higher education, the Commission put forth its reasonable and constructive suggestions.

On a perusal of the Report, it will be evident that the Commission had been influenced, to some measure, by the Haldane Commission on London University. The organisation of 'University colleges', 'constituent and incorporated colleges, the 'Academic Council', institution of 'Readership', and 'Halls' for the residence of students in India had been modelled on the recommendations and suggestions of the Haldane Commission on London University.

It is, however, an admitted fact that in spite of the high aim of the Commission, some of its recommendations were premature. The proposed working of the Calcutta University on the pattern of Oxford or Cambridge University was not suitable to the practical needs of the time, howsoever efficient it might be. Transferring of the control over primary education from the Department of Education to the Boards was done earlier than the time was ripe for it. Experimentation in the sphere of Intermediate colleges was also not successful. It is eminently proved by the fact that now many States are realising the need of recorganising Higher Secondary education to enable it to achieve its cherished objects. But all these defects are insignificant and cannot lessen the importance and value of the Report. It was on the lines of its recommendations that residential universities were established at different centres of the country *i.e.* Mysore, Patna, Benaras, Aligarh, Decca, Lucknow, and Hyderabad, and Secondary and higher education was organised. It will always be regarded as an epoch making Report in the History of Indian Education.

C. Educational Progress (1905-1920)

University Education

The Indian Universities Act of 1904 sought to reorganise the five universities of the country. Senates and Syndicates were constituted a new and term of office of Fellows was fixed for a period of five years only instead of whole life. Besides internal administrative improvements in the Universities, satisfactory amelioration had been effected in the mode of examinations, method of teaching and curriculum. The universities having been empowered to inspect the affiliated colleges, the standard of education and administrative conditions in these colleges consequently shot higher. Signs of all-round development of colleges were unmistakably manifest. It is, nevertheless, true that owing to the strict control the number of Arts Colleges sank from 145 in 1902 to 140 in the year 1912, but the number of students increased. The number of students in the colleges of Assam and Bengal too increased considerably. In 1910, an Islamic college was founded at Peshawar.

The aim of collegiate education did not remain only obtaining Government services because the number of the educated persons was on the increase in the country. There being no other alternative of employment and earning livelihood, students began to seek refuge in college education and consequently the number shot upward. Owing to the scarcity of technical colleges or those imparting vocational education, most of the students sought admission to Arts and Science colleges. Such increase in the number of aimless students was far from being a sign of healthy growth; on the other hand, it was a clear symptom of disease.

Much improvement was to be seen in the financial position of the colleges of this period. The Government had also increased grant-in-aid for them. Formerly the Punjab University received an aid of Rs. 30,000/- per annuam for the faculty of Oriental Learning. The State consented to the sanction of an additional annual aid of five lakhs of rupees for the progress of Indian universities. Some specific sum out of it had been earmarked for the expansion of affiliated colleges. During the period between 1907 and 1912, a further annual grant-in-aid of Rs. 2.45 lakhs was sanctioned for the affiliated colleges. Satisfactory increase in the income through fees produced a healthy effect on the financial position of the institutions. Besides this, the Central Government sanctioned a grant of 27.5 lakhs of rupees for the purpose of construction of buildings to house the period between the years 1904 and 1912. After 1912 the Government made liberal grants for the construction of buildings.

From the viewpoints of efficiency in the method of teaching and suitability of curriculum, progress consistent with general expectations was achieved. The Act of 1904 had directed the Universities to undertake teaching function. The Calcutta University focussed her attention on the post-graduate teaching. The Bombay University provided for Honours courses. The Universities organised the system of Extension Lectures by the External expert; and eminent educational celebrities like Sir. T. Holland, Prof. Ramsay Muir, Dr. Daniel Jones and Prof. Armstrong were invited for special talks during winter season. Special provision was made for research work in such subjects as Science, Commerce, Economics and Experimental Psychology.

Following the Resolution of 1913, the Act of 1915 brought the Benaras Hindu University into existence and it began to function well by 1917. The credit of founding this University goes specially to the Late Pt. Madan Mohan Malviya. Following it other universities were established at different places: the Mysore University (1916); the Patna University (1917); the Usmania University, Hyderabad adopting Urdu as medium of higher education (1918) and the Decca, Aligarh and Lucknow Universities (1920). Thus the number of the Universities rose from 5 in 1916 to 12 in 1921. Most of these universities are residential where there is the arrangement for both the residence and education of students.

Thus it is quite evident that the establishment of teaching. Universities contributed much to the improvement in the sphere of higher education. In fact the importance of residential Universities for the immense educational requirements of such a vast country as Indian cannot be overestimated. But owing to the paucity of funds, the necessity of the existence of affiliating universities, will continue to exist for a long time to come.

Secondary Education

Owing to the educational policy of Lord Curzon, the State control over secondary education had increased considerably as a result of which efficiency improved though quantity suffered. All sorts of institutions—private and Government aided ones, were given recognition by the Government. Besides the recognition of the Department of Education, that of the University concerned had to be sough if the pupils were to be sent for Matriculation examination. This dyarchical system of administration impeded the growth of secondary education to a considerable measure. The Secondary schools were entitled to grant-in-aid subject to the recognition of Education Department; the students were eligible to appear in Government Entrance examination and they could also receive government scholarships. At the same time the students studying in the unrecognised schools were forbidden to be transferred to recognised ones. This put a check upon unrecognised institutions. In fact, Lord Curzon put the secondary schools under state control entirely by eradicating the long-standing '*Lassez-Faire* policy' in the field of education. These measures were vehemently opposed by the Indian opinion and they were associated with the political stratagems of the government. The free and unstinted growth of Secondary education in poor and dependent country like India had been obstructed. The State institutions, it is true enough, were granted liberal financial aid. Nonetheless, it will have to be admitted that the greatest benefit of this policy was the introduction of efficiency and improvement in education, because the unrecognised institutions began to improve their condition with a view to obtaining recognition and State grant-in-aid. Thus between 1904 and 1912, the number of students in secondary schools increased, but satisfactory increase was not brought about in the number of Secondary schools themselves. As a result of educational policy adopted by the State in 1913 the Secondary schools multiplied in number abnormally. The number of pupils was rising to an extent that the pre-existing institutions could not cope with the situation. In the year 1917, the number of state schools was 237 for boys and 20 for girls. At the sametime the issue that the State should either close Govt. High schools or transfer them to private control so that a vast amount of money might be free to help the expansion of education through private enterprise, became very urgent compelling immediate attention. But this demand still persists unfulfilled. In each district, there still runs a Government high school which cannot assert any claim for especial treatment from the viewpoint of quality and efficiency. Not only that; it is also a truism of be acknowledged that some of the provincial Governments show preferential treatment towards State schools in comparison to private institutions. The question of medium of education in Secondary schools had not been settled finally. The vogue of School Final examinations had increased. On account of rigidity and inflexibility and want of choice and variety in the Matriculation curricula, different provincial governments formed the schemes of 'School Final Examinations' to be conducted by the Education Department. The scheme was very popular in Bombay Province. The U.P. government too organised the 'School Leaving Certificate Examination.' Similar schemes were formed in the Punjab, Bengal, Madras, Burma, and Central Province in the 1911. Education in Science and Commerce was also stressed. In 1913, in the Province of Bihar and Orissa, a similar plan was chalked out but it could not be materialized.

Primary Education

As we have seen, the Government of India had been making plans for the development of primary education since 1854, but expected results had not been achieved in this direction as yet. Towards the close of 19th century, famine and earthquakes had diverted the attention of the Government from education and hence its growth had suffered during that period. In the year 1904, according to the proposal of Lord Curzon, the Government of India conferred that "the rapid spread of primary education is one of the foremost duties of the State". Therefore, introducing improvement in the Local Boards, their efforts were concentrated exclusively on primary education. The effect of Lord Curzon's educational policy was that primary education began to show marks of rapid growth; and innumerable Upper and Lower Primary schools sprang up. the Government of India increased the grant-in-aid from Rs. 40 lakhs in 1905 to 75 lakhs of rupees and in addition to that they consented to pay annual recurrent grant of 35 lakhs of rupees. The natural result of it was that the number of primary schools between 1902 and 1912 was doubled.

The harmful system of "Payment by Results' was annulled in 1906 as a result of the recommendations of the Resolution of 1904 and amendments in the rules of grant-in-aid were introduced. Heretofore, the grant-in-aid was one-third of the whole expenditure, but Lord Curzon made one-half of the total sum spent on primary education. This improved both the quality and quantity of primary education. Besides these. Lord Curzon contributed much to the promotion of primary education by improving curriculum and method of teaching as well as through proper training of teachers.

The introduction of compulsory primary education in Baroda State in 1906, political awakening among the masses and the Swadeshi Movement were among the main factors helping the rapid growth of elementary education in the country. The people had begun to realize that they could not progress without raising the percentage of literacy and education. The efforts and the historic Bill of Sri G.K. Gokhale had made in the problem of primary education one of magnitudinous importance. Though the Bill had been turned down by the Government, yet she could not ignore the propriety and ever-growing need of elementary education for the public. Hence she extended liberal grants-in-aid for primary education. The number of children attending primry education grew from 4 lakhs to 5 lakhs between 1907 and 1912. Primary education became free practically in all the provinces.

When controversy over Gokhale's Bill was raging fiercely. His Majesty King George V, in the Delhi Durbar in the year 1911, announced an annual grant of Rs. 50 lakhs from the Royal Exchequer for primary education considerably helping thereby its rapid growth.

The Educational Resolution of 1913 too gave priority to the mass education in the country. According to its recommendations, most of the Lower Primary schools were developed into Upper Primary ones; and Boards too established more primary schools. Provision was made to improve the condition of the teachers and to provide them training. The result of the educational policy adopted by the Government in 1913 was that primary schools under Boards were established by 1917 nearly in all the provinces viz. Bombay, U.P., Punjab, Madras, Central Province, N.W. Frontier Province and Assam. Separate schools were provided for the girls. The Board schools did not make much progress in provinces like Bengal, Bihar and Orissa and Madras. Only private institutions were predominant there. The Bengal Government made the plan of establishing *"Panchayati Schools"* according to which a model school was established for an area of 104 square miles. In U.P. one primary school was to serve an area of 25 square miles.

Thus we see that though primary education made progress in some measure but it was not adequate, and satisfactory. The unfinished work of Sri Gokhale was taken up by Bal Gangadhar Tilak and Vithalbhai Patel. Shri B.G. Tilak put forth the demand for free and compulsory education through his paper *'Kesari"* in very effective and forceful words. By 1917 only 33 per cent of the children of school-going age were attending primary schools. During the quinquennium of 1912 and 1917, on average one boy attended school in an area of 8 square miles.

After 1918, elementary education began to progress again in the country. The impediments that had checked its growth during the World War I, had now disappeared. In 1918, the Bombay Government passed "the Bombay Primary Education Act" which authorised the Municipalities to start compulsory education for boys of the age between 6 and 11 years. Similarly, other provincial Governments promulgated like measures and by 1919, the Governments of the Punjab, U.P., Bengal and Bihar-Orissa brought into force the "Primary Education Act". In 1920, Madras and Central province too followed suit and passed similar Acts.

Conclusion

The political agitation during this period affected the education in general and primary education particularly. News about Russian Revolution in 1917 travelled to India and it deeply influenced Indian education. Besides all these, education in India had been influenced by multifarious other factors such as, the passing of Rowlat Act in 1919 and its vehement opposition and boycott by the Indian masses, atrocities perpetrated by General O. Dyer in Jalianwala Bagh, high prices and unemployment following in the wake of War and the most significant event *i.e.* 'Non Co-operation Movement' launched by Mahatma Gandhi in 1919-21etc. Seeing all this agitation and turmoil, the Government of India had realized that "the inevitable result of education in the history and thought of Europe is the desire for self-determination; and the demand that now meets us from the education classes of India is no more than the right and national outcome of the work of a hundred years." All this resulted in Montague-Chelmsford Reforms in 1919 and amendment in Indian constitution. A description of the progress made by education in the light of Montague-Chelmsford reforms will be given in the following pages.

REFERENCES

1. *Gikhale's Speeches* (1920 Ed.) pp. 618-19.
2. Dumbell. Page 94. Quoted by Dr. Zellner: *Education in India*, pp. 146-47.

6

Growth of Education (1921-37)

MONT-FORD REFORMS

Introduction

In 1917, Mr. Montague visited India with the then Viceroy Lord Chelmsford and having studied the political and constitutional circumstances, submitted their joint Report in 1918. The reforms embodied in the Report were referred to and approved by British Parliament and came into force in 1921. Through an act passed by the Parliament in 1917, Dyarchy was introduced into the provincial administration. Formerly the Central Government used to exercise her control over the provincial governments in matters of issues affecting the whole of the country and appoint different committees and commissions in this connection. In the sphere of education too, the Central Government would introduce new reforms. But Mont-Ford Reforms brought a change in the existing state of affairs. The provincial subjects were divided into two parts: the Reserved and the Transferred. Departments of Health and Education were transferred to the control of provincial ministers. These ministers were responsible to Legislatures. This was the first lesson to Indian Ministers in the field of autonomous rule. Though education was transferred to the control of provincial governments, the Government of India retained under their immediate control education of certain areas centrally administered viz. N.W. Frontier province, Ajmer Merwara, Coorg, Delhi, Baluchistan etc. The Princes' Colleges, and the Universities of Delhi, Aligarh and Banaras remained under the control of Central Government.

The Mont-Ford Reforms pushed the growth of education upward. The Indian Ministers zealoully took the reins of the expansion of education in their hands. The provincial Legislative Assemblies too fulfilled readily the demands pertaining to grand-in-aid and undertook the responsibility of spreading education amongst the masses. The responsibilities of Local Boards also increased and primary education was transferred to their hands nearly in all the provinces. It was admitted in the Mont-Ford Report concerning the contemporary state of affairs in India in the following words:

"Our educational policy in the past aimed at satisfying the few who sought after English education, without sufficient thought of the consequences which might issue from not taking care to extend instruction to the many. We have, in fact, created a limited intelligentsia, who desire advance; and we cannot stay their progress entirely until education has been extended to the masses.... We have not succeeded in making education practical.... We must admit that the educated Indian is a creation peculiarly of our own; and if we take the credit that is due to us for his strong points, we must admit a similar liability for his weak ones".

Some Obstacles

The Mont-Ford Reforms introduced dyarchy in provincial administration. The responsibilities of education rested upon the Indian minister, but he did not possess any power thereabout. The subject of finance was treated as Reserved. The Revenue Department was under the control of English ministers who were answerable only to the Governors of their provinces. Under this arrangement the Education Ministers were not free to spend necessary amount on educational plans. This rendered their projects futile and meaningless.

Secondly, the Central Government discontinued to give any portion of their revenue to provincial governments for educational purposes causing thus much financial loss to them.

Thirdly, the powers of Governors were abnormally large and in the words of Dr. Zellner, they used 'Veto' power unexceptionally and they could reject any Bill pertaining to growth of education as 'unnecessary' according to their sweet will.

The forth complication was that high ranking I.E.S. officials of Education Department were under the direct control of the Secretary of State for India. There would always remain a gulf between the Indian ministers and these officials and they would not look eye to eye with each other upon any issue whatsoever. The result was generally that most of educational plans ended in fiasco. Hence in 1924, recruitment to Indian Education Service was stopped.

Besides, people had no faith in the constitution of India framed in 1919 owing to national movements. They regarded it as a mere humbug. In some cases, the Educational minister did not duly represents the Indian masses, hence he did not get the support of the Legislature. In the absence of Central control over education, many problems of all-India and inter-provincial importance remained unsolved and the Central Government could not formulate any uniform policy pertaining to it. This brought about not only a severance of relation between the Central and provincial governments, so far as education was concerned, but harmonious relations amongst the provincial governments themselves also deteriorated. Thus the Indian education ministers of different provinces working under dyarchical system of administration, had to fight against odds in bringing about improvement in the field of education. Consequently no marked progress could be achieved during this period.

Effect of National Movement

It has been indicated in the previous chapter that at the end of World War I, the British Government had amply remunerated war services of the Indians in terms of inordinate firing at Jalianwala Bagh, Martial Law in the Punjab, country-wide repression and the constitution of 1919. All these events stimulated national consciousness in the hearts of the Indians. In 1921, Mahatma Gandhi launched the Non-cooperation Movement and many students leaving their schools and colleges joined the movement. They did not like to receive education in such institutions as imparted education in exotic learning and foreign culture and language and crushed thereby all national sentiments. As such the English schools began to be boycotted openly.

But it was the paramount duty of national leaders to provide proper facilities for the education of such students. Therefore, within a short space of time a number of national schools and *Gurukulas* and *Vidyapiths* (National Universities) sprang up in the country. From amongst these, the *Vidyapiths* at Poona, Ahmedabad, Lahore, Patna and Banaras as well as the Jamia Millia at Aligarh, which had been transferred to Delhi in 1925, are very important. A description of these national institutions will be given at proper place later on.

Thus the number of students in the Government schools or those recognized and aided by the State, dwindled considerably. "In 1921, the percentage of decrease in attendance for the whole country was 8.6 (colleges), 5.1 (high schools), and 8.1 (middle schools)". This involved, moreover, financial loss owing to decrease in income through tuition fees and examination fees.

From another point of view this Movement proved beneficial also in the field of education, because it aroused national awakening amongst the masses. People began to show keen interest in education. The wealthy class of the country was inspired to grant endowments to educational institutions for the purpose of educational advancement of the country. People were filled with zeal, hope and high ambitions and were inspired by the sentiments of sacrifice for the progress of education. By that time Indian National Congress had become the foremost political organisation of the country. In the Karachi Session of Indian National Congress held in 1931, our leaders supported the principle of free and compulsory primary education. In 1937, Mahatma Gandhi worked out Wardha Scheme of Education with a view to making primary education for general masses inexpensive, practical and beneficial. The scheme embodied the principle of the primary education through some basic handicrafts. Though the movement was semi-political in character, it helped a lot in moulding the educational system of the country according to the needs and spirit of times, changing it and making it more universal. The glaring defects of modern system of education were clearly brought to light and people realized that mere literary education, which proved quite futile in practical life, should positively be altered. Indian youth also realized that they had to contribute their share to the task of building up and regenerating their nation.

At last, it needs, however, to be remembered that provincial education ministers also got inspiration from these movements. They passed bills in relation to rendering elementary education free and compulsory in different provinces. Secondary schools and other universities to be referred to in course of time, came into existence. The Simon Commission was appointed in 1927 in order to study political and constitutional circumstances born of the constitution framed in 1919. This Commission was asked to submit its report on Indian education. In order to achieve this objective, the Commission formed an Auxilliary Committee with Sir Phillip Hartog as President who had been one of the members of the Sadler Commission and ex-vice Chancellor of the Decca University in 1921. This Committee is known as the 'Hartog Committee'.

Hartog Committee Report (Recommendations)

The Hartog committee submitted its Report in September 1929. It contains a vivid description of all aspects of Indian education. The Committee had admitted that during the decade between 1917, and 1927 education made considerable progress. The quality of education improved *pari passu* with its expansion. "Education has come to be regarded generally as a matter of primary national importance, an indispensable agency in the difficult task of national building'. The attention given to it by Legislative Councils is both a symptom and evidence of this recognition. The transfer of the Department of Education to popular control, as represented by a Minister has both increased the public interest in it and made it more sensitive to the currents of public needs and public opinion. Nor is it only the authorities and the well-to-do classes that have welcomed and encouraged the spread of education. Communities which had for long been educationally backward, like the Mohammedan community, have awakened to the need and possibilities of education for their children. The movement was spread to the depressed classes and even to the tribal aborigines, and has stirred a much larger proportion of the people than before to demand education as a right."[1]

Primary Education

Though education was making progress, yet the Committee was not satisfied with the scanty growth of literacy in the country. In its opinion, much 'wastage' and 'stagnation' had crept into education. Too much attention was devoted to higher education and primary education was being entirely neglected. On account of certain difficulties in the way of rural education, progress of literacy was extremely dull and slow. The main difficulties were: poverty of the villagers, ignorance, lack of means of transportation and communications, seasonal diseases caste barriers and religious conservatism and above all, premature engagement of children in agricultural occupations etc. In the opinion of the Committee, another important reason hampering the expected growth of literacy was that provincial governments were not taking any concrete steps in the direction of compulsory primary education.

As regards the primary education, the Committee further observed : "In the Primary system which from our point of view should be designed to produce literacy and the capacity to exercise an intelligent vote, the waste is appalling. So far as we can judge, the vast increase in number of primary schools produces no commensurate increase in literacy; for only a small proportion of those who are at the primary stage reach class IV, in which the attainment of literacy may be expected.... It is to be remembered that under present conditions of rural life, and with the lack of suitable vernacular literature, a child has very little chance of attaining literacy after leaving school; and, indeed, even for the literate, there are many chances of relapse into illiteracy" Thus in the opinion of the Committee, one should necessarily devote at least four years to become literate. But on account of certain unforeseen circumstances, the child generally left the studies after passing I and II class in British India out of every 100 students reading in class I in 1922-23, only 19 students remained in III or IV class after the expiry of three years. The Committee attributed this decrease in the number of students to the above-mentioned two factors i.e. 'wastage' and 'stagnation.' By 'wastage' they meant premature withdrawl of children from any stage before the completion of primary course. According to the views of the Committee, whatever money and time was spent on them, was nothing short of 'wastage' because they could not even attain literacy. 'Stagnation' meant the detention of a child in the same class for more than one year.

In the case of the education of girls too, the Committee made complaints of wastage. Only 14 girls out of every hundred reading in class I could reach the stage of class IV. In other words, our 80 per cent educational efforts were merely wasted.

In the opinion of the Committee, the problem of primary education in urban areas was not very urgent but it admitted that "in rural area school units are usually small; adequate staffing is more expensive; and conditions of life are not attractive to teachers unless they are specially selected and trained; women teachers cannot, as a rule, live in villages unless circumstances are exceptionally favourable; the teachers are isolated and the difficulties of administration, supervision and inspection are much greater; and it is more difficult to secure regular and prolonged attendance of children." The problem of primary education at such places was very crucial. This must necessarily have involved wastage.

The main reasons of this wastage were : (i) stagnation: (ii) Relapse of the literate into illiteracy owing to their leaving off in the middle of primary course; (iii) want of proper and adequate facilities for adult education ; (iv) uneven distribution of schools so that "there were large areas without a school, while in others were many little schools indulging in cut-throat competition for the children' ; (v) The difficulty of providing schools to villages with a population of less than 500 inhabitants; (vi) Inability to draw utmost utility out of the existing schools which meant that in spite of the existence of schools in large number in many provinces, a large number of children failed to attend them ; (vii) Single-teacher schools i.e. schools having only one teacher for each school who could not do full justice to every child in every subject; (viii) want of proper training of teachers; (ix) want of adequate inspection; (x) unsuitable curricula—such curricula as are not related to practical aspects of life; and (xi) existence of primary schools of ephemeral character.

The Committee made following recommendations with a view to remedying all these defects in primary education. They are briefly put forth as follows:

(i) A policy of consolidation should be adopted in place of expansion of education;

(ii) Four years should be the minimum duration of primary education;

(iii) The standard of general education of primary school teachers should be raised. Proper facilities should be

provided to them for their training and refresher courses. Educational conferences should be held for an increase in their knowledge and their salary should be increased and service-conditions improved in order to better their condition;

(iv) The curriculum of primary teachers should be sufficiently liberalised and be made more suitable. "A well attended school directly related to the surrounding conditions can do much towards training the younger generation in ways of hygiene, physical culture, improved sanitation, thrift and self-reliance;"

(v) School hours and holidays should be adjusted to seasonal and local requirements;

(vi) Special attention should be paid to the lowest class in primary schools and whatever wastage and stagnation is rampant there, concrete and intrepid efforts should be put forth in order to remove it;

(vii) The work of rural uplift should be undertaken and it must be associated with school work;

(viii) The problem of primary education being of national importance, the Government should herself assume the responsibility of its expansion and should not feel contented by handing it over entirely to the local bodies;

(ix) The government inspection staff should be increased;

(x) Hasty steps in the direction of making primary education compulsory, are always detrimental. Hence it is necessary that work should be begun only after preparing the ground for the purpose.

Secondary Education

Having gone through every aspect of primary education, the committee undertook the examination of Secondary education. With regard to Secondary education, it was the opinion of Hartog Committee that it had made satisfactory progress. "In the sphere of Secondary education, there has been an advance in some respects, notably the average capacity of the body of teachers, in their improved conditions of serving and training, and in the attempt to widen the general activities of school life. But here again there are grave defects of organisation. The whole system of Secondary Education is still dominated by the ideal that every boy who enters a secondary school should prepare himself for the University: and the immense number of failures at the Matriculation and in the University examinations indicate a great waste of efforts." This wastage is attributed to two main factors:

1. Laxity of promotion from one class to another in the earlier stages; and
2. Prosecution of higher education by incapable students in too large a number.

The remedies suggested by the Committee for the reform in secondary education included setting up of diversified and varied curricula in middle schools meeting the requirements of majority of students at that stage. The Committee further suggested "the division of more boys to industrial and commercial careers at the end of the middle stage for which provision should be made by alternate courses in that stage, preparatory to special instruction in technical and industrial schools."[2]

University Education

The committee was satisfied with the progress made by University education. But it found certain defects in it too. "Many of the universities and colleges show marked improvement in their methods of teaching and in the amount of original work which they have produced; and in some of them there is undoubtedly a better training for corporate life than formerly. But, the theory that a university exists mainly, if not solely, to pass students through examinations still finds too large acceptance in India; and we wish that there were more signs that the universities regarded the training of broad-minded, tolerant and self-reliant citizens as one of the primary functions. They have been hampered in their work by being over-crowded with students who are not fitted by capacity for university education....

The Committee, therefore, put forth suggestions for the improvement of universities. The Universities should maintain a high standard of education and candidates appearing at the Entrance examinations should strictly be dealt with, so that under serving students might be debarred from entering the universities. Besides, the Committee also recommended the institution of Honours courses and establishment of good libraries and beginning of tutorial classes.

Education of Women

As regards the education of girls, the Committee felt that the condition was unsatisfactory. There was no proper provision for their education in rural areas. There was enormous disparity in the proportion of education of girls and boys. The sphere of Secondary education for girls was awfully limited. There was conspicuous scarcity of capable and trained women teachers. The Committee made recommendations in this direction also. The curriculum for girls should be consistent with and suitable to their requirement. There was the need of increased number of primary and secondary schools for them. There should be adequate number of women teachers and inspectresses. Primary education should be made compulsory gradually for girls as well. Girls are would be mothers of the country and hence they should be given preference.

In the end, the Committee also realized that transferring of control of education by the Central Government to provincial governments was too hurried a step taken by her. As a matter of fact, the Central Government can never afford to absolve herself of the responsibilities of the education of the country. It pointed out the need of setting up a Central Education Committee at Delhi. The Committee was not niggardly in its appreciation of the work of Directors of Public Instructions. It suggested that there should be an increase in the staff at headquarters and that more inspectors and sub-inspectors were needed for the assistance of D.P.I's. It made further recommendations that in the Centrally Administered Areas, an Education Secretary should be appointed in place of Education Commissioner and that Government of India should convene regular educational conferences of Directors of Public Instruction in order to discuss current problems pertaining thereto.

Criticism

The Report of Hartog Committee holds a unique position in the history of Indian education. In fact, it gave a permanent shape to the educational policy of that period and attempted at expanding and stabilising education. In official spheres, the Report was heartily welcomed and it was hailed as the torch-bearer of State efforts. The committee's suggestion about improvement in quality in comparison to quantity of education, was much credited. In fact, the Report represented the educational policy of the government officials. Thus the wide expansion of education was consciously suppressed in different provinces under the pretext of raising the standard of education.

But the non-official view made scathing criticism of the Report. It was criticized as a political device to check the expansion of mass education. On account of national awakening, every government policy began to be viewed with suspicion and disturst. The national leaders gave priority to educational expansion by holding that standard of education could be raised after its wide diffusion. The real need of the country according to this view was universal literacy, hence it was felt that the policy of consolidation would run counter to the national interests. Besides, the authenticity of certain statistics provided by the Committee was also doubted.

The Effect of the Report

It is, however, beyond doubt that the progress made in the quinquennium of 1922-27 could not be maintained after 1927. One of the main reasons of it was the universal economic crises of 1930-31 which adumberated the budget of Government of India Consequently, the Central and Provincial Governments had to make

Year	*Government Expenditure (in lakhs of Rs.)*
1926-27	11,93
1930-31	13,61
1931-32	12,46
1932-33	11,35
1933-34	11,47
1934-35	11,59
1935-36	11,84
1936-37	12,36

ruthless curtailment in the budget assigned to the plans of nation building, and work of reconstruction. The following statistics show how the Government curtailed expenditure on eduction, having increased it in the beginning which could be augmented only in the end:

These statistics show that in 1930-31, the expenditure on education decreased and continued to decrease till in 1937 it was below the expenditure incurred on education six years ago. But whereas Government expenditure on education was decreasing, that of private enterprise was increasing. This goes to prove invincible zeal among the people who were ready to make the greatest sacrifice for the noble cause of education, as is evident from the following figures:

	Expenditure in Lakhs of Rupees				
Source	*1901-02*	*1916-17*	*1921-22*	*1931-32*	*1936-37*
Government	103	392	902	1,246	1,236
Non-Government					
(a) District Board	59	174	168	280	257
(b) Municipalities	15	49	79	158	178
(c) Fees	127	319	380	623	711
(d) Other sources	97	195	308	412	424
Total	401	11,29	1,837	2,719	2,806

N.B. (The figures are for British India only.)[3]

It is, however, true that in spite of financial difficulties, education was advancing in the country. The recommendations to raise the standard of education and to consolidate it did not affect private enterprise in the field of education. Their efforts to make education universal persisted. Consequently the number of private institutions in the fields of primary, secondary and collegiate education increased considerably, as is manifest from the following table of figures:

Thus we come to know that between 1922 and 1937, the number of schools and students was constantly on the increase, but

Type of Institutions	*No. of institutions*		*No. of Scholars*	
	1921-22	*1936-37*	*1921-22*	*1936-37*
1. Universities	10	15	Figures not available	9,697
2. Arts colleges	165	271	45,418	86,273
3. Professional colleges	64	75	13,662	20,645
4. Secondary schools	7,530	13,056	11,06,803	22,87,872
5. Primary schools	1,55,017	1,92,244	61,09,752	1,02,24,288
6. Special schools	3,344	5,647	1,20,925	2,59,269
Total for Recognised Institutions	1,66,130	2,11,308	73,96,560	1,28,88,044
7. Unrecognised Institutions	16,322	16,647	4,22,165	5,01,530
Grand Total	1,82,452	2,27,955	78,18,725	1,33,89,574

N.B. (These figures are for British India only).[4]

considering the population of the country, the number was not adequate. At the same time no attention was paid to some of the valuable recommendations of Hartog Committee such as increase in the salary of teachers, appointment of more inspectors, improvement in the curriculum and provision for adult education etc. They remained mere pious hopes.

The Central Advisory Board

The Central Advisory Board was established in 1921 with a view to co-ordinating the educational policy of the Central Government with that of other provinces and providing advice on many important educational problems. But owing to the financial crisis it was dissolved. As a result of the recommendation of the Hartog Committee, the Central Advisory Board was revived in 1935. This Board consisted of members of all provinces. At the first meeting of the Board in 1935, it considered almost all the vital problems of education of the country and passed resolutions in order to bring about some radical changes in educational system. It sought to reorganize the classes and stressed the need of industrial and vocational education in place of pure literacy education. It was stated in the resolution that in order to bring about revolutionary changes in the field of education, it is of paramount necessity that students should be given not only vocational education and that helping them to get admission in the university, but also that sort of education which may enable them, at the time of having attained to the proper stage, to join some technical institution or undertake some particular profession. In this connection that Board suggested the following stages:

(i) The Primary Stage

Its aim should be to provide a minimum of general education and to ensure permanent literacy.

(ii) The Lower Secondary Stage

It must have self–sufficient curriculum for general education . It must form the basis of higher secondary education and vocational training.

(iii) The Higher Secondary Stage

It will include institutions with varying length of courses according to the needs of individual institution. These schools will be chiefly of five kinds:

1. Preparing students for admission to universities in Arts and Science;
2. For training teachers for rural areas;
3. For the training in agriculture;
4. For clerical training;
5. For training in selected technical subjects to be chosen in consultation with the authorities.

Besides, these, the Board advised through a resolution that at the end of the lower secondary stage, a public examination should be held. The Government was requested to invite the advice of educational experts in order to construct and reorganize this scheme.

Wood-Abbott Report

According to the last proposal of the Central Advisory Board that expert advice should be sought for educational reorganization, Messrs. A .Abbott who was formerly Chief Inspector of Technical schools, Board of education, England and S.H. Wood, Director of Intelligence, Board of Education, England were invited to India for the purpose. They made a tour of India in 1936-37 and submitted their report in June, 1937 which is divided into two parts. Mr. Wood made a close study of general education and its organisation ad put forth his suggestions; whereas Mr. A. Abbott who was a world famous expert on vocational and technical education, analysed very minutely the state of affairs in India and her vast resources and gave some practical and valuable suggestions.

With regard to general education, Mr. Wood recommended that provision for trained teachers should be made for primary schools and special attention should be paid to the education of girls. There was need of much change in the curriculum of primary schools and education of children in primary schools should be based upon the activities of the children more than upon bookish learning. Moreover, the curriculum of middle schools in rural areas should be related to rural environments and needs; the medium of instruction should be the mother tongue and English should not, as far as possible be taught in middle schools. English should be treated as compulsory subject in secondary school necessarily. Arts and Crafts should be encouraged and included in the curricula of primary and secondary education. Capable teachers should be appointed in High schools to teach these subjects. A training course of the duration of three years should be prescribed for the teachers of primary and middle schools after they had passed middle class.

Thus Mr. Wood made valuable recommendations for the reorganization, control and curriculum of secondary education.

Writing about the reorganization of vocational and industrial education, Mr. Abbott recommended that the nature of vocational education should be determined by the prevailing circumstances in view of multifarious needs of the place. He also observed that technical education should keep pace with industrial development of the country in order to check all possibilities of unemployment. He held that like general education, technical education also brings about a harmonious development of physical, mental and spiritual aspects of the personality. As a matter of fact general education is but the counterpart of technical education. The latter is, however incomplete without the former; and all the vocational subjects begin in general schools. Despite this similarity, the aims and means of both the types of education differ considerably. Therefore, there should be separate schools for them.

From this viewpoint it is clear that vocational education should be preceded by general education. The industrialists should extend their co-operation for the organisation of industrial education. Besides these, there should be adequate provision for training in technical education in cottage industries and agriculture.

Mr. Abbott observed that there was the need of training of three types of employees for the organized large-scale industries in India (i) Managers (ii) Supervisors (iii) Operators. He held that training of supervisors is of vital importance and training centers for the purpose should be provided sufficient in number. The operators of machines should receive their training during off-hours.

The Report recommended the establishment in each province for Advisory Council for Vocational Education. The Council should appoint sub-committees dealing with Education for Engineering, the Textile industries, Agriculture,. Small-scale and cottage industries and Commerce. These sub-committees should be entrusted with the entire responsibility of organizing vocational education and prescribing curricula for them in each province.

Vocational education should have general education as its basis. The students seeking admission to junior- vocational schools should be required to have passed middle examination, whereas those seeking admission to senior vocational schools, an examination parallel to Higher Secondary school examination. Students receiving education in junior vocational schools with a course of two years would be treated as equal to those receiving higher secondary education. Students having passed the examination of junior vocational school should be eligible to admission to senior vocational school or be entitled to special training in some particular vocation.

Those students who have passed Senior Vocational School Examination would be treated as equal to students having passed Intermediate Examination. Their curriculum also would cover a course of two years. They also suggested that part-time schools should be provided for further education of persons already in employment.

As regards education in agriculture, the Report suggested that there should be a limited number of schools for the purpose. Subject of agriculture should be treated as optional at primary and secondary stage of education. Similarly commerce could be made optional subject.

The Report recommended the establishment of a single Polytechnic School where training in many vocations should be given, instead of special individual schools for the training in individually different vocations.

Besides these, education in Arts and Crafts was emphasized and the establishment of a Vocational training college at Delhi was also recommended.

This the Wood-Abbott Report fulfills a special demand, considering the circumstances and substantial needs of the country.

After having described the important historical land marks during the period under review now we shall make a study of the growth of education of the country in the light of these Reports and other changes as a consequence of various movements.

PROGRESS OF EDUCATION 1921-37

University and Higher Education

A satisfactory improvement and expansion in University education took place during this period. Establishment of Inter-University Board and five new Universities; reorganization of the existing universities; provision of research facilities and that of Military education and emergence of some national universities are some of the important features which throw some light on the evolution of higher Education.

Inter-University Board

With the growth of Universities in India it was felt essential that for the purpose of establishing harmony and mutual co-operation among the universities, there should be constituted some such body as might bring about uniformity and co-ordination in the working of different universities. The Calcutta University Commission had emphasized its need, the Congress of the Universities of the British Empire held in 1921 and the Lytton Committee constituted for the benefit of Indian Students in England had also supported the idea of its establishment. The first All India Conference of Indian Universities was held at Simla in 1924 and an Inter-University Board was established. Its Head Office was at Bangalore.

There are representatives of all the Universities on the Board. After its establishment, the British has solved many an intricate and significant problem pertaining to University education. Its annual meetings are held at different educational centers. Besides these meetings, a quinquennial conference of the Board is also held in order to provide solutions for knotty problems about higher education. It publishers "A Handbook of Indian Universities, which is very important to provide a close knowledge about the working of Indian Universities.

In brief, the functions of the Board are as follows:

To act as an Inter-University organisation and bureau of information, to facilitate the exchange of professors to bring about mutual co-operation and co-ordination among the Indian universities, to provide information to Indian students about foreign universities and to assist Indian universities in obtaining recognition for their degrees in other countries; to send Indian representatives to Imperial or International Educational Conferences and to do other necessary helpful activities in the interests of universities. It is, nevertheless, true according to the views of Sri Radha Krishnan that the Board has discharged its functions as Advisory body but its influence has not been as forceful and strong as it should have been. "The universities have not always been inclined to follow the advice given by the collective voice of the Vice-chancellors which, in effect, the Board has become."[5]

Establishment of New Universities

According to the policy of establishing at least one University in each province and from the viewpoint of residential universities, five universities were founded during this period: Delhi (1922, Nagpur (1923), Andhra (1926), Agra (1927) and Annamalai (1929).

(i) Delhi

The University of Delhi had been established originally as an affiliating university having St. Stephen's College, the Hindu College and Ramjas College under its jurisdiction. In 1927, an especially appointed committee considered the question whether it should be an affiliating university or a Federal one. At last the Government of India decided that it should be developed as a Federal University. But certain Colleges remained affiliated to it.

(ii) Nagpur

The Nagpur University had been established for the Central Province in 1923. It was originally an affiliating university, but in due course of time it introduced teaching classes and incorporated a Law College. It still functions as an affiliating University.

(iii) Andhra

The Andhra University was founded mainly for the northern parts of Madras province which is now called Andhra Pradesh. In 1920, the principle of establishing a university on linguistic basis had been accepted by Madras University. The people speaking Telugu were raising a constant demand for a separate university for themselves. Therefore, by an Act of 1926, the Andhra University was incorporated as a unitary and residential university with jurisdiction over the Telgu-speaking areas "to serve the interest of Andhras who were proud of their achievements in Art and Architecture, Music and Painting". It provided higher technical education. A special feature of its constitution is the election of the vice- chancellor. The constitution lays down the use of mother tongue as medium of instruction and examination but it has not been brought in force fully. The issue of its site has always remained a most controversial point on account of local patriotism. Formerly, it was at Vijayawada whence it was transferred to Waltair in 1930. In 1942 consequent on the dislocation caused by war conditions, headquarters were temporarily shifted to Guntur. Four years later the University was moved back to Waltair.

(iv) Agra

The Agra University was established in 1927 to take over the affiliating functions of the Allahabad University. The sphere of jurisdiction of the Allahabad University had become very large, therefore, the colleges affiliated to that University were transferred to the jurisdiction of the Agra University. Degree colleges at Ajmer, Gwalior and those of Rajputana were all brought under its jurisdiction. But owing to the establishment for a separate university of Rajputana, its field has now become narrow and confined. Well-nigh all the Degree Colleges of U.P. (excepting the colleges under the jurisdiction of residential universities) are affiliated to the Agra University. Though the purpose of this University was "to provide for instruction in such branches of learning as the University may think fit and to make provision for research and for the advancement and dissemination of Knowledge", but it is, in a way purely an affiliating University. Nearly all the Degree colleges under it in U.P. have Intermediate classes the examination of which is conducted by the Allahabad Board.

(v) The Annamalai University

The Annamalai University had been founded in 1929 at Annamalai Nagar, Chidambaram in South Madras. It owes its existence to the generosity of Late Raja Sir Annamalai Chettiar, who had handed over three collegiate institutions together with a benefaction of 20 lakhs of rupees to Madras Government for the foundation of this University. It is a teaching and residential university. The special feature of this university is that it provides education and research facilities in Oriental languages, Tamil, Sanskrit, Indian History and Indian Music. Its special attractions are the Raja Annamalai Music College and Oriental Training College. In 1934, provision was made for research work in Tamil. Its constitution is similar to that of other universities.

Other Reforms and Growth of University Education

Besides the establishment of these new universities, some improvements were introduce in the older existing universities also during this period. The constitution of Madras University was revised in 1923 and 1929. According to the amendments, it developed as a teaching university. Research facilities were provided in Economics, Zoology, Chemistry, Botany, Mathematics, Indian Philosophy and History and Oriental Research Institute was established for the sake of research work in Oriental languages such as, Tamil, Telugu, Malayalam, Kannad, Sanskrit, Arabic, Persian and Urdu. The Bombay University was reorganized in 1928 as a result of which facilities for higher education and research work were increased. The Patna University was reformed through an Act of 1932. The Allahabad University now began to function as a purely teaching university. An amendment in its constitution had been introduced by an Act of 1922. Similar changes and improvements were brought about in the Punjab and Calcutta Universities by amending their constitutions.

The number of affiliated colleges too increased vastly during this period. The number of Faculties in Universities also increased. As regards the number of affiliated College is rose from 207 in 1922 to 446 in the year 1937 and that of students shot from 66,258 to 126,228. Heretofore the Universities were not educational centres in the right sense of the term. They existed merely to conduct examinations and confer degrees; but the main function of most of them now became teaching and research work. Provision for rich libraries was made to facilitate the research work of students and they were encouraged in their venture by awarding scholarships to them. Most of the universities were housed in their own vast and beautiful buildings. Harmonious relations among the different Indian universities developed and elaborate provision was made for the physical well-being of the students by providing them with regular games, sports and physical exercises as well as medical test. Students Unions and other welfare organizations established for the sake of engendering a spirit of co-operation and self–reliance among the students. As a result of the Indian Territorial Army Act of 1920, the vogue of military education (U.O.T.C.) increased in the Universities. It was established at each university and degree colleges affiliated to them. Military education promoted both their health and character.

Thus higher education evolved and advanced appreciably. But it was not wholly immune from certain defects. Standard of education was lowered and mere bookish learning flourished. Consequently owing to inadequacy of vocational education and want of employment many educated young men wandered aimlessly. Efficiency of administration suffered with the rise in the number of students. Universities could not materalise their development plans owing to paucity of funds.

Other Centres of Higher Education

In addition to regular universities, there were certain such educational centers in India as provided higher education in different special subjects. These institution could neither properly be called universities nor were they affiliated to any university. The following institutions are worth mentioning out of them.

(i) The Bhandarkar Oriental Research Institute, Poona (1917); (ii) The Bose Research Institute Calcutta (1917); (iii) The Harcourt Butler Technological Institute, Kanpur (1921); (iv) Imperial Agriculture Research Institute, New Pusa, New Delhi;[6] (v) Indian Institute of Science, Bangalore (1911); (vi) Indian School of Mines, Dhanbad (1926); (vii) Indian Womens' University, Bombay (1916); (viii) Vishwa Bharati (1922); and (ix) Serampore College (1918).

These institutions had been conducting higher education freely, Majority of them, as is indicated by their names, had been established for providing education in science, vocations and industries. Some of them were Government institutions and some private ones.

Besides, there were functioning some national universities in the country. As has already been pointed out, this period was characterized by political upheaval in India. National sentiments were overwhelming the people. Hence boycotting English institutions, those based on national traditions were established in their stead. From amongst these the Vishwa-Bharati of Rabindra Nath Tagore, Sewagram, the Pondicherry Ashram, Darul-Ulum of Devband and the Jamia Milia of Delhi are worthy of note.

The Vishwa-Bharati was founded by Dr. Rabindra Nath Tagore on May 6th, 1922 at Bolpur, a place situated at a distance of some hundred miles from Calcutta. He named it as 'Shanti Niketan' (the abode of peace). Upto 1948, the Vishwa-Bharati functioned without Government financial aid. The chief aim of Dr. Rabindra Nath Tagore in establishing it was to harmonise Oriental and Occidental systems of education, their culture and civilization. The classes were conducted in open air or under the trees. As a matter of fact, it is an experiment in a new method of education in modern times. According to the system of co-education boys and girls together receive education in arts, literature, philosophy and science. The main departments of the institution are:

(i) Vidya Bhavana where facilities are provided for research in Sanskrit, Pali, Prakrat, Hindi, Arabic, Persian, Urdu and other languages as well as in Indian philosophy, Buddhism and in the Vedantic philosophy.

(ii) Cheena Bhavana where Indian students are provided facilities to study Chinese culture and civilization and vice versa.

(iii) Shiksha Bhavana; (iv) Kala Bhavana; (v) Sangit Bhavana; (vi) Sriniketan, and (vii) Shilpa Bhavana.

After the freedom for the country, however, the Government devoted her attention towards this great institution and recognized it as a University. Since 1951, the Vishwa-Bharati is under the control of the Central Government and it is a unique institution of its own kind attracting students not only from different parts of higher education in different subjects.

Here it would be legitimate to say a few words about the Jamia Milia. Its meaning is the National Mohammedan University. It was founded by Maulana Mohamad Ali in 1920 at Aligarh for the education of nationalist Mohammedans; but in 1925, it was shifted to Delhi and Dr. Zakir Hussain was appointed as its Vice- Chancellor. It provides higher education in arts and science, besides conducting secondary education on sound lines. Basic education is imparted in primary schools through crafts. For this purpose it has a Basic Training Department. The arrangement of hostels is praiseworthy. After the independence of the country, the National Government has taken it under her control and sufficient funds are being expended on its advancement.

Secondary Education

Progress in the sphere for secondary education was quite satisfactory during this period. The number of students increased with that of the institutions. Private venture made appreciable progress in the field of education despite the meagerness of State aid, a phenomenon only to be explained by country wide national awakening. The number of recognized secondary schools rose from 7,530 in 1921-22 to 13,356 in 1936-37 and the number of students also rose from 11,06,803 to the stupendous figures 22,87,872. High Schools sprang up in big villages and towns too besides the cities. Some middle schools were recognized as high schools. Secondary education made progress among girls as well and backward classes of the society availed themselves of the advantages of secondary education for their children. Individual benefactors made liberal donations for the establishment of secondary schools. At places, the spirit of emulation too helped the establishment of a sister institution. But it is a deplorable fact that communal institutions bearing the name of Castes and sub-Castes were greatly encouraged during this period. Different communities collected subscription on organized basis and started their own institutions. Thus the Indians who had already been manacled in the fetters of communalism and caste rigidity, instead of eradicating this evil, fostered the sentiments of communalism through the establishment of communal institutions. It is, indeed a pity that these sentiments are still being fed fat under the pretext of nationalism and a kind of vain patriotism used in the narrowest sense. The Government has been extending recognition from day to day to the communal and sub caste institutions and thus she has been promoting discord among the Indians. Needless to say, these communal institutions are the centers of conspiracy, communal favouritism and nepotism and thus tend to bring about more evil than good. This is an instance of distorted patriotism. "These difficulties are accentuated by the fact that privately managed schools are almost invariably of a Communal type. The rapid multiplication of these schools had not only resulted in unnecessarily amplication and extravagance, sometimes in a weakening of discipline, but also in stimulating the unfortunate Communal Controversies which mar the progress of India, especially of the Punjab. It cannot be beneficial that boys should spend the impressionable years of youth in the narrowing atmosphere of a communal institution and that they should be denied intimate association with boys of other countries."[7]

The villagers were much benefited by the expansion of secondary education in rural areas during this period. Formerly, they had to send their children to some town for education, fighting against odds; but the percentage of village students in secondary schools was on the increase owing to partial availability of secondary education in villages.

The growth of secondary education is, as has been mentioned above, attributable mainly to private efforts. Whereas the number of Government Schools for boys was only 379 in 1921-22 and that of girls schools 115 rising to 436 and 207 in 1936-37 respectively indicating thus a total increase of 149, the total increase in private schools was abnormally large i.e. 1,836 out of which 315 schools were unrecognized. This increase in the number of secondary schools had been persisting for long.

Even after 1930, despite the economic crisis, India made satisfactory progress in secondary education. In 1937, the private venture was so active that the problems of Secondary Education as such became the problems of private secondary schools. The progress of secondary education can well be understood from the figures of the following table:

Year	*Number of Secondary Schools*	*Number of Students in Secondary Schools*
1881-82	3,916	2,14,077
1901-02	5,123	5,90,129
1921-22	7,530	11,06,803
1936-37	13,056	22,87,872

From the viewpoint of medium of instruction, this period was notable. Nearly in all the provinces, medium of instruction was made either Hindi or other provincial languages. In practice, however it brought about some difficulties. The main reason was that on account of English being the medium of instruction in universities some persons thought that secondary education was merely a part of university education and not an independent and self-contained unit; hence students were to be much profited later on if they were taught English in secondary schools. This argument was quite absurd in as much as it hampered with the growth of regional languages besides presenting countless difficulties before the students at the Secondary level. English was preferred as medium of instruction also because of the ambition of most of the young students to speak English and the wish of their parents to see their children speak it; and the desire to make English strong on account of its being the medium of answers in the competitive examinations. There were certain other limitations of the mother tongue depriving it of its recognition as medium i.e. the difficulty of script, lack of scientific technical words, and dearth of good text books in the beginning. But by 1937, most of these handicaps were removed and mother tongue began to be used as medium both in principle and practice.

There was also some improvement in the training for teachers, conditions of service and their salary. There was scarcity of trained teachers in secondary schools at that time. Hence untrained teachers had to be appointed under the circumstances. In fact, the number of training colleges in the country was so small that it could not meet the necessary requirements. The percentage of trained teachers in Bengal, Assam, Sindh and Bombay was 20.7 per cent, 39 per cent, 16.5 per cent and 22.8 per cent respectively. The figures in U.P., Madras, Delhi, Punjab, N.W. Frontier Province, Central Province and Bihar, however, were respectively 67.2 per cent, 84.7 per cent, 82.8 per cent, 89.7 per cent, 80.3 per cent, 70.2 per cent and 54.4 per cent. Rest of the teachers were untrained. This dealt a severe blow to efficiency in teaching. The condition of teachers in private secondary institutions was very deplorable. They had usually to fall a prey to the unhealthy petty politics of the management.[8] Their services were very often temporary. The scale of salary was very low and in most of the provinces there was no provision for old age. Generally the financial position of private institutions would always remain unsound, hence they could not get the services of able and eminent teachers. This brought about a fall in the standard of education. This problem soon diverted the attention of provincial governments, and constructive steps were taken in this direction. Needless to say that most of the problems confronting teachers in 1837 are still persisting. Not only that the situation has deteriorated in certain matters. A teacher who is the real nation builder and forms the spinal chord of the whole educational organism is discharging his duties listlessly as an ordinary labourer considering it to be a lifeless activity.

The other defect of secondary education was that although the vocational education made some progress during the period, it was quite inadequate in view of the needs of the country. Secondary education was tending to become bookish and theoretical, and as such unemployment was raging at its fiercest. Therefore, it became almost indispensable to include vocational and industrial education in the curriculum of secondary education. In Bombay, Madras, Bengal, U.P, the Punjab and in Central Province, such optional vocational subjects as spinning, weaving, crafts, bookbinding, agriculture, commerce, and making of toys were included in the curriculum. Theoretical education of agriculture was also included in the curriculum of high schools. On the recommendations of Wood-Abbott Report also, propagation of vocational education had been effected all the more.

Primary Education

The growth of primary education in the first decade following 1921 was satisfactory but it slackened at length. Hitherto the policy of Government in connection with primary education of general masses was always vehemently criticized. But all the Commissions and Committees since the Despatch of 1854 till Hartog Committee had recommended the universal expansion of mass education along with its being made compulsory, but no concrete step had been taken in this direction upto that time. In the decade between 1917 and 1927, some constructive schemes were framed and Bills enforcing compulsory primary education were passed by different provincial governments. The passing of such Bills was a strong retort to the defeat of Sri G.K. Gokhale. The Bombay Municipality has passed an Act in connection with compulsory primary education as early as 1918. After the Mont-Ford Reforms, a tide of such acts overflooded the sphere of primary education. In 1919, the Bengal Government passed this Act for urban areas. Next year, an attempt was made to include rural areas under this Act by amending it, but it was only in 1930 that the Bengal (Rural) primary Education Act could be passed thus fulfilling a long-cherished hope. It was in the same year that the Punjab, U.P. Bihar and Orissa Governments also passed similar Acts. The U.P. government passed. "The District Board Primary Education Act in 1926 for rural areas. Similarly, the Madras, Bombay and Assam Governments passes such Acts respectively in 1920, 1923 and 1926 to make primary education compulsory with, of course, some limitations.

These Acts placed primary education entirely under the control of local Boards-District and Municipal Boards. Each Board made a thorough study of the condition and needs of its own educational field and accordingly made schemes to promote primary education. The local boards were entrusted with the responsibility of defining the sphere wherein compulsory education was to be introduced in each province. They were empowered to levy educational cess, though this power could not be fully utilized. Provincial governments too consented to sanction grant-in-aid in connection with the expenditure on education. Compulsory primary education was in force in every province with the exception of the Punjab and Bihar and Orissa where it was applicable in case of boys only.

Ordinarily, where the primary course covered four years, the system of compulsion in education was applicable to children of ages between 6 and 10 years. Where the course was of the duration of 5 years, it was applicable to children between 6 and 11 years of age. In the Punjab it was between 7 and 11 years. Children were forbidden to be employed in any service. The guardians of children not complying with the law of compulsory education were liable to be punished. This sort of education was, generally, free or a nominal fee was levied for the purpose.

The object of compulsory primary education Act in all the provinces was the same i.e. eradication of illiteracy through compulsory education and vesting of this power in local boards.

The reaction of these Acts was wholesome. The new education ministers formed their educational schemes and enforced them in a vast sphere. The provincial Governments too tried to fulfil the demands of education ministers by sanctioning liberal grants-in-aids for educational purposes. Consequently, the number of primary schools was 1,55,016 in 1921-22 rising to 1,84,829 in 1926-27 and expenditure rose from Rs. 3,94,69,080/- to Rs. 6,75,18,802/-. Similarly, the number of children attending primary schools shot upward. But in the following quinquennium, this progress slowed down owing to economic crises and to the views of Hartog Committee Report Mr. Hartog had opposed further expansion of Education and had emphasized the improvement in quality and its solidarity. The education authorities complied with the recommendations of Hartog to the last letter. This explains the fact that primary education has not been made compulsory as yet in the country. Whatever Acts had been passed by provincial governments with regard to making primary education compulsory, proved nugatory and void for some reason or the other and they could nowhere be applied in true sense. In fact, this movement itself proved unsuccessful. This shows that in spite of all the schemes for the expansion of primary education formed during the last hundred years, and all controversy over this issue, the problem has not been solved substantially and entirely even upto this time.

The attitude of Hartog Committee Report proved very detrimental. it gave undue encouragement to provincial governments who closed many elementary schools down on the grounds that they were running under very precarious condition, that they had no funds and building or their efficiency of working was below the norm etc. The non-official views were against this attitude and policy of the government. According to them quantitative improvement was much more necessary than qualitative improvement because the country was shrouded in the dark veil of ignorance at this time and the percentage of literacy had increased from 3.5 in 1881 to only 8.0 in 1931. In other words 92 per cent of Indian population was groping in dark for want of light. The public wanted that nectar of education should fall in torrents instead of falling drop by drop.

In spite of difference of opinion and controversies over this issue, educational progress remained far from being satisfactory and heartening during the decade 1927-37. It is quite evident from the

	1921-22	*1926-27*	*1931-32*	*1936-37*
(i) No. of recognized primary schools	1,55,017	1,84,829	1,96,708	1,92,244
(ii) No. of Pupils	61,09,752	80,17,923	91,62,450	1,02,24,288
(iii) Total of Direct expenditure (upon primary education)	Rs. 4,94,69,080	Rs.4,75,14,802	Rs. 6,87,95,236	Rs. 8,13,38,015

figures in the following table that there is a very slow rise in the number of students and institutions between the years 1927 and 1937 so much so that the number of institutional had fallen by 4,464 from 1931-32 to 1936-37:

The reasons of educational demotion were very many besides economic crisis in India and the policy of Hartog Committee. As a matter of fact, the local boards could never take the problem of expansion of primary education seriously. These places were vitiated by mutual rivalty, partisan spirit and low politics.. The members of local boards did never levy education cess for fear of their discomfiture in the following elections. The local boards, therefore, remained financially impoverished. The members generally did not understand the significance of education. Lack of proper inspection can be cited as one of the strong factors which have checked the growth of primary education. The inspectors while going to inspect the schools in rural areas, would carry with them an air of superiority complex, and behave the poor school teachers drily and impolitely instead of proving their friends or guides. They would thus go about from place to place aimlessly making a formal inspection; and after an outing of a few days would come back to towns. Similarly, in urban areas inspection was inefficient and insufficient. Owing to carelessness of Attendance Officers, primary education could not be made compulsory in the proper sense of the term in urban areas well. It is still a cherishable vision for us.

Moreover, the plight of village school teachers—low salary, little education, inadequate training—was also one of the reasons causing a lot of harm to primary education. The curriculum, being quite divorced from the practical needs of life, could never inspire the boys. Their tender brains were subjected to the abstract bookish learning. The wide-spread economic crisis impoverished the masses utterly. Hence the poor parents, instead of sending their children to schools considered it to be more profitable to send them to fields or on some other employment in order to keep their body and soul together. They would thus get their daily meager wages in terms of a few coppers. This tendency also contributed much to the decline in the number of students. One of the evil consequences of widespread poverty was that it encouraged child labour. A few copper pieces which the child would get as remuneration for tending the cattle or doing some other similar service, would help the family budget considerably. Under such financial circumstances, there were very few parents who, forgoing the meager income, could have sent their children to school.

Conclusion

It is, however, a truism that with the enforcement of constitution of 1935 in India, the Provincial Governments were given full autonomous powers. Consequently, the representative Indian ministers took the administrative reins in their own hands. The education minister too availed himself of the opportunity of materializing his educational plans. All these events produced a very wholesome effect on education and it began to make an all round progress. The following pages will be devoted to this end.

REFERENCES

1. Hartog Committee Report; p. 31.
2. Report p.107.
3. Nurrullah and Naik: *History of Education in India;* p. 691.
4. Ibid: p. 619
5. Report of the Universities Commission (1948-49) Vol. I, p. 29.
6. This institute was formerly situated at Pusa (Bihar); but after the earthquake in 1934, it was shifted to Delhi. It maintains an agricultural farm at Delhi.
7. Quinquennial Review of the Progress of Education in India 1927-324 Vol. I, p. 106.
8. Efficient and capable teachers are sometimes victimised, not through any fault of their own, but because they had incurred the displeasure of the management by failing to cater to the whims of those who have gained for the time being the upper hand in the administration of the institution" *Progress of Education* Quinquennial Review 1927-32. Vol. 1. p. 106.

7

Education Under Provincial Autonomy (1937-1955)

Introduction

The Constitution of 1935 laid the foundation stone of autonomous rule in India. In 1937, a system of administration known as Provincial Autonomy came into operation in II Provinces seven out of which had Congress Ministries. The powers of these ministers were very large. They got an opportunity to materialise unhindered all their plans of nation-building. By this time the importance of education for the regeneration of the country had been accepted in all quarters. The country, moreover, had produced a number of eminent educationists and leaders who understood educational problems fully well and were in a position to put certain concrete suggestions to solve them.

A wave of enthusiasm spread in the country as a result of this political change of historic magnitude. Education began to be overhauled and reorganised in each province. The Congress Ministries were engaged in finding proper solutions for multifarious problems of the country by operating their plans. An era of educational renaissance was, as it were, ushered in. Literary movement, Adult education movement, education of women and the untouchables—these and a number of similar other projects were launched with great vigour and zeal. In 1937, Mahatma Gandhi infused a new life in primary and secondary education by finding the formula of Basic Education at Wardha. This strengthened the hope for the enforcement of free compulsory primary education in the country.

Meanwhile in 1939, owing to the outbreak of the World War II, and as a protest against the Government's policy of compelling India to participate in War, Congress Ministries tendered resignations, Thus the rising tide of educational expansion was for the time being stemmed by these circumstances. Later on, in 1942, the world-famous 'Quit India movement broke out in the country. The British Government repressed the movement brutally. The tales of British atrocities are sufficient to make one turn away from them in sheer disgust and shame. The Indian leaders were placed behind the bars as a result of the movement; thus an irretrievable harm was caused to educational movement as well as to national movement. The Central and Provincial Governments devoted their entire efforts to war. This should have been resulted in scarcity of funds for educational purposes. As a matter of fact the five years may well be called the 'dark period' for the education of the country. Educational institutions were kept merely alive. This led to stagnation in their growth.

With the sure indications for victory for the Allies, in the beginning of 1944, post war reconstruction projects began to be chalked out. In the sphere of education too, a post-war development plan ' Sargent Plan" by name was submitted by the Central Advisory board which will be mentioned shortly afterwards in this chapter.

On the basis of Sargent Plan reorganisation of education began to take place in the country and during the period following 1945, education began to make advancement. The fury of political movement was raging in the country. The position of England had become quite weak after the war. She was too weak politically to keep India under subjection any further. The Indians were struggling hard to achieve freedom. At length on August 15, 1947, India was divided and became independent. After 1945, a separate Education Department was established under the Central Government and its responsibilities were entrusted to a member of the Central Executive. In 1946, the University Grants Committee was also appointed. Now during the post-independence period the plans for the reform and development of education are making appreciable headway and their number is multiplying. Today both the Government and public are engaged in the task of solving this important problem.

The independence of the country has brought in its wake many problems in the sphere of education. The percentage of literacy is shamefully low even today. Only six crores of people out of a vast population of 37 crores are literate, which means that only 17 per cent persons of the whole population are literate. Under these circumstances the country is confronted with a responsibility of magnitudinous importance i.e. to make the vast population consisting of teeming millions literate and to provide them with such an education as may serve their practical ends in life. We see that proper steps have been taken in this direction. Considering the grave defect of Indian system of education i.e. the predominance of mere bookish learning, more importance is being attached to scientific technical and vocational education so that permanent and solid foundation might be laid for the reconstruction of the nation by moulding education into a new form.

Acknowledging the importance of education as the *sine qua non* of national progress, both the Central and Provincial Governments have begun to materialize various development plans with a view to providing education to maximum possible number of people. Many scientific and technical institutions have been started in the country. The number of universities, secondary schools, primary and basic schools is increasing from day to day. Moreover, diverse plans have been put into operation under the first five-year Plan of the government for the sake of bringing about a co-ordinate progress of all the aspects of the education. Progress is being made in the field of social education to make innumerable adults literate and make them acquainted with the attributes of good citizenship. The Government of India has begun to award scholarships to Indian students going abroad for special training and to foreign students to enable them to receive education in Indian universities. Special educational facilities are being provided to the backward classes as Harijans and tribal races etc, and to persons handicapped physically and mentally i.e. the blind, deaf and imbeciles. An account of it will be given in the following pages.

Besides, the Central and Provincial Governments have made a thorough examination of all educational problems in their entirety with the aim of reorganising education at all stages by appointing commissions and committees of educational experts to this end. A University Commission, for instance, with Shri Sarvapalli Radha

Krishan as its Chairman, was appointed in the year 1948. It had submitted its detailed Report in 1949-50. According to the suggestions of this Report, efforts have been made to solve the problems of University and collegiate education in a novel way. In July, 1952, the Secondary Education Commission under the Chairmanship of Dr. Lakshman Swami Mudaliar, the Vice Chancellor of the Madras University, was appointed for the purpose of reorganising Secondary Education. The Commission submitted its comprehensive report before the country in August 1953. We can mention the U. P. Secondary Education Reorganisation Committee (1953) with Acharya Narendra Dev as its Chairman and the Allahabad University Inquiry Commission under the Chairmanship of justice Mootham from amongst the committees appointed within different states. A detailed account of these commission will be provided in course of time.

Besides these, basic education has been recognised at primary and secondary stages of education. Many Basic Training colleges are being established for the training of Basic teachers. Reference to all these developments will be made in detail at the proper place.

From the viewpoint of medium of education, Hindi has been recognised as the National language by the Indian Constitution and efforts are begin made to bring it into force by 1965 at primary, secondary and university levels. In different States, provincial languages will be used as media of instruction at primary and secondary stages.

So far as the question of organisation and administration is concerned, we see that since 1947, Education Department in the centre has developed into fullfledged Ministry under the Central Government. The States are entirely free in the sphere of education. The responsibility of educating the people of the States is devolved upon them. The Central Government looks only to the national aspect of education and tries to solve problems related there to of all India importance and magnitude. It is the duty of the centre to see whether or not the standard of education is equal at different stages in different states.

The Government of India is directly responsible for the education of the people of parts 'C' and 'D' states viz. Ajmer, Coorg, Andaman and Nicobar, Kachachha, Manipur, Tripura and Bhopal.

The power of control and administration of education has been partly transferred to Universities, Secondary Education Boards, District Boards, Municipalities and Cantonment Boards and similar other local bodies as well as to other philanthropic, religious and private institutions.

The Central Educational Ministry consists of an Education Minister and for his assistance an Educational Adviser, two Deputy Educational Advisers and four Assistant Educational advisers who are responsible for educational responsibilities of different branches. In addition to these there are Educational Secretary and Under Secretary who execute the Government policies. The Central Advisory Board of Education is the main body to provide advice on educational problems of country-wide importance. It consists of the representatives from different States. The Board has rendered valuable services in connection with bringing about a co-ordination among educational systems of different provinces and effecting a uniform educational policy. The Central Government has established an Overseas Information Bureau which gives information to the students desiring to go abroad for further studies and furnishes valuable information to the Universities of different States. In the States, besides the Education Minister, there are one Director of Public Instructions, or Director of Education, Deputy Directors and Inspectors to assist him. There are in the State Governments Education Secretaries and Under Secretaries to execute the State duties about education.

The following statistical table throws sufficient light on the educational progress of the country.[1]

Thus we see that India is on the way to progress in educational field. The Government is trying her best to provide ample opportunities to the masses for their education. In spite of the sincerity of the Government efforts in this direction, we find that the problem is so gigantic and difficult that it baffles all solutions. Hence the steps directed toward this side are far from being satisfactory and adequate. Today we hear all the eminent educationists and political leaders of the country observe that the educational system of India is defective and quite unsuitable to the spirit of time and place. No doubt, the statement contains some truth in it. But today we are a

Kinds of Institutions	No. of Institutions	No. of students in thousands	Expenditure (in lakhs)
1. University	30	26	466
2. Board of Secondary and Intermediate Education	12	-	75
3. Science & Arts Colleges	579	347	833
4. Vocational and Special Education Colleges	311	71	520
5. Secondary Schools	22,500	5,648	3,340
6. Primary Schools	2,14,862	18,901	4,015
7. Pre-primary Schools	331	23	15
8. Vocational and Special Education Schools	51,999	1,484	544
Total	2,90,264	26,500	9,808[2]

free nation and we have all the powers, resources and opportunities to mould educational system according to our own ideology and pattern. Why then are the educationists and Government of India inactive to remedy all these defects which have crept into the educational system? As a matter of fact, we can make bold to say that the educationists have not clearly visualized any definite shape of the future educational system which might be put before the country. We have been following the educational system and traditions born during the British period and still advancing the old pattern further. We shall have to sketch out a new picture and apply new colours to it. This is quite impossible in the absence of any systematic plan. There are a number of remedies worthy of prescription which can bring Indian educational system on a par with those of other nations by removing the inherent defects from it. The suggestions are mainly:

(i) To mould the curricula according to the needs of the country by introducing radical changes in it;

(ii) Attaching sufficient importance to Primary and Secondary education and making the method of teaching scientific;

(iii) Making the university curricula more suitable to the needs of life and country by the inclusion of more subjects of practical utility in the syllabus;

(iv) Emphasising the need of technical and vocational education;

(v) Provision of adequate and special facilities for the education of women;

(vi) Establishment of special institutions for the purpose of social education;

(vii) Improvement in the conditions of teachers and teaching at all stages; ensuring of academic autonomy to the teachers;

(viii) Provision of all the facilities for research work and environment and encouragement to teachers to qualify themselves better.

Now we shall undertake a thorough examination of the growth of education after 1937.

Wardha Scheme of Basic Education

With the establishment of popular Governments in the Provinces in 1937, an important event in the history of Indian education took place and that was the introduction of the Wardha scheme of education. Mahatma Gandhi, as a matter of fact, had been expressing his views on education through the articles published in the 'Harijan.[3] In the Educational Conference held at Wardha on 22nd and 23rd October, 1937, he put forth his ideas in the form of a systematic educational plan. It was the time when Indian leaders were dissatisfied with the contemporary educational system and were eagerly endeavouring to nationalise it and thus make it more useful and effective.

On October, 2, 1937, Gandhiji published an article in the 'Harijan' embodying his desire of calling a Conference of National Education on 22nd and 23rd October of the same year. He put forward four main problems pertaining to education in the following words:

(i) English holds a prominent place in the present educational system; hence knowledge cannot percolate to the masses;

(ii) The course of primary education should at least be extended to seven years;

(iii) Education should, as far as possible, be imparted through the medium of profit yielding craft for the all round development of the children; and

(iv) Higher education should be entrusted to private enterprise. Universities were to manage higher education.

Accordingly, on the occasion of the silver jubilee of "Marwari Shiksha Mandal", the Wardha Conference was called under the presidentship of Mahatma Gandhi. Sri Shrimannarayan was the convener of this conference. Several educationists from different parts of the country and all the provincial education ministers participated in it. In his presidential address delivered at the Conference, Mahatma Gandhi presented his plan. He observed:

"The views I wish to place before you possessed and occupied my mind for long, though the way of their presentation is somewhat novel. The proposal I am putting forth is related both to the primary and college education but the former should have more claim upon our attention. I am including secondary education with the primary education because primary education is available only to a negligible section of the villagers, as I have found during the course of my tours throughout the country since 1915....

"My conviction is that we shall have to combine primary and secondary education together, if we aim at improving the condition of the villages. Hence the educational plan we are going to implement should essentially be rural in character.... If we succeed in tackling the problem of primary education satisfactorily, the problem of college education can easily be solved.

"I am fully confident that the present primary educational system is not only wasteful but, on the other hand harmful too. Generally, the children are rendered of no practical use to their parents and cannot, moreover, undertake their hereditary occupation.

More often than not they contract many vices of city life. Whatever partial knowledge they acquire cannot be called education whatever else it might be. Now the question arises: what should then be the form of primary education? The only remedy, in my opinion is that of imparting education through crafts and occupational activities. I have the experience of my children and other children being taught through the wood-work and leather work in the Tolstoy Farm....

"The aim of my educational plan is not merely to teach some handicrafts to children along with the so called liberal education. I wish that entire education be imparted through the medium of some handicraft or industry. It may be argued that during the medieval age, students were educated in handicrafts alone; but the aim of occupational training was not educational at that time. These handiworks were taught mainly for occupational purpose alone and no endeavour was made for the mental development of the students....

"Improvement in education can be expected only when the art and science of some vocation is taught through practical education and it is made the basis of the entire educational system. For instance, while teaching the art of spinning with the *'Takali'*, other correlated subjects *i.e.* kinds of cotton, suitable soil in Indian provinces for its production, a history of downfall of cotton industry, the political reasons of it including the British rule in the country and mathematics etc. should also be taught to the students. I have been doing this experiment upon my grandson who even does not feel whether or not he is being taught. I am laying particular emphasis on the *'Takali'*, because I am conscious of its force and 'romance'. It can be used for manufacturing cloth in this country. It is, moreover, quite cheap. Taking into consideration the pitiable economic condition of the country, the *'Takali'* alone is the possible solution of our problems.

"I have submitted this plan to the ministers. It is upto them whether or not they accept it. My advice is that *'Takali'* should constitute the nucleus of the primary education.... The *'Takali'* would be helping production, because the cloth made by children will be much in demand. I have thought of a seven year course which will aim at giving practical education in spinning, weaving, dyeing and making designs.

"I have the problem of meeting the expenses of the teacher in my view. It can be solved by selling the commodities made by children. Otherwise, there is no other way of catering to the educational needs of hundreds of thousands of children.... The primary education embodies the principles of self-help and filial piety along with the sanitary rules and dietetics etc. Children of the present generation are not familiar with the sanitary rules and the virtue of self-reliance and they are physically weak too. I am, therefore, in favour of giving them compulsory education along with music drill.

"The critics of my scheme affirm that I am opposed to literary education. It is far from being true. I am simply paving the way for such education. The argument is advanced that while we should have spent crores of rupees on education, we, on the contrary, are thinking of exploiting children. It is also feared that the plan will entail much wastage of time and money. But the practical experience proves all such fears to be baseless. So far as the question of exploitation of children and subjecting them to work is concerned, my answer is whether rescuing them from utter ruin means their exploitation. *'Takali'* is a kind of toy for children; does it lose its utility as a toy by being a means of production? Even today children do help their parents in one way or the other.... Thus when the child will be taught spinning and helping their parents in agricultural occupation, a feeling will be engendered in his heart that he belongs not only to his parents but to his village and country as well and that he ought to absolve himself of the debt due to them. This is the only advisable course open to us. I shall advise the ministers that giving financial aid to the education of children is tantamount to rendering them helpless and depended on others. If, on the other hand, children earn enough to meet their educational expenses, they would grow into self-dependent and brave persons. The formula is applicable to all alike be he a Hindu, Mohammedan, Parsi or Christian. Some people ask why I do not emphasise religious education. My answer is that my aim is to teach them the practical religion of self reliance."

Gandhiji then referring to the appointment of teachers observed that they ought to volunteer their services to the country. He also said, "The test of the success of this educational scheme lies in its being wholly self-supporting. Children should meet the expenses of their education at the expiry of seven years and be earning factors."

Concluding his address, Mahatma Gandhi observed in the end: "If we sincerely wish the abolition of communalism and international dissensions, its foundation should be laid solidly and the new generation should be educated according to my scheme. The origin of this scheme lies in the principle of non-violence.... We are to make our children the true embodiment of our culture, civilization and national glory. It is impossible so long as we do not give them primary education based on the principle of self-reliance. Europe cannot serve as our model. Since her educational schemes are based on violence.... If India has pledged the vow of abstaining from violence, only the proposed educational scheme can be the sole means of its fulfilment. We are told that large sums are spent on education in England and America, but we forget that this sum is obtained through sheer exploitation of the masses. The art of exploitation has assumed the form of science in these countries. We can neither think of exploitation nor shall ever do so. Hence there is no other alternative for us except an educational system thoroughly steeped in the principle of non-violence."

Following the presidential address of Gandhiji other learned educationists like Dr. Zakir Hussain and Prof. K.T. Shah etc. expressed their own views about the envisaged scheme. Education Ministers from different provinces while appreciating the scheme threw light on some of its drawbacks and put forth certain difficulties. Gandhiji gave satisfactory replies to all the critics and put forth suggestions for its experimentation. Leaders such as Acharya Vinoba Bhave, Kaka Kalelkar, Mahadev Desai, B.G. Kher and Pt. Ravi Shankar Shukla supported the scheme. At length four resolutions were passed.

Resolutions

(i) That in the opinion of this Conference free and compulsory primary education be provided for seven years to all boys and girls on a nation-wide scale;

(ii) That the medium of instruction be the mother tougue;

(iii) That the Conference endorses the proposal made by Mahatma Gandhi, that the process of education throughout this period should centre round some

productive form of manual work, and that all other abilities to be developed or training to be given should, as far as possible, be integrally related to the central handicraft chosen with due regard to the environment of the child; and

(iv) That the Conference expects that the system of education will be gradually able to cover the remuneration of the teachers.[4]

With the passing of the above resolutions, a Committee under the presidentship of Dr. Zakir Hussain, the then principal of Jamia-Millia, Delhi, was appointed with a view to giving a practical shape to Gandhiji's scheme and for preparing a detailed syllabus. There were nine more members on it including Sir Aryanayakam (convener), Sri Vinoba Bhave, Kaka Kalelker, J.C. Kumarappa, Sri Mashroowala and Prof. K. T. Shah, to name only the prominent ones of them. They were empowered to co-opt some other members. On December 2, 1937 and in April 1938, the Committee submitted two Reports. The first Report embodies the fundamental principles underlying the scheme, prevalent educational system, Gandhi's leadership, Crafts in schools, stress on the cultivation of the qualities of good citizenship and the self-supporting aspects of the scheme. Moreover, it also gives a brief outline of the syllabus of basic education for seven years and that of educational organisation and administration throwing light simultaneously on the aims of the scheme, training of teachers, inspection and rules of examination. It includes a detailed curriculum of the main handicraft of spinning and weaving. In its second Report, the Committee included other basic crafts also such as agriculture, metal-work and carpentry and submitted a comprehensive syllabus and method of instruction. It has, moreover, sought to establish natural points of correlation between these basic handicrafts and other subjects. The Zakir Hussain Report was submitted in February 1938, before the Haripura Congress Session for discussion. Subsequently, the congress accepted the scheme officially. The Scheme having been published, it was spread in the country. It received criticism from different quarters of the country. Gandhiji replied to the criticism and set all doubts at rest through the 'Harijan'. Thus having emerged in its pure form, the Basic Educational Scheme was experimented in U.P., Central

Province, Bihar, Orissa and Bombay. As indicated above, the scheme remained incomplete consequent upon the resignation of Congress in the year 1939. Later on, the authorities abolished it considering it to be detrimental and impracticable. It, however, remained in effect in well nigh twenty seven centres of Champaran in Bihar.

Some Important Features of the Wardha Scheme

The Wardha Scheme introduced a new system of education viz. Basic Education in the country. Prior to our understanding of the fundamental principles and features of the Scheme, it is necessary to discern the significance of the word 'basic' as related to education. Primarily, education has been termed as basic, for it will form the basis of our national culture and civilization. Every child belonging to any class will get the opportunity to adopt it without any distinction. It will be compulsory in character. The next reason of its being called as 'basic' is that it will have as the centre of instruction some such basic craft as might form the basis of Indian economic life. Besides, the scheme envisages the full development of the fundamental creative faculty of the child. The handicraft will fully cater to the creative feelings and the child will show a keen interest in the acquisition of knowledge. Hence basic education will, to a considerable measure,, meet the fundamental requirements of life—social, individual, economic and intellectual. It would, verily, form the solid plane sustaining the existence of our children, society and nation.

Here it is essential to describe the main elements of basic education briefly:

(i) *Basic Craft as the Medium of Instruction:* The special feature of basic education is that it is imparted through the medium of some useful basic craft. All the modern educationists are unanimous on the principle of educating children through the medium of some suitable form of productive work. Thus education will essentially be related to real life. Whereas the problem of employment will also be fully developed and his creative and productive faculties will be fostered to a large degree. It has been mentioned in the Zakir Hussain Report that psychologically, the adoption of crafts as medium is desirable because it rescues the child from the bondage of a purely literary and theoretical instruction against which its spirit has always put forth vehement protest. It will educate both the mind and the body of the child. Its aim will not miserably be confined to superficial literacy, on the other hand, it will instruct the child to use his hand and intelligence for some constructive purpose. Its prime objective would be, if the use of the phrase may be permitted "the education of the whole personality."

The Report further states the basic education will level down all the social distinctions and prejudices; and thus the wide gulf between the intellectual worker and manual worker will also be bridged over. The children thereby will realize the dignity of labour.

Economically considered, the scheme will, if carried out intelligently and efficiently, make the child self-dependent; and education will also become self-supporting. "Knowledge will thus become related to life, and its various aspects will be correlated with one another."

The centre of basic education will, therefore, be craft. But, as has been said in the Report, "the object of this new educational scheme is not primarily the production of craftsmen able to practise some craft mechanically, but rather the exploitation for educative purposes of the resources implicit in craft work." It necessarily implies two conditions. "First, the craft or productive work chosen should be rich in educative possibilities. It should find natural points of correlation with important human activities and interests, and should extend into the whole content of the school curriculum.

The craft thus will not only form a part of the school curriculum but will also form the centre of other subjects and be related to them. According to the views of Gandhiji "every handicraft will be taught scientifically, not mechanically as is done today so that the child may learn the relation between cause and effect on each process.". If spinning and weaving were to be taught like other subjects, it would be suicidal to the entire scheme itself. In fact no single craft exclusively serves as medium of instructions. Every craft has its own limitations. Hence social and natural environments too, in addition to the craft has been kept in view. Thus a particular subject "what cannot be correlated through craft work will be correlated through physical and social environment of the child in which he is as keenly interested as in craft work."[5]

(ii) *Cultivation of the Ideal of Citizenship:* Child of today is the citizen of tomorrow. The aim of education, therefore should essentially be the development of the qualities of citizenship. The rising generation should realize its duties towards the society and country. In modern age every citizen should be a useful and productive unit of the society. Gandhiji had fully recognised that the current educational system of the country had been producing a class of exploiters who led a parasitic sort of existence upon the means of others. Hence it was thought essential that some such kind of educational system should be evolved as might convince the children of the true dignity of labour and make them self reliant. Basic education fulfils this aim to a major extent. Under this system every child has compulsorily to do some manual work. All children of the class, irrespective of social distinction, do work collectively. Thus sentiments of co-operation along with those of independence and dignity of labour are naturally inculcated in their minds. They develop their love for the country and the nation and learn the concrete lesson of corporate life, being inspired by the feelings of social service. Hence the formation and development of character that take place during the childhood and adolescence is reflected in later period in practical life.

The sentiments of co-operation are absent usually in common schools; but immense encouragement is given to these feelings in basic schools. A child engaged in his creative and productive activities feels proudly that he forms an important limb of the nation and that he learns the lesson of nation building and its well-being.

(iii) *Self-supporting Aspect of the Scheme:* As a matter of fact, this is that aspect of the Scheme which has been much criticised throughout the country. Prof. K. T. Shah opined that we would make the slave of a child by subjecting it to the training in craft and exploit it by placing the economic objective before us. The child, forgetting higher aims of education, would work as professional artisan—mechanical and insensate. It was also contended that basic education would convert schools into factories where it would be expected that the salary of the teacher should be paid off from the child's production. The teacher too would extract maximum work from the child. Besides these objections, some persons expressed their doubts that the articles produced by the children would be too clumsy to have any sale value and that much raw material would go waste in the beginning. "An attempt to make the schools self-supporting would mean converting the institutions in to centres of production; and the success of any school will be reckoned not by its education but by the production of the saleable commodities."[6] Again, children are entitled to get education form the state; why should they depend for their education upon their productive resources, etc. etc.?

Viewed critically, it would be, however, manifest that all these contentions and doubts are baseless and pessimistic. In fact, there is a great misunderstanding about them. The self-supporting and independent aspect of the scheme means that on the one hand the salary of the teacher may partly be met by the productive labour of the child; on the other, the pupil also may get productive means of his livelihood in later life after education. The scheme does not aim at producing merely artisans. The Committee in its Report has made this point clear that "even if it is not 'self-supporting' in any sense, it should be accepted as a matter of sound educational policy and as an urgent measure of national reconstruction". So far as the issue of expenses is concerned, the scheme will meet daily expenditure by producing things incidentally. In its support, the Committee has also proved by giving statistics of spinning and weaving that the scheme can be self-supporting.

So far as the question of the reply to the above-mentioned objections is concerned, Gandhiji has made them clear in the Harijan at intervals. He wrote that the salary of teachers and the expenditure of basic craft could easily be met by the seven years' labour of the children. The raw material might go waste only in the beginning; but, later on, it would cease to be so. It is natural that capable teacher can stop the wastage. The articles produced by the children would be bought by the Government. The citizens too would feel happy and elevated by purchasing at higher rates goods produced by the children.

So far as the question of competition in the market is concerned, only those articles which admit of no competition will be produced in schools such as course cloth, indigenous paper and raw sugar from date-palm etc. In similar way, Gandhiji has refuted other objections too. He was of the opinion that any craft could thoroughly be taught within the span of seven years. Thus unemployment would be abolished and virtues of self-reliance and nation-building would be engendered among the pupils.

Gandhiji also believed that elementary education should be developed in the country, as soon as possible and for this purpose it was impossible to wait for state help any longer. Hence it was essential that education should be made self-supporting. "The educational system of this sort can certainly be self-supporting and it should be so; as matter of fact, self-sufficiency is the only test of its reality."[7] So far as the question of regarding basic schools as 'factories' is concerned, Gandhiji told that holding of such views was nothing short of being blind to facts, for factory had for its objective, exploitation. No attention is paid there to the principles of education whereas to sole aim of basic schools would be education. Handicrafts would remain mere medium and not the aim of education.[8]

In the end of the Committee's Report a warning has been given against the danger of teachers sacrificing cultural and educational aspects of the scheme to the economic aspect and devoting their time and energy to seeing that the students were earning money through maximum production. The only remedy against it is that teachers should, during the course of their training, be advised well and inspectors be required to see that pupil's labour might not be exploited in any way.

(iv) *Child as the Centre of Education:* Though the teacher holds an important place in the basic educational system and the pupil cannot be active without his proper guidance, yet the child remains the centre of activity. Education in the basic school is what happens, primarily to the child and thus it is grounded in his activities. Hence unless the child takes active part in the activities of the school, it cannot progress educationally. The Basic system regards the child as the "educational consumer"; its needs, therefore, have to be studied, understood and catered to.

The system is not in any way an innovation. Throughout the world, a move is afoot to establish schools where special stress is being laid upon the development of the child's personality and it is regarded as the centre of education. During the nineteenth century, in Western countries, educationists like Rousseau, Pestalozzi, Froebel and Herbert emphasized the importance and value of activity in education by 'psychlogising' it and thus made an attempt to understand and develop the individuality of the child. They held that the 'present' of the child was more important and it should, therefore, be kept in view ignoring the possibilities of the future. In modern times as well, these principles have been supported by John Dewey, a famous American educationist. He was of the opinion that the child's personality should be as much respected in the school as that of the adult in society.

The Basic system of education also regards the child as the centre of activity and develops its individuality. Sometimes, its is contended by some critics of the scheme that it is 'craft-centred' instead of being 'child centred'. The critics hold that when every subject is taught through the medium of some craft work and the articles made by the children are sold in order to meet the expenditure of the institution, the interests and natural abilities of the children would be exploited to raise the standard of production both in quality and quantity. But these objections have adequately been met by Dr. Zakir Hussain and Mahatma Gandhi. As a matter of fact, craft work will remain only a means and not an end and only that craft will be selected which is rich in educative possibilities. It will have natural points of correlation with important human activities and interests. The basic scheme is one of education and not of production. Its chief aim is to utilize the resources implicit in craft work for educational purposes and the development of the child's individuality; it does not seek merely to produce craftsmen at the age of fourteen.

In India where education exists but for the 'examination' and entire system is dominated by various subjects and text books, the Basic system holds a very important place. According to ordinary educational system the child receives from teachers and books information and knowledge as a passive listener of those incidents which are considered to be possibly related to the future life. Whatever is learnt by the child is expected to be repeated by him. Both the teacher and the child remain constantly horrified with the idea of examination. How can one imagine of the development of the child's personality under these circumstances? The basic system on the other hand, seeks to eliminate both these defects. According to it child takes initiative himself and progresses under the guidance of the teacher. The teacher gets ample opportunities to supervise the work and judge the fundamental capacity of the children. Hence it is evident that the child is the centre of education under this scheme.

(v) *Knowledge as One Unified Whole:* Under the ordinary educational system, the children are taught different and mutually exclusive subjects in the schools. The child, therefore, instead of regarding knowledge as one unified whole, considers it to be a collection of varied and unrelated events. It is difficult for the child to establish any relation between and multifarious subjects owing to their being taught separately. The teacher pours factual knowledge into the willing or reluctant heads of pupils and they to themselves try to store it by rote memory till they are called upon to pour it back in an examination. Whether such knowledge helps develop their latent powers and faculties or whether it is related to their future life or not, is regarded to be no concern either of the teacher or the school.

According to the Basic system, children are no longer regarded as plastic material capable of being moulded at will or as empty vessels to be filled with the factual knowledge of varied subjects by the teacher. In fact, craft being the medium of education, all the subjects are taught through the medium of it. An attempt is made to correlate the study of all subjects to it. The child thus understands knowledge to be one unified whole. The curriculum no longer means a mere scheme of studies or a list of subjects and text-books, but in the entire range of activities and experiences wherein the child keeps himself engaged under the supervision of the school. The curriculum does not follow a narrow rigid pattern, but is, on the other hand, sufficiently flexible and grows and changes *paripassu* with the growth and development of the child. On account of the predominance of 'activity' instead of 'subjects' in the child's education, he assimilates easily the knowledge and experience gained through it. For instance, the teacher during the course of instructing the pupil to spin on the '*Takali*' can impart to him knowledge of such things as cotton and the need of proper soil and water for its production, development of cotton industry, advent of the Britishers in India and the determining of the price of cotton. Thus the child can easily learn geography, chemistry, history and arithmetic along with spinning. Thus explains why knowledge in regarded as one unified and integrated whole under the basic system of education.

(vi) *More Freedom for Teachers and Pupils to Work:* Both the teachers and pupils enjoy grater freedom to work under the Basic system. 'When the aim of education is conceived to be the fullest possible growth and development of the young through self-activity, spontaneous and creative, the pupils must have a larger measure of freedom to think for themselves, to plan their work according to their choice and interest and to carry out their plans at their own pace."[9] We cannot expect self-expression and creative activity from the child under the present educational system where excessive stress is laid on mere rote memory and mastery of facts within a prescribed span of time for the sake of passing the examination. The object of Basic school, on the other hand, is to provide ample opportunity to work, acquire knowledge through useful work and display his interests. Here attention is paid to the child's individual difficulties and needs, and he is made to feel that the school exists and works for him.

In like measure, the teacher too enjoy comparatively greater degree of freedom. He is not required to follow an inflexible and rigid syllabus incapable of being, if need be, alternated by him. Nor is he at all worried about finishing courses and text-books for the examinations. In fact, he can think and make experiment for himself and work out such methods of teaching as may be more convenient and useful both for himself and pupils and be best suited to the conditions of the school. He is free to modify the work and change text-books in the light of his accumulated experience. He does no longer feel that he is a helpless tool in the hands of those who draw up the syllabi, prescribe text-books, frame timetables and conduct examinations. It should not, however, lead us to surmise that under. The Basic system there is no fixed and definite curriculum or there are no fixed text-books. The only difference is that this system is much more flexible and the teacher is empowered to exercise personal choice and make changes in his daily work. It the teacher enjoys considerable measure of freedom to experiment his knowledge and methods in the class room, he can, no doubt, use it for the good of pupils. But if, on the contrary, he remains frightened, suppressed like some bond slave, be can never inspire his pupils with the noble virtues of self-confidence, courage and initiative. It is only a free teacher who can engender among the pupils the qualities of free thinking, planning and undertaking responsibilities. Basic education provides ample opportunities for these purposes.

Thus it is evident that Basic system possesses all these educative possibilities whereby there can be fullest physical, intellectual and moral development of the child. It is by virtue of these special features implicit in Basic system that it can stand shoulder to shoulder with the important modern systems of western counties *i.e.* Project Method, Kindergarten, Montessori system and Education through activity etc.

Curriculum

There will be a plan of seven-year course for the Basic schools, *i.e.* children of the age between seven and fourteen years will study therein. Upto class fifth, there will be co-education. Thereafter, in spite of the similarity in the curricula for boys and girls, the only difference will be that girls will be required to study Home Science instead of General Science. In brief, the outline of the curriculum is as follows:

1. Basic Crafts

   (a) Spinning and weaving

   (b) Carpentry

   (c) Agriculture

   (d) Fruit and Vegetable gardening

   (e) Leather work

   (f) Making of toys and pottery

   (g) Fisheries

   (h) Domestic arts for girls

   (i) Any other craft according to local and geographical conditions.

2. Mother tongue
3. Mathematics
4. Social Studies (History, Geography and Civics)
5. General Science (Nature study, Botany, Zoology, Physics, Hygienic and Chemistry) Physical culture has been associated with Hygiene.
6. Arts: Drawing and Music etc.
7. Games, sports and physical exercise.
8. Hindi (where it is not the mother tougue)

English has not been given any place in the Basic system of education. It has been replaced by Hindi which will be taught instead of English. In different provinces local mother tongue will be taught in place of the main language. At places, Hindi will be taught only at the stage of fifth of sixth class. The knowledge of mere writing and reading Hindi has been considered as needful. According to Gandhiji the curriculum of Basic education will be of the standard of current High Schools except in point of English. Though some people regard it with doubt, yet it is a subject worth experimentation.

No place has been given to religious education in this curriculum, because Gandhiji sought to teach the moral lesson of self-dependence to the people. Though not against religion as such, Gandhiji did not want to include the teaching of any particular religion or creed in the system of education; because he feared that the present religions would create a feeling of separation and disunity instead of co-coperation and unity in the minds of the children. At the same time he believed that the substance of all the main religions must be included in the system; but that substance cannot be learnt through words or books; it could rather be learnt from the daily life of the teacher himself.

Training of the Teachers: The Basic educational system attaches much importance to the teacher. Infact the success or failure of the scheme rests upon the individuality of the teacher. Two kinds of curricula, therefore, have been prescribed in the scheme for the training of the teachers—long term curriculum and short term curriculum. Teachers teach not only common subjects but crafts also.

Hence they have needs to master the knowledge of those crafts by getting training in them.

The minimum qualification required of the trainees for being admitted to training colleges is matriculation or two years teaching experience after passing the Vernacular Final Middle or Junior High School Examination.

The duration of the course of long-term training is three years. This curriculum is very comprehensive and includes all the important and necessary subjects. Though this course appears to be somewhat lengthy, yet it can be completed by being regular and working with devotion. The necessity of short-term training was left mainly because the scheme had to be brought in force forthwith. Hence its duration was kept one year only. The curriculum too, in brief, remained the same as it was in the beginning. The teachers are compulsorily to reside in hostels during the period of their training.

Method of Teaching: Method of teaching has been attached much importance to under Basic system. Any form of education becomes futile and useless in the absence of proper and efficient method of teaching in spite of the curriculum being of best nature. The method of teaching and approach to the subject under the Basic system differs widely from those of common and popular educational system. Under the former system no subject is taught as an exclusive and separate unit, but it is taught by making the centre some such developed activity as might be co-related to other subjects. The teachers, therefore, make a plan of all those closely co-related subjects and thus an indissoluble link is established among "the life, knowledge and activity."

The entire curriculum of Basic education is divided into seven successive classes. In the class first, the child aquires oral knowledge of the Mother Tongue then learns reading and in the end writing along with some basic craft. Thus he makes progress from stage to stage. As he progresses, the co-relation of the basic craft with other subjects such as mathematics, language, arts, history, geography and science grows deeper gradually. This basic craft, as a matter of fact, serves but as medium to impart instructions in other subjects. Thus by the end of seven years the child acquires knowledge of necessary literary subjects along with acquiring proficiency in that special basic craft. The entire method is founded on the productive basic craft based on psychology.

Spinning and weaving mainly form the basic crafts; but according to the views of Mahatma Gandhi other crafts too can be included in it. No craft can serve as a perfect and ideal medium; but only that aspect of it can be used which may be practicable. As for others, different other methods can be followed.

Natural environment, social environment and craft are the only three means by which a particular subject can be co-related to another and a child can be capacitated to mould himself according to the circumstances wisely and actively. Thus the entire curriculum is child-centred' and not 'activity-centred'.

The child works with the hand and uses simultaneously his mind and imagination. Children possess a natural creative instinct which is fully exercised under this system. His individuality and character also develop along with his physical and mental growth and he begins to regard himself as an important link of them nation and society.

Under the Basic system the child can remain no longer merely a passive listener as in the case under common educational system. The Basic schools are those spheres of activity and centres of experiments and investigation where the child always remains alert. Curiosity and hope of achievement and success push him forward. According to the views of Zakir Husaain Committee so far as the curriculum is concerned stress has been laid on the principle that teaching should be based on the realities of life related to some craft and social and physical environments of the child so that whatever knowledge he acquires might be harmonised with the progressive activities of his life.[10] Under this system the principle of "learning by doing" is also kept in view. The child learns craft while playing and acquires knowledge of other subjects without boredom or *ennui*.

The Basic System emphasises the mag.. ude of inspection work life teaching work. For t! s purpose, there is the need of capable and experienced persons who should not only inspect but guide too.

The present educational system is very defective and puts obstacles in the way of the development of the child's personality. Under the Basic system, the mode of examination has completely been reoriented on scientific basis by effecting a revolutionary change in it. The teacher holds a prominent place in such a mode of examination.

Progress of the Scheme: Many modifications had been made in the scheme according to the report of Zakir Hussain Committee. Thus rules pertaining to the self-supporting aspect of the scheme were relaxed. The sphere of basic craft was also enlarged and the entire experience of the children began to be utilized for educational purposes. India is proceeding with swift strides in the sphere of primary education on the lines of the scheme.

The scheme had been accepted officially at Haripura Congress Session. The Congress Ministries experimented it in different provinces. Its pace assumed swifter speed with the establishment of the "Hindustani Talimi Sangh". After 1938, it was officially applied in Central Provinces, U.P., Bombay and Bihar-Orisssa. New training colleges and schools were established and teachers began to be sent for training. The Central and Provincial Governments evinced a keen interest in the scheme. The Wardha Normal School was promoted to Vidya Mandir Training School and ninety-eight other Vidya Mandir schools were opened. The U.P. government on her part did not lag behind and introduced the scheme in the Province immediately. The new Education Minister patronised the scheme well and a special official was appointed to supervise the Basic education; there was established, moreover, a Basic Training College. In Bihar, the scheme bore fine fruits. But a terrible blow was given it in 1940 at the hands of political disturbances.

In 1938 and 1940, respectively; the Central Advisory Board of Education appointed two committees under the chairmanship of Sri B.G. Kher. These Committees expressed their careful and studied views about Basic education. As a result of their views the Basic education was completely overhauled and reorganised in the country. The committee put forth the following recommendations:

(i) The scheme of Basic Education should first be introduced in rural areas;

(ii) The age range of compulsion should be six to fourteen years, but children can be admitted to the Basic school at the age of five;

(iii) Diversion of students from the Basic school to other kinds of schools should be allowed after the fifth class or about the age of eleven plus;

(iv) The medium of instruction should be the Mother Tangue of the pupils;

(v) A common language for India is desirable. This should be Hindustani with both Urdu and Hindi scripts. Option should be given to the children to choose the script and provision should be made for teaching them in that script. Every teacher should know both scripts, viz Urdu and Hindi;

(vi) No external examination need be held. At the end of the Basic course a School Leaving Certificate based on an internal examination should be given.[11]

The Central Advisory Board of Education accepted many recommendations of the Report of Kher Committee and tried to give them a practical shape in the Sargent Report of 1944.

In the beginning of 1945, a meeting of the Hindustani Talimi Sangh was again called at Wardha. In this meeting, the entire educational system and the progress of the scheme were thoroughly examined and discussed. The value and importance of the Scheme was recognised in this meeting too and in view of its being founded on Gandhiji principles it was named the 'Nai Talim' or New Education. The Nai Talim was classified into four divisions—Pre-Basic, Basic, Post Basic and Adult education. The Pre-Basic education was meant for the children of the age between three and six years, and Post-Basic education included higher education.

Even prior to this, in the year 1944, the Central Advisory Board of Education had supported the plan of expanding the basic education. The National Planning Committee which had been appointed by the Congress for the purpose of giving its report and suggestions concerning multifarious problems of the country, also approved of Basic system of education. In 1947, the Hindustani

Talimi Sangh Wardha drew up a comprehensive syllabus which had been applied nearly in all the provinces. The Post-Basic Secondary education received meager attention under the plan. The main media of these Post basic secondary schools are such crafts as agriculture, dairy, masonry, smithery, carpentry and weaving etc. It is on the basis of these crafts that plans for the reconstruction of villages are thought out and framed. The Post-Basic colleges are likely to be organised, as Sir Radha Krishnan Commission Report has recommended, on the lines of the People's Colleges of the Scandinavian countries.

Nearly in all the provinces the move to propagate and expand the Basic education has been started. The movement has been accorded a cordial welcome in all the quarters of the country owing to the independence of the country and the growing demand for education among the people. There are two main tendencies prevalent in this sphere; first, the provision for free and compulsory primary education, and secondly, the conversion of the existing primary schools in to the Basic Schools. It has been laid down in the Constitution of India in 1950 that every effort will be made to give the benefit of free compulsory primary education to children of the age between six and fourteen years within the span of 10 years. Even before the Constitution came in force in 1950, steps in this direction had already been taken. On the recommendations of the Central Advisory Board of Education, the government had already admitted that the education of the country should be reorganised on the Basic pattern. The independence of the country kindled the hearts of the countrymen with new a zeal and desire to educate their wards even upto the primary stage. People now realize that education is their fundamental human right. This sort of desire and zeal is manifest even at those places where there were no educational facilities before 1947. For instance, before 1947 there was not even a single school in the tribal area of North East Frontier Agency; but by the end of 1953, as many as 1900 schools had been established there, and fresh ones are constantly emerging.

So far as the question of the conversion of existing primary schools into Basic Schools is concerned, some progress has been made in this direction too. But in the absence of trained teachers, proper buildings and paucity of funds, the progress is not satisfactory; moreover, no significant improvement has been made in the nature and quality of education.[12] The main cause has been the utter difficulty to get able and contended teachers. The Basic education while it is simple and easy for children, is comparatively more difficult for the teachers. But wherever teachers have worked with devotion and assiduity the scheme has borne fine fruits.

People entertain different views about the Basic education. In the Province of Bihar where the scheme has achieved success, people have admired it and accorded a sympathetic welcome to it. Similar is the case in Madras, Bombay and Tribal areas. But at some other places, people have not only regarded it with disdain but also opposed it strongly and actively. Under these circumstances, the quality of education in these areas has positively deteriorated instead of improving.

When the Basic education had been introduced in the country, the basic crafts as spinning, weaving and agriculture served as medium of education. But they are far from being adequate. In different provinces, local crafts are in vogue. We can find out educative possibilities in all these crafts. For example, Kashmir has always been renowned for such crafts as embroidery and woodcarving. Spinning and weaving of silk is the craft of nearly all the houses in the province of Assam. It is, therefore, quite manifest that every province can adopt local handicrafts. Progress made in this direction is conspicuous and gradually new crafts are being adopted in the Basic education.

The independence of the country brought in its wake many political, economic and natural adversity. India persisted in her efforts to make progress in educational sphere in spite on the partition of the country, scarcity of foodgrain, floods and other adverse circumstances. The progress can rightly be calculated by statistics. On 31st March, 1948, in the states of the category A, the number of primary schools was 1,40,121 attended by 1,10,00,964 students. On the same date in 1953 the above-mentioned number rose respectively to 1,77,285 and 1,56,65,056. Thus we see that during the first quinquennium of our independence the numbers of schools and students increased by 37,000 and 46.00,000 respectively in the A states. In 1953, the total number of primary schools throughout India was 2,21,082 and that of the students attending them was 1,92,96,840. From literacy point of view too, the progress is quite evident. Barring the children under five years, the percentage of literacy in 1941 was 14.6. It rose to 18.3 in 1951 at the time of final census, and on 31st March, 1953, it reached the level of 20.0. Nevertheless, the percentage is quite insufficient and unsatisfactory in view of the vastness of the population of the country and urgency of educational need.

Similarly, from the standpoint of expenditure we find that after the independence of the country, there has been 87 per cent increase in the expenditure on primary education. On 31st March, 1953, the estimate budget of primary education throughout the country was calculated to be four hundred and thirty seven million rupees.

So far as the question of the training of teachers for the Basic schools is concerned, the greatest obstacle in the way of the progress of the Basic education is, as has already been indicated above, the lack of trained teachers. Efforts are being made throughout the country to meet this demand. Some institutions prominent among which are as follows, have been working very efficiently:

Nai Talim Bhavan, Sevagram; Jamia Millia Islamia Teachers' Training Institute, Delhi; Sri Ram Krishna Mission Centre, Coimbatore. (It includes the Gandhi Basic Training Vidyalaya Teacher's Basic Training School and Vidyalaya Teachers' College which have been working creditably); Graduate Basic Training Centre, Dhabaka (Bombay): Vidya Bhavan, Shanti Niketan; Vidya Bhawan, Udaipur; and Sarvodaya Mahavidyalaya, Tarki (Bihar).

Besides these, there exist training centres nearly in all the provinces giving proper training to the teachers to the Basic schools.

The Guru Training centres of Assam have been converted into the Basic Training Centres. Bihar is conducting the work of training the teachers very efficiently. The number of the teachers in the training institutions of Bihar rose from 235 in 1946-47 to 3,326 in 1951-52 including 190 women teachers. All the teachers of the Basic schools in Bihar are properly trained. The facilities of basic training are being provided to the teachers of ordinary primary and Middle Schools. At Narsinghnagar (Tarki, Muzzafarpur), in 1951, a Basic Training College has been founded for the training of higher educational officers in the Basic system of education. It has now been nomenclatured as the Sarvodaya Mahavidyalaya.

In Bombay Province, there are well-nigh seventeen government training centres where nearly 3,000 teachers receive training in Basic system every year. There is separate arrangement for the training of the graduates. Teachers and educational officers are sent to Sevagram for higher training. Similar provisions have been made for training also in U.P. the Punjab and Madras etc. At Delhi, in addition to Jamia Millia, two more schools, one for men and other for women have been opened. In different provinces, short-term "Refresher Courses" have been organised for the teachers of primary schools.

Now many experiments are being made throughout the country to raise the Basic system of education to the level of Secondary and Higher education. In this respect, Bihar is the pioneer of other provinces. There in selected areas only, social education is being introduced on the lines of Basic system. In order to fulfil the aim of expanding social education, a plan has been worked out during last five years by some institutions as Sarvodaya Mahavidyalaya Basic Training College. 19 Basic Training Schools and 13 Post-Basic schools. But the scheme has not attained adequate success owing to the lack of disinterested workers and teachers as well as funds. During the quinquennium between 1947-52, the Bihar Government spent nearly three lakhs of rupees on this experimentation. In July 1954, the Executive Committee of the Bihar Basic Board of Education decided to found nearly six Post-Basic Colleges for the sake of those students who had passed the Post-Basic School examination. The Board by passing a resolution had put forth a demand to the Bihar Government to open a community college at Tarki (Muzzafarpur). Consequently work has been started in August after the foundation of the College. Similarly there is a plan of opening one College at each of the places Nalanda. Nagarpara (Bhagalpur), Kolhand Patory (Darhbanga) and Bakhari (Muzzafarpur). Another subsidiary aim of establishing these rural Basic Colleges is the possible establishment of a rural university there within the span of the three years.

Besides, recognition has been granted to Private Sarvodaya Schools along with the Government Sarvodaya Schools in Bihar. Formally, the Sarvodaya Schools were under the direction of

Government alone. The Board of Basic Education has decided to improve the Basic education, expansion of social education and condition of the basic teachers in Bihar.

In the same way, the Punjab Government have decided to raise the Basic education from the primary stage to the Secondary level. For this purpose, in October 1954, a Senior Basic College has been established at Chandigarh. It will admit only the graduates.

In Travancore Cochin, decision has been taken in 1954, to convert all the primary school into Basic Schools and thus impart encouragement to the Basic system of education. In the first instance, the scheme will be applied to the first three primary classes. Subsequently with the successful experimentation of the scheme, it will be applied to other classes.

The U.P. State is progressing on the way to reorganising the entire primary education on the Basic pattern. Since 1948, as many as 12,350 primary Basic schools have been opened in the State. Under the Second five-year Plan, there is the provision for the further establishment of 9,650 basic schools at a cost of three hundred and forty millions of rupees.

In fact, the Central Government is very eager to organise primary education of the country on the Basic pattern. On January 18,1955, in the 60th Congress Session held at Avadi, the following resolution had been passed:

Far-reaching changes in the existing educational system are absolutely essential for achieving the national aims and social objectives of Free India and in particular to train the right type of personal for the speedy execution of the developmental plans....

The Planning Commission and the Government of India have already accepted the policy of introducing basic education as the future pattern of primary as well as secondary education in India. Since basic education uses the medium of productive activity and co-relates academic subjects to different crafts and to the social environment, it is eminently suitable for the needs and conditions of India. The Congress calls upon all the State Governments to further, as early as possible, this policy so as to implement it fully both in rural and urban areas in a systematic and well-planned manner within a period of ten years.

Thus we see that Basic system of education despite its limitation is growing in importance for India. Under the first Five-Year-plan, the Indian Government had incurred an expenditure of sixty lakhs of rupees within three years on the experimentation about effecting improvement in the Basic system of education; they have decided to spend even more in the remaining period. If the Scheme were to be well worked out in all the states, it was hoped that by the end of 1955-56 as many as 38,059 additional schools inclusive of the Basic schools would be opened to be attended by some forty lakhs of additional students. By the end of 1953, the number of the schools was 16,276 and that of the pupils was nine lakhs. So far as pure Basic schools are concerned upto the end of 1953 some 2,179 schools had been established from amongst the 9,471 schools proposed under the First Five-year Plan.[13]

It can be held on the basis of government reports that the Basic education is making satisfactory progress in the states, especially in Bihar and Bombay. These schools established in the neighbouring villages are amalgamated into a solid unit. One "Janata College" which provides lodging and boarding for the student hailing from rural area, and where education is imported in handicrafts, sanitation and fundamental elements of social life; one Basic Training College where to Basic schools are attached and a library which provides visual aids—these are the institutions which constitute the Basic experimental unit. Though this work had been begun very enthusiastically in Delhi also, but no remarkable success was achieved in the venture. The object of this experimentation is to acquaint people with the principles of Basic education and prepare efficient workers.

With a view to expanding the Basic education in the country, the Central Government has agreed to meet 30 per cent of that expenditure which the State governments have to incur in opening new Basic schools or converting common primary schools into Basic schools. This grant-in-aid has been sanctioned on the basis of the recommendations made by Kher Committee. The central Education

Ministry has decided to publish a booklet with the sole purpose of defining the principles and system of the Basic education.

The target which has been fixed with regard to the establishment of the Basic schools in the Five Year Plan includes also the plan of conversion of the existing primary schools into the Basic ones. At some places only usual primary schools are being established and the plan of the establishment of Basic schools is being postponed on the grounds of possible excessive preliminary expenditure on the scheme. The progress of the primary Basic schools is very slow owing to the scarcity of efficient trained teachers, a system of basic training commonly approved and a total lack of such literature as might guide the teachers. But every state adopted the policy of bringing the Pilot Project in force the Five Year Plan with the aim of meeting all those scarcities had limitations. Under these Pilot Projects, the entire Basic education will be put into action in a definite, solid and substantial way from the primary stage to the Post-graduate Training and a proper technique will be evolved through this experimentation. All these schemes have not so far been acted upon fully in any state, though preliminary steps have been taken in this direction.

The Central Government has extended financial help to the State for the sake of giving practical shape to the Pilot Projects. This help will be utilized for the following purposes:

(a) to convert existing primary schools into Basic school;

(b) to establish fresh Basic Schools;

(c) to help those Basic schools having inadequate equipment and staff;

(d) for the training of craft-teachers and to introduce crafts in schools; and,

(e) to prepare those things which may be utilized in teaching in the Basic Schools.

From this point of view the Central Government has realized that those experiments which have been made in Denmark in the sphere of rural education can be helpful in the reorganisation of rural education of India. Hence the Indian Government has sent a group of eighteen educationists to Denmark for the purpose of studying the various systems of primary, secondary, adult and social education.[14] In this connection, the tour of Dr. Peter Menish, a Danish expert of rural education, to India on the invitation of the Indian Government its worth mentioning.

Thus we see that Basic education, as a matter of fact, is assuming magnitude as the very basis of national life and inspiration and not merely that of Indian system of education. It is expected that in future its form will still be more comprehensive and universal. Only then the views of Gandhiji, originator of the scheme, about education will be fully objectified. The primary education which had been treated with indifference and negligence during the British regime in India, could not lie under a cloud in free India. If India has to compete successfully with the civilized nations of the world, she will have to eradicate her 90 per cent illiteracy. It is, no doubt, quite true that we can wash away ugly stigma of illiteracy by means of proper curriculum, efficient teachers, skilful organisation and administration, economic stability and untiring perseverance and by making primary education compulsory in the proper sense. When America, Russia, China and Turkey etc. have attained marked success in this experiment, is there any thing which cannot be accomplished by free India with all her noble ambitions and higher aims?

The fact that proper importance is not being attached to primary education in India, admits, of no doubt during the hundred years between 1854 and 1954, the Government has confessed theoretically several times that the spread of primary education is one of her most important duties. According to the 45th clause of the new constitution of India, it is the duty of the Government to impart free and compulsory education to all the children between six and fourteen years upto the year 1960. But inadequate advertence has been paid in this direction. The Government is concentrating her attention and energies upon the improvement of university and Secondary education. Manifold problems thereof have been fundamentally and comprehensively analysed by the Central Government from time to time. But the government of independent India has not been able to realize so far that a similar commission to examine the problems of primary education ought to be appointed forthwith.

Hence it is of utmost necessity that the Indian Government should appoint a primary education Commission for the purpose of studying all its problems on all-India basis and providing concrete suggestions for their satisfactory solution.

Further, we have to consider the question of the improvement in the financial condition of primary-school teachers. It is a well-known fact that the teacher of Indian primary schools gets very low salary. Hence he leads a very miserable life full of wants, being always haunted by financial worries. The Government too, considering him to be quite helpless and poor can conveniently afford to neglect and ignore him. The authorities too attend to the grievances of the university teachers more readily than to those of the teachers of primary schools, because the former are more forceful and can convey their complaints to the higher authorities, and possess the power to fight for their rights and claims. The primary school teacher who is better than a common drudge in no wise, on the other hand, carries on his teaching profession without hope or inspiration. So long as the condition of primary education is not improved, the foundation of education in India will always remain weak. It naturally leads us to the inevitable inference that so long as the financial position and working conditions of the teachers of primary schools are not improved, all hopes about the educational improvement would remain but vain and futile. In comparison to the ordinary primary teachers, the lot of basic teachers is still harder. The period of their training is longer and expenditure larger; their teaching-work is much more irksome and tiring. Hence it is natural that the scale of their wages should be higher than that of common primary-school teachers. The Madras Government has diverted her attention in this direction to a certain measure, but other states have ignored this problem altogether.

Another major problem which confronts the primary or basic education is the scarcity of school buildings. It is, indeed, a pity that we do not provide the future citizens of the country with proper place where they might learn the first lessons of their life. Nearly in all the parts of the country most of the primary schools do not possess their own buildings. If at one place, the children receive education in dilapidated and tottering houses, at others sitting under trees they are exposed to rains, sultry heat of the sun, biting cold of the winter and other tyrannies of nature. Indeed, scarcity of school buildings is a crucial problem. It is, in all respects a ridiculous and ignominious state of affairs demanding immediate and proper attention.

Besides these difficulties, there are many more which may also be mentioned here. There are many other factors which impede the swift career of primary education in the country; they are failure of the Government to apply the principle of compulsory education throughout the country; lack of good text-books and other reading material; curricula defects, want of facilities for the training of teachers, inefficiency and inadequacy of inspection; petty politics in local boards immolation of primary education under these boards and reigning poverty among the masses. So long as these obstacles are not removed from the way we cannot, in any way, improve primary education, which includes Basic education also.

Sargent Report (Post-war Development Plan)

At the end of the World War II, a new educational scheme popularly known as the Sargent Scheme was submitted to the Indian Government. John Sargent who was the then Educational Advisor to the Government of India, was asked to draft such a memorandum as might contain an outline of the plan for post-war educational expansion. The Central Advisory Board of Education accepted this memorandum during the course of their meetings in 1943 and 1944. The memorandum was based on all those reports which had been published by the sub-committees appointed by the Board for the different aspects of education. Therefore, the Scheme was named after John Sargent. The Report published by Central Advisory Board of Education has an immense value and importance in the post-war schemes. The Report contains a detailed account of education from Nursery stage to University level; it throws light upon its organisation, defects, methods of improvement and other future suggestions. In a way, it is the first report of its kind which seeks to examine and study the entire national education so comprehensively and minutely.

The Sargent Report has taken into its purview every aspect of education by dividing into twelve chapters. They are, in brief, as follows:

(i) Provision of universal free and compulsory primary education for the children between the age of 5 or 6 and

14 years. This education will be sub-divided into two heads: Junior Basic (6-11); and Senior Basic (11-14). The former type of education will be compulsory for all while the latter form of education will be meant only for those who do not intend continuing their studies in high schools;

(ii) Provision of pre-primary education for children of the age between three and six years. The main aim of it would not be to give ordinary education, but to give them lessons in social behaviour and discipline;

(iii) High School education for the selected children of the age between 11 and 17 years. Only those students, who will evince interest in further studies, will be eligible to be admitted to these schools. Normally the number will be 20 per cent. These high schools will be divided into two classes: (I) Academic High Schools; and Technical High Schools. In the former institutions, subjects of arts and science *i.e.* mother tongue, English, History, Oriental languages, modern languages, Geography, Mathematics, Science, Hygiene and Sanitation, Agriculture, Music, Economics and Civics etc. will be taught. In the latter ones, vocational and commercial subjects such as metal and woodwork, Engineering, Drawing, Book-Keeping, Short-hand, Type-writing, Accountancy and Business Method etc. will be taught. The medium of instruction will be mother tongue and English will be second compulsory language. In the Girls' Schools, Home Science will be taught in place of General Science. The candidates desirous of being admitted to high schools should necessarily have attained to the age of II plus year and they should have completed junior Basic Course. Every student in it will be of the age under 14 plus. Fifty per cent students will receive free education. Facilities for higher studies will be provided to able and intelligent students;

(iv) Provision of High School education for the selected students after completing their Intermediate course in existing institutions. By abolishing Intermediate classes,

the first year should be transferred to high school and second year to degree classes. The report throws light on the defects of modern university education. Restrictions have been imposed upon admission to them. Only one out of every fifteen Matriculates should be given admission to the University. Personal contact must be developed between the teachers and students. Improvement should be made in the working conditions and salaries of teachers. An Indian University Grants Committee should be established for the purpose of effecting co-ordination among the curricula of different universities;

(v) Provision should be made for technical, commercial and Arts education to which full-time and part-time students should be admitted in adequate number. Four kinds of workers will be needed for Indian industries: (I) Chief Executives: These persons will get admission to the Technological Departments of the Universities after finishing their courses in Technical High Schools. Strictness will be observed with regard to their admission. (2) Minor Executives: It will include the Foremen and Charge hands etc. Students having completed Technical High School-courses will do that work. (3) Skilled craftsmen: These students will be taken from Technical High schools at the completion of their Senior High School courses. (4) Unskilled Labour: These persons will directly be admitted from Senior Basic Middle Schools where they might have learnt some craft work. They can be included with skilled artisans after gaining sufficient experience;

(vi) Proper arrangement should be made for the education of the adults between ten and forty years. The education in their case should be both commercial and general. "The main emphasis in this country must, for some time to come, be on literacy, although from the very beginning some provision must be made for adult education proper, so that those made literate may have an inducement as well as an opportunity to pursue their studies". There should be separate classes for boys and elderly persons.

Special attention should also be devoted to women-adult education. In order to make adult education more interesting and effective, the use of magic lanterns; Cinema, Gramophone, Radio, Folk dances, music and dramatic performance should largely be made; besides, public libraries should be organised which must take a maximum period of twenty years only;

(vii) Full provision for the proper training of teachers should be made for the implementation and continuation of the scheme. It has been laid down in the scheme that in the Pre-Basic and Junior Basic Schools one teacher for every thirty children: in Senior Basic Schools one for every 25 children and in High Schools one teacher for every 20 students will be needed. Thus the entire scheme will need 22,17,733 teachers (*i.e.* about 20 lakhs non graduates and 1,81,320 graduates). The graduates will be trained in Training Colleges and the non-graduates will be given three kinds of training for Pre-primary teachers, Basic teachers and non-graduate teachers for High Schools. There is the need of Refresher Course for trained teachers at different intervals. No special Training Colleges are needed for the training of technical and commercial teachers because they will have their training in technical and industrial institutions. There should be increase in the scale of salaries in order to provide inducement to able and efficient teachers;

(viii) Proper provision should be made for compulsory physical education, medical inspection and treatment of the students in order to keep them physically fit. A thorough medical test of the health of the children should be made at the age of six, eleven and fourteen years. There should be maintained a record of the students' physical state, height and weight. Immediate and proper medical treatment must be given to the students in case of any defect after the medial test. Students should be provided with literature on dietary, sanitation and physical culture. The classrooms should be well-ventilated, clean and well-equipped with furniture;

(ix) Special institutions should be provided for the education of physically and mentally handicapped children. These two categories include imbecile, blind, dumb and deaf children and those suffering from some other similar physical handicap;

(x) Employment Bureaux should be established;

(xi) The institutions should provide for social and recreational activities on a fairly large scale;

(xii) Well-organised Education Departments should be established at the Centre and in the states. Thus education should be entrusted to those expert who understand the secrets of it. Entire education except University education should remain under the direction of the States. The organisation of University activities should be on an all-India basis.

Criticism

Merits: In brief, it is the Sargent Plan. Seeing the high standard of education in other progressive countries, it was essential to frame a comprehensive and all-embracing educational plan in order to enable the country to stand shoulder to shoulder with other countries. The scheme thus holds a very important place in the educational planning of Post-war India. It is much more universal than all other plans introduced hitherto. It contains an analytical account of all the aspects of education. It has sought to solve finally and decisively problems related to education such as that of the introduction of compulsory education in the country. The scheme affords ample scope for free all-round development of the child's individuality.

The exponents of the Scheme had fully well realized that the teacher formed the nucleus of the all-educational plans. Howsoever attractive and beneficial any scheme might be, it can never be successful if we have no efficient, capable and contented teachers for the purpose of implementing it. Keeping this point in view, the scheme lays special emphasis upon the improvement of the scale of salaries of the teachers of all classes *i.e.* primary schools, secondary schools and universities.

The report has brought to surface all the inherent weaknesses and defects of the present educational system of the country. For example, it has been admitted in the scheme that undue emphasis is laid on examinations engendering in the students bookish narrowness. They dwell in the world of imagination loosing all contact with the realities and hard facts of life. High School education has hitherto been regarded as complementary to university education. It is not sufficient in itself. Moreover, university education also lacks systematic planning. There is no proper and adequate provision for the training of teachers etc.

Demerits: It is not at the same time true that the scheme is quite immune from defects and limitations. It has been assumed that if the scheme were to be operated for a period of forty years, education in India could reach the level of that in England. But it has been forgotten that England will not sleep over that period; but on the other hand, she will continue to progress and India will lag behind by well nigh half a century. Again, the period of forty years is also considerably large. The whole plan covering forty years has further been divided into five-year programmes. "The first five" as the report says, "should be devoted to planning, Propaganda and particularly to the provision of the institution necessary for training teachers and that thereafter the actual carrying out of the scheme should be divided into seven five-year programmes, during each of which an area or areas should be fully dealt with. The size of these areas in the case of each Province will be determined during each programme period by various factors, of which the supply of teachers available will be the most important." This shows that the period of forty years is more than required and India is not in a position to wait so long for the reconstruction of her education. Further, the scheme will be experimented in the areas one by one. It may also be noted that the scheme will require 313 crores of rupees annually of which 277 crores will have to come from public funds. Considering this, the scheme is immensely expensive for a poor country like India.

The Sargent scheme has neither thrown any light upon nor made any provision for certain vital problems of Indian education such as, rural education, women education and the place of religious education in our educational organisation. The method of selecting students is also undesirable. It limits the scope of every student to receive higher education.

The self-supporting aspect of the schools as laid down in the Wardha Scheme has totally been discarded. Further it does not provide for any proper and strong government machinery in order to force compulsory education in the country. To regard the educational level in England as the standard for India is also not proper and desirable at all.

Progress of the Scheme: Having analysed the merits and demerits of the Sargent scheme, it appears that despite its shortcomings and limitations, it is a big epoch-making plan. The Central Government have accepted its major recommendations and established a separate Education Department at the Centre in 1945.

In 1944, the Central Government asked the provincial Governments to draw up their five-year programmes on the basis of the Sargent Scheme. Many such programmes during the quinquennium between 1947-52 were framed. The scheme had been put into operation even as early as 1946. The Central Government had agreed to sanction a sum of forty crores of rupees as financial help during 1947-48. These provincial five-year programmes include improvement in the scale of teachers' salaries, free compulsory Basic education applicable to children between 6 and 11 years in the first instance to be extended to children of the age between 11 and 14 years, improvement in university education, special provision and facilities for technical and adult education, special arrangement and facilities for scientific investigation etc. Further, the period of forty years has been reduced to sixteen years.

Besides, on the recommendations of the Report an All-India Technical Education Committee has been instituted and a Poly-technical College has also been established in the metropolis of India. In 1945, the Educational bureau and in the following year, the University Grants Committee have also been established. The question of foreign education of Indian students has been taken up by the Central Education Department.

Progress of Secondary Education (1937-55)

During the period following the year 1937, the number of secondary schools and the students attending them increased astonishingly. The attention of the Provincial Governments was also shared by the secondary education along with the improvement and expansion of primary education. The increase in the number of institutions and students is attributable also to the growing demand of secondary education specially English among the Indian masses. But the progress of secondary education was considerably hampered by the resignation tendered by popular Provincial Governments and disturbances of war-period and ratio did not appreciably increase in spite of the increase in number. The number of the secondary schools in United India during 1936-37 was 13,056 falling to 11,907 in post-partition India in 1947. Rest of the institutions went under the possession of Pakistan. In the past decades, secondary education has constantly redoubled itself but it could not happen during this decade. There are mainly two reasons responsible for such a slow growth: the first is the check on the progress of primary education, and second is financial crisis brought about by war. The number of the students decreased during the War period owing to the economic crisis affecting the persons belonging to the middle class, for it was this particular class where from the main supply of students was drawn for secondary education. On account of education being extremely expensive, secondary education became a thing of luxury for the students belonging to poor indigent stratum of society.

It is, however, true that at the expiry of war period, education began to progress in the country. With the advent of independence of the country in 1947, a reviviscence has taken place in the sphere of secondary education. Owing to the spread of primary education among the masses, secondary education rose in demand. Education which was hither to unavailable for the children of peasantry, itself began to knock at their door with the flood of secondary schools affecting prominent villages and neighbouring towns. Women education also was awakened from torpor with the wave of political and social consciousness running through the entire fabric of Indian society. Consequently, satisfactory increase has taken place in the number of Secondary schools for girls. Other sections of society such as the untouchables, aborigines and backward classes could not escape the overwhelming tide of secondary education and they took fullest advantage of it. Impetus to the progress of Secondary education has been given by the mother tongue serving now as the medium of education.

The U.P. Unemployment Inquiry Committee had recommended to reorganise the secondary education. It had been fully realised by now that the only and narrow aim of current secondary education was to prepare candidates for the High School Examination and admission to the Universities. It was not a self-sufficient and independent unit by itself. Under these circumstances, there was the need of effecting necessary changes in it.

In 1938, the Bombay Government formed a committee for the reorganisation of Secondary education; it drew up a curriculum covering a period of four years. It was to be used after a primary curriculum of the duration of seven years. This four-year syllabus had been sub-divided into scientific and general curricula. Both these curricula were further sub-divided into three groups each. Under the general curriculum were included (i) Literary (ii) Arts (iii) Commerce; and under the Scientific curriculum were included (i) Agriculture (ii) Commercial and Technical (iii) Scientific and Vocational curricula. Experimental education was included in every curriculum besides literary one. The entire course which can be compared to High School curriculum, covered a period of four years. It was thus a sufficiently progressive plan.

Besides this Committee of the Bombay province, in U.P. too a Primary and Secondary Education Reorganisation Committee was appointed under the chairmanship of Acharaya Nerendra Dev. Similar Committees were established in Delhi and Madras also.

The Acharya Nerendra Dev Committee U.P. (1939)

The U.P. Government with a view to reorganising the primary and secondary education of the province, appointed a Committee which submitted its Report in 1939. Other prominent members of the Committee were Sri Kane, Dhulekar, Kumari Williams, Mrs. Uma Nehru, Acharya Jugul Kishore, Mohammed Ismail Khan, Begum Azizul Rasool, Sri R.S. Pandit, Sri Ram Ugra Singh, and Dr. Zakir Hussain, etc. Arter submitted its Report on primary education, the

Committee submitted its Report on Secondary Education and put forth valuable recommendations. They are in brief as follows:[15]

Recommendations

(i) The first defect in the modern system of education is that it does not meet the multifarious requirements of life. Moreover, it does not make any provision for the solution of the problem of unemployment rampant among the masses and their varied interests;

(ii) It is merely complementary to the university education;

(iii) Secondary education should be complete and solid, the curricula should be self-sufficient and independent units;

(iv) Secondary education should be for children of the age between 12 and 18 years;

(v) All the Secondary institutions will be called "colleges" the standard whereof will be higher than that of the existing Intermediate colleges;

(vi) The curriculum of the first two years in these colleges will be similar to that of the highest two classes of the Basic Schools. Less emphasis may be laid on crafts, English would remain compulsory subject;

(vii) The syllabus would include the following Subjects:

(a) Language, literature and Social Science;

(b) Natural Science and Mathematics;

(c) Art;

(d) Commerce;

(e) Technical and Commercial subjects;

(f) Home Science (for girls).

(viii) Admission will be made two times. First after the Basic education second after the curriculum of seven years;

(ix) The terms "High School" "and Intermediate" will be removed;

(x) Hindustani should be the medium of education;

(xi) Experts should be appointed to draw up the syllabi. The curriculum should be real and practical and should symbolise the needs of the time and nation;

(xii) English should be treated as compulsory subject; besides, Physical Science and General Knowledge will be other compulsory subjects;

(xiii) Advisory Boards should be appointed for the purpose of opening all kinds of colleges. Their duty would be to advise the government in connection with the curricula and collect funds from Trade and Industry for the college;

(xiv) Colleges for Home Science should be established for girls;

(xv) Adequate library facilities should be provided in each college;

(xvi) For the sake of improving the character of the students and engendering the sentiments of citizenship, democracy, self-reliance, leadership and social justice in their minds, it is essential that such extra-curricular activities, as Scouting, Debating Societies. Dramatic performances, Social Service, Co-operative Societies. Consumers' stores and similar other association should be organised. These activities should be emphasised like regular curricular activities.

Besides these recommendations, the Narendra Dev Committee expressed its opinion on and put forth many constructive suggestions about a number of important problems *i.e.*, women education, vocational education, training of teachers and improvement in their service conditions, agreement form of service for teachers, improvement in text-books, improvement in the method of examination and education organisation as well as discipline. It also recommended the establishment in the province of a Central Pedagogical Institute to which should be attached a library and a reading-hall.[16]

After the War

In addition to this Committee, the Central Government and different Provincial Governments appointed similar other Committees regarding Secondary Education. All these Committees were of the opinion that the curriculum of High School should be multifaceted and one of its aims should be University education. By abolishing Intermediate classes, first year class should be transferred to High School and the 2nd year class should be joined to the Degree classes thus increasing its course to three years. The curriculum of Secondary education should cover a period of six years to be taken up by the student in the sixth class at the expiry of his five-year primary course, and to continue upto eleventh class. Variety should be introduced in the curriculum after the eighth class *i.e.* after finishing eight years of education. Upto the level of eighth class all the subjects should briefly remain compulsory so that when the student reaches the IX class, he may choose any subject according to his taste and aptitude. Commerce should be introduced at the level of IX class.

As a matter of fact, the above-mentioned plan had been framed by one Sapru Committee. It was consequently approved by the Inter-University Boards, the Central Advisory Board and the Central Government. It has been acted upon first by Delhi Province and later on by U.P. All the High Schools in Delhi have been converted into Higher Secondary Schools which conduct education upto eleventh class. Similar experiment is being done in Uttar Pradesh too; according to the Scheme, primary schools form 1st to fifth class, Junior High Schools from 6th to 8th class and Higher Secondary Schools from 9th to 11th class are proposed to be established. All the High Schools are now called the Higher Secondary Schools and every year some High Schools are granted recognition to start 11th class. The Government High Schools too are being converted into Higher Secondary Schools. The results and progress of this change are being observed with keen interest by the educational experts.

In the light of the post-war Sargent scheme of Educational Development, secondary education, as has already been mentioned, is being reorganised in different provinces.

In the year 1948, the Indian Government had appointed a Committee in connection with the Secondary education. Its Report had been discussed by the Central Advisory Board of Education in the meeting held at Allahabad in 1949. It had been decided in this meeting that a student should have completed the four-year secondary education course in order to be eligible for admission to degree classes. National language should be made compulsory in Senior Basic classes and it should be treated as optional in Higher Secondary classes. In Universities too, at the end of the career of English as medium of instruction, national language should be adopted as the medium. Besides, the Higher Schools should be multilateral; but unilateral institutions should also be encouraged according to the local conditions. An examination would be held at the end of Secondary education. Universities can frame independent regulation with regard to admission to them. Students of outstanding merit should be accorded financial help. In the Secondary schools, different useful institutions and associations should be organised for the improvement in the social life of students. The Committee accepted all the recommendations put forth by the Central Advisory Board of Education with regard to the improvement of teachers' service condition and their scale of salary in those institutions. Lastly, recommendation was made for the appointment of a Provincial Board of Education to advise the education authorities on the problems of Secondary education.

The Secondary Education Commission (1953)

Appointment: The Central Advisory Board of Education, in its 14th Session held in January 1948, had made recommendations to appoint a Commission in order to examine the prevailing system of Secondary Education and suggest measures for its re-organisation and improvement. The Board reiterated its recommendation in the year 1951. The Government of India too realized the magnitude of Secondary Education. Sufficient survey had been made in the spheres of primary, University and Vocational education in the foregoing years, but no such step had hitherto been taken in the sphere of Secondary Education on all-India level. As a matter of fact, it is a stage where most of the Indian students finish their academic career. Further, the Matriculates specially either undertake the teaching work in Primary schools or go to Universities for higher education. Thus Secondary education considerably influences the standard of education both at the stage of Primary as well as University education. Keeping all these considerations in view, the Government of India appointed the Secondary Education Commission on September 23,, 1952.

Dr. Lakshmanaswami Mudaliar, the Vice-Chancellor of Madras University was appointed the Chairman of the Commission. That is why it is also called the Mudaliar Commission. The Commission was asked to submit its Report and suggest recommendations on the following problems of Secondary Education:[17]

(a) to enquire into and report on the present position of Secondary Education in India in all its aspects; and

(b) suggest measures for its reorganisation and improvement with particular reference to:

(i) the aims, organisation and content of Secondary Education;

(ii) its relationship to Primary, Basic and Higher education;

(iii) the inter-relation of Secondary Schools of different types; and

(iv) other allied problems sc that a sound and reasonably uniform system of Secondary Education suited to our needs and resources may be provided for the whole country.'

The Commission made a tour throughout the country and having studied and examined the educational problems at different places, submitted its Report on August 29,1953. It was discussed by the Central Advisory Board of Education at Delhi on November 9th and 10th, 1953. The Board authorised its Chairman to appoint a Committee to give suggestions about the immediate implementation of the recommendations of Report after their thorough examination. In February 1954, the suggestions of the Committee were discussed. The recommendations of the Secondary Education Commission were thus accepted in their original form by the Government of India.

Recommendations

The important recommendations of the commission are, in brief, as follows:

1. Secondary Education should commence after four or five years period of Primary or Junior Basic Education. It must include different curricula *i.e.* Language, Social Studies, General Science and Handicrafts. The work of prescribing textbooks should be undertaken by some strong Committee. Students should be given opportunities to avail themselves of proper advice and guidance in matters of choosing their subjects;

2. The mother tongue or the regional language should generally be the medium of instruction. During the Middle School stage, the child should be taught two languages: one Federal and the other some foreign language;

3. As a rule the total number of working days in a year should not be less than two hundred; the working hours per week should be at least thirty-five periods of about forty-five minutes each;

4. Due consideration should be given to the class room work done by student throughout the session while passing him in the examination or promoting him to higher class;

5. Multi-purpose Schools should be established in order to encourage technical education at the lower stage;

6. Teachers of Secondary Schools and Graduate teachers should be trained. Special attention should be paid to physical education;

7. Secondary Education Board, Teacher's Training Board and State Advisory Board of Education should be established. With a view to rendering administration more efficient, the Central and State committees should call joint meetings. Thus a co-ordination in their activities should be established. Persons of exceptional merits only should be appointed in the Department of the Directors of Education;

8. There should be a Managing Board of every School duly registered under the Companies Act. The Headmaster of each School should be the *ex officio* member of the Managing Board of his school;

9. The School buildings should be clean and well-ventilated possessing spacious playgrounds;
10. In the interest of the training in agriculture, industry, commerce and citizenship, the Central Government should provide resources for raising funds for the purpose.

Besides these recommendations, the Commission put forth various other constructive and practical suggestions pertaining to multifarious educational problems such has establishment of libraries, measures to check growing indiscipline among the students, partial religious education either through the willingness of the student himself or the permission of his parents, improvement of the health or students, inculcating in the students of such virtues as self-reliance and ideal citizenship, improvement in the mode of examination, improvement in the service conditions of teachers, lastly improvement in the financial condition, administration and organisation of schools and the like.

Criticism

By full examining the recommendation of the commission it appears that the Report has attempted to examine all the fundamental problems of Secondary Education and solve them. We find these recommendations to be more practical and sound than those made by other Commissions appointed in the past.[18] The Commission has put forth sincere efforts to remedy all those defects which had hitherto persisted in Secondary Education *i.e.* predominance of bookish and literary knowledge, lack of vocational and technical education, defective mode of examinations, defects inherent in the Managing Bodies and Organisation of schools, indifference towards the teachers and difficulties about their training etc.

The suggestion for the establishment of multipurpose schools is entirely an original one implying possibilities of sufficient improvement. In the opinion of the Commission, our schools should not be 'single-track' institutions; on the other hand, they should be 'multipurpose' ones catering to the needs of students full of various ambitions, tastes and aptitudes.[19] The development of agriculture and industries is one of the most vital problems confronting the country at present. Under these circumstances, the Commission has performed a creditable duty by including these subjects in the curriculum of Secondary Education and emphasising the education in them.

In connection with the improvement of the methods of examination the Commission's views are: "If examinations are to be of real value they must take into consideration the new facts and test in detail the all round development of 'pupils," The validity of current pattern of examination admits of doubt from the viewpoint of the real test of the intellectual attainments of students. This mode of examination leave so much scope for the subjectivity of the examiner that cannot be safely relied upon to a considerable measure. Under these conditions, the recommendation which emphasises the class-room work of the student done throughout the session to be taken into consideration, is a proper and essential one. In the opinion of the Commission external examinations should not be too many. The defects and limitations inherent in essay type examinations should be eliminated. For this purpose Objective Tests have been recommended. The questions to be set in the examination papers should be such as might not encourage the evil and much prevalent tendency to memorising by rote. Similar recommendations have been made for the improvement of internal examinations.

In connection with the improvement of teachers' condition, the commission has admitted that "the most important factor in the contemplated educational reconstruction is the teacher—his personal qualities, his educational qualifications, his professional training and the place that he occupies in the school as well as in the community". The Commission, therefore, has recommended that 'if the teachers' present mood of discontent and frustration is to be removed and education is to become a genuine nation-building activity, it is absolutely necessary to improve their status and their conditions of service."[20]

The Commission has given practical suggestion in order to effect improvement in this direction. Further, its recommendations in connection with the reorganisation of schools and improvement in the Massaging Committees, are also very useful and valid. If Secondary education in India be reorganised and reconstructed on the basis of the Commission's various recommendations, there is all possibility of its inherent defects being remedied soon.

The recommendations of the Commission, in spite of their value and validity, however admit of certain limitations which should be examined briefly. As a matter of fact, the Commission has endeavoured to mould the pre-existing pattern of Secondary Education according to the needs of the country by effecting a patch-work improvement in it. It needed, on the other hand, a complete overhauling, even a revolutionary change. The manifold suggestions of the Commission in connection with the improvement in the mode of examinations, rendering the curriculum 'multi-purpose', improvement in the service conditions of teachers and improvement in the private Managing Committees etc. are but traditional. They cannot eradicate the fundamental defects in these spheres root and branch. The recommendations of the commission in connection with the control of education are quite lifeless and conventional. In fact, the Secondary Education should immediately pass under the State control. It is an established fact that irregularities rampant among the Managing Committees are very pernicious to the healthy growth of the Secondary Education. The only remedy to remove all these defects is the nationalisation of Secondary Education.

Besides these, the Commission has ignored and attached no importance to the education of women. The suggestion pertaining to the training of teachers are also not very original. Lastly, the Commission's recommendations with regard to the sanction of grant-in-aid by the Central Government to the State Governments for the purpose of improving the Secondary Education are also inadequate and unsatisfactory.

Despite these defects, on the whole we find that the Commission's recommendations are immensely beneficial and are of magnitudinous importance for the improvement and reorganisation of the Secondary Education in India.

Present Progress: With the advent of independence, the Primary Education is continuing to spread so universally that its influence on the Secondary Education is but natural and inevitable. Consequently during recent past years, the number of the Secondary Schools has considerably increased. But the rise in number of students attending them has surpassed even that of the institutions. The number of schools did not increase as had been expected owing to the lack of funds had able and trained teachers; but with the ever-increasing demand for the Secondary Education in cities, rural areas even in tribal areas of the country, the number of students attending the pre-existing institutions has doubled itself during the last decade.

In the year 1948, in the bigger States of the country the total number of the Secondary Schools inclusive of Middle and High Schools was only 12,693. In 1953, it rose to 18,497 *i.e.* it became one and a half times greater than the original number. An increase of 77 per cent has taken place only in the number of High Schools during all this time. On March 31st 1953, the number of the Middle Schools and High Schools throughout the country were respectively 15,232 and 8,633.

The student cannot cherish the possibility of securing employment soon after finishing his primary education. But this possibility increases after passing the High School examination. This is why the number of students in High Schools is on constant increase. In the a year 1948, the numbers of students in Middle Schools and High Schools were respectively 11,67,283 and 17,86,712. These numbers in 1953 rose respectively to 15,21,903 and 29,12,232. This clearly shows that during the first six years of independence of the country, there has taken place an increase by 30 per cent and 60 per cent respectively in the number of students seeking admissions to Middle Schools and High Schools. If the number of the students belonging to smaller states be added to the above mentioned numbers, the number of students attending all kinds of Secondary schools of the country was 59,06,666 on March 31st, 1953.

So far as the question of expenditure on Secondary Education is concerned, we find that in 1948, the direct expenditure on Secondary Education in the bigger States amounts to 13 crores and forty-eight lakhs of rupees. In 1953, this sum redoubled itself : *i.e.* during the span of six years it rose to 28 crores and 68 lakhs of rupees. On 31st March, 1953, the total expenditure on the Secondary Education throughout the country was 36 crores and 85 lakhs of rupees.

These figures, though large, can never be regarded as satisfactory. When we take the vastness of the dimensions and population of the country into account, these figures are dwarfed into insignificance. Nevertheless, it can safely be held that the Secondary Education is on the way to progress.

The Central Advisory Board of Education discussed the Report of the Committee appointed by the Central Government to examine and discuss the Report of the Secondary Education Commission at its 21st session held on February 7, 1954. In this connection, the Central Education Minister accepted the following three suggestions:

1. The Secondary Education should be so patterned that it might be, for most of the students, an education complete in itself. Its aim should not be mere admission to universities, but it should be a final and complete stage in itself;

2. Its form and syilabus should be of such a kind as might fulfil the needs of students having different interests and aptitudes. It should never be placed in the water-tight compartment; and

3. As we have selected the Basic Education as the foundation of education in the preliminary stage, the Secondary Education should be so moulded that it might help perfect the educational system adopted at the preliminary stage by carrying it further and produce such citizens as might posses the capacity to discharge their civic obligations and responsibilities. Thus the recommendation emphasising some craft in the curriculum of the Secondary Education is appreciable.

One of the significant recommendations made by the Committee appointed in connection with the Secondary Education Commission was that the duration of the Primary Basic Education should be eight years, that of the Secondary Education four years and that of the University three years.

The Committee considered also the recommendation of the Commission that under the curriculum of the Secondary Education. Languages, General Science, Social Studies and a handicraft should be treated as co-subjects. Besides this, the Committee set much stores by such subjects as Humanities, Sciences, Technical subjects,

Commerce, Agricultural subjects, Fine Arts, and diversified curriculum of Home Science etc.

The Committee also suggested that an examination should be held after the completion of the Secondary course. Moreover, special importance should be attached to the monthly tests and the record of the regular progress of students. The Training Colleges should impart free training to teachers. The teachers should receive full salary during the period of their training in order to meet their expenses. It also recommended that Higher Secondary Education Examination should be regarded as the minimum qualifications for most of the government services.

Lastly, the Committee suggested that nearly 50 per cent of the existing Secondary Schools should be converted into Multipurpose schools within next two years and the remaining 50 per cent schools should also be converted into the same within next five years.

Thus it is evident that measures are being adopted to introduce radical changes in the fabric of the Secondary Education and make it suited to the needs of students and the country. The Central Advisory Board has accepted well-nigh all the suggestions of the expert Committee. The Board had also recommended that those schools which desired to be converted into Multipurpose institutions, should be given financial help by State Governments and the Central Government. Provision was made for the special scale of salary for the teachers teaching the technical subjects. The Board further suggested that the State Government should not extend recognition to any school which does not start education in the practical group besides general literary group. For the establishment of libraries in the Schools, the Board recommended the sanction of an incipient grant-in-aid of a sum of Rs. 5000/- to very school to be granted by the Central Government and State Government in the ratio of 1:2 respectively.

On the basis of above recommendations, a scheme of an expenditure of five crores of rupees has been made for the last two years of the First Five Year Plan. Under this plan, five hundred multipurpose schools will be established wherein education in various subjects will be given to the students according to their diverse aptitudes and interests. An opportunity to receive higher technical education in the Polytechnical colleges will be provided to those students who finish their education in those schools.

Another scheme of the Planning Commission in this respect is that all the existing Secondary Schools in the country should introduce the subject of General Science positively within the next seven years. For this purpose special grant-in-aid will be sanctioned to the schools in order to establish laboratories and purchase scientific apparatus and other paraphernalia. Similar special grants-in-aid will be sanctioned to five hundred Multi-purpose schools and fifteen hundred other schools for the purpose of establishing libraries. The third aspect of this plan is the starting of education in handicrafts and improving them. All these improvements are being made with a view to materialise the recommendations of the Secondary Education Commission.

The 22nd session of the Central Advisory Board of Education was held at Delhi on January 12, 1955. Again the problems of the Secondary Education were discussed by the Board and the progress made by it on the basis of the recommendations of the Commission was reviewed. Expressing his views in this meeting Maulana Abul Kalam Azad, the Central Education Minister has confessed that "the Secondary Education is the weakest link of the Indian education". Further, submitting the Government Blue Book to the Advisory Board, he expressed similar views on Secondary Education. According to the views of Maulana Abul Kalam Azad, "the Secondary Education is that stage to attain which opportunity should be given to all. In short, it is that stage and will remain for long where most of the children of the country end their academic career. Hence this education should be of such a nature as might prepare them for practical life. But a it is pity that Secondary Education at present is not fulfilling this aim".

The Education Minister told in this session of the Central Advisory Board of Education that the Central Government was thinking seriously of establishing a Council for Secondary Education on the lines of All-India Technical Education Council. This Council will make periodical reviews of the progress made by the Secondary Education in the country and will advise the Government for the improvement and expansion of education. It was also decided by the Board that on the basis of the recommendations of Radha Krishnan and Mudaliar Commissions, the Course of the Secondary Education should further be increased by one year. This, on the one hand, will raise the general standard of education, of the other, will relieve Universities of excessive burden.

The Board, having accepted the recommendations of the Mudaliar Commission concerning the establishment of multipurpose schools, has decided to take immediate and precipitate steps in this direction. Though the Government have already directed their attention towards that side, nearly all the Secondary Schools in all the states are academic in character even today. The main reason is the utter lack of efficient teachers, paucity of funds and want of necessary equipment and paraphernalia. The plan of the Government is that five hundred multipurpose schools should be so distributed throughout the country that there should necessarily be at least one such school in each district.

Thus majority of the Board's recommendations are nothing more than mere repetition of the recommendations of the Secondary Education Commission and those of the Board's made at its 21st session. Under the Five Year Plan the Secondary Education is making progress gradually; but it is moving, surprisingly enough, at the snail's pace. The fact is that in spite of the State efforts and the recommendations of the Secondary Education Commission, the framework of the Secondary Education is still old and traditional. No appreciable change has been introduced in its aims, means, control and organisation, curriculum and method of teaching, the mode of examination, the training of teachers and their social and economic status. Whatever state efforts are directed to eliminate all these fundamental defects, come to an end during the period of experimentation and are consigned to oblivion gradually. The major number of recommendations of the Commissions and Committees are never fully implemented. Some of the main problems of the Secondary Education may be analysed briefly. They are as follows:

Some Problems of the Secondary Education

Aim: The main aim of the establishment of English Schools in India had been from the very beginning to prepare and train educated officials and clerks for conducting administrative work. Unfortunately, the aim persists to remain more or less the same. As a matter of fact, the Secondary Education in India suffers from aimlessness even today. Its sole purpose is only to prepare the child for entrance into the University for clerical jobs. This is why we usually find the Indian colleges full of such students as do not have an inkling of the ultimate object of their education or of the profession they are being prepared for. Most of them attend schools for the simple and good reason that they are sent by their parents to schools for studies. At schools, according to their own convenience or the opinion of their friends, they choose those simple and easy subjects by devoting less energy and time to which they might at least get through the examination. They can probably never realize what the aim of their success of this type will be or what position they will hold in their life in future.

As a matter of fact, the Secondary Education should be a self-sufficient and an independent unit in itself and not merely complementary to University education. A hint thereabout has been given in the preceding pages. At the completion of the Secondary Education course the student should be able to feel confidentally that he has attained a definite stage in his academic career and the he is comparatively capable to undertake some independent work. He must feel that he has been prepared for life and not for university. The aim of such education should be both economic and cultural.

The educationists fully well realise the importance of adolescent period with regard to the formation of character and life-long habits of a person. The period falling between eleven and eighteen years is the formative period in a student's life and it is during this period when he receives his Secondary education. The main aim of Secondary Education is the fullest physical, mental and moral development of the child's personality so that the sentiments of leadership might be engendered in him and might lead the country confidently on the way to progress in future. "The High School is in onesense the backbone of a national educational system for it is to the High School that the country must look for the preparatory training of its leaders and experts in all walks of life.[21]

India is a free country today and democratic form of Government secular in nature has been established here. The new

India is confronted by diverse problems—economic, social, political and cultural. Hence there is the need of setting not merely a general and theoritical aim of the Secondary Education, but on the contrary some such aim as might be consistent with the changed conditions. "This means that the educational system must make its contribution to the development of habits, attitudes and qualities of democratic citizenship and to counteract all those fissiparious tendencies which hinder the emergence of a broad, national and secular outlook"[22].

Under such conditions, the aim of the Secondary Education in India should be four-fold, first the formation of students' character so that they might actively help build a democratic social order as responsible and free citizens; secondly, to increase their utilitarian and productive efficiency so that they might make the country prosperous through the economic reconstruction of it; thirdly, an all-round development of students' personality *i.e.* the development of their literary, aesthetic and cultural aptitudes which are quite indispensable for their self-expression and full development of their personality; lastly, development of the qualities of leadership, The Secondary Education should, therefore, seek to fulfill all these many sided aims of education and prepare students by developing their faculties as perfect units so that they might make their own contribution to the prosperity and enrichment of national life in all possible respects.

It is unfortunate that most of our present Secondary schools are not fully conscious of their essential duties and fall short of our expectations in fulfilling those aims. Hence it is of primary importance that we should make not only the students realise but also their teachers and guardians the supreme significance and magnitude of those aims.

Curriculum: If we go through the curriculum of the Secondary Education of our country, we find that probably the problems has not been tackled radically and no corresponding steps have been taken to improve it for a century. Many political, economic and industrial changes of magnitudinous importance are happening in the country at different intervals; but our education in general and Secondary Education in particular is unable to keep pace with the changing times. The curriculum does not appear to be related in any wise to the real and practical life of the child or his environments.

He reads the pre-determined and traditional curriculum mechanical without curiosity, interest, understanding or appreciation, for his immediate aim is to get through the examination and be admitted to higher classes or prepare himself for some clerical job. Needless to say that on account of the unsuitability of the curriculum, huge waste of human energy is taking place in the country, In the absence of proper education of various subjects, we are producing young persons, all of the same kind like the factory manufactured goods lacking in originality and inventiveness. When the child faces the real and practical world at the expiry of the Secondary Education career, he finds himself a total stranger in an environment quite maladjusted to him.[23]

Various Education Commissions have pointed out this defect in the curriculum at different intervals, but even today it exists as before to a considerable measure. Though some of the important technical and vocational subjects have been introduced into the curriculum of the Secondary Education, yet the efforts are far from being satisfactory and adequate in view of the large requirements of the country. The need of the hour is that the curriculum of the Secondary Education should be vast and varied and children should be encouraged and trained to choose subjects according to their tastes and aptitudes, having found out these tastes and interests through the help of psychological experts.

Nearly 85 per cent population of India dwells in rural areas, Hence our curriculum should be so formulated as to be related to the main rural occupations *i.e.* agriculture, dairy, animal-husbandry and other cottage industries. Moreover, there should be proper provision for training in modern industries. We can ill afford at the same time to ignore the liberal literary education. As a matter of fact, the curriculum which had been set up for the Post-Basic education, is suited to present requirements.

Discipline: The problem of discipline should not be regarded as that of Secondary Education exclusively; on the other hand, it is a country-wide problem of the entire students' community. Though the problem of discipline is not directly related to educational organisation, yet Indian system of education; educational organisation, method of teaching and the mode of examination indirectly exercise a profound influence upon the question of discipline as a whole among the students.

The question arises: what are the prominent reasons of the growing indiscipline among students ? The answer to the query is not far to seek. The student receives manifold social influences indirectly and unconsciously. Our country seems to have lost sight of higher spiritual values on account of the degenerating moral standard. Majority of the students, teachers and guardians forgetting higher aims and values of life have grown irresponsible and undisciplined.

Further, the political revolutions that occurred during the last few decades can also be held responsible to some extent for the indisciplined state among students. The political leaders encouraged and even instigated students to participate prematurely in political movements or observe strikes during the course of launching the movement for freedom of the country. Those very tendencies and sentiments are still active even today when the country has achieved independence.

The third cause of indiscipline is the defective mode of examinations. Students today do not hesitate to adopt the foulest means in order to pass the examination. Thus tendency leads them sometimes even to the prepetration of such atrocious crimes as murder. Carrying of books in the examination hall, copying, talking and seeking the help of some corrupt teachers fearlessly—these and other similar nasty practices have become quite commonplace features of examination system in the country.

The fourth reason is the wretched economic condition of teachers and the resultant deterioration of the sense of responsibility and morality in them.[24] It is indeed a lamentable fact and we have to swallow the bitter pill of the fact that the teacher of today has deviated from his duty on account of the terrible blows of economic difficulties. He seems to connive at and at times even unconcerned at the unpleasant incidents occurring in the school and the growing indiscipline among the students. He finds himself unable even to create a sense of goodwill and self-control among the students or to place before them the ideal of disciplined behaviour. There is no reason why indiscipline should continue to persist if the teachers make earnest efforts to eradicate this evil.

Besides these, there are some other factors which go a long way in explaining the causes of indiscipline among the students such has negligence shown by the guardians or the parents of children in matters of the formation of character and good habits in their wards, some unwholesome influences *i.e.* Cinema, teachings of the teacher-politicians and the emergence of such organisations and play upon the tender dispositions and feelings of children during the most impressionable period of their life and thus exploit them to serve their own interests. Other factors responsible for the same evil are frustration among youths, lack of extra-curricular activities, absence of an ideal of social and corporate life growing corruption in society and lastly communal prejudices which help the growth of indiscipline among the students.

At times, the learned persons and educationists of the country have thrown light upon this problem and warned against it. It appears that if no proper remedy is invented to counteract the tide of this malady prevalent among to students, the very aim of education is likely to be defeated.

The Secondary Education is that foundation upon which we errect the mansion of the future career of students. The development of character of creation of correct habits of behaviour usually takes place during children's adolescence. Hence it becomes the duty of all concerned to engender in them higher and noble virtues of humility, politeness and discipline.

Private Management and Administration: The secondary schools are controlled and managed by different types of Bodies *i.e.*, Government; Local Boards (District Boards and Municipal Boards) as well as private managing committees at places.

From the very beginning it has been the policy of government to withdraw itself gradually from the sphere of the Secondary education, and larger scope has been given to private venture.

In majority of the cases, the Secondary Schools are managed by Boards and private Managing Committees. The policy of establishing at least one Government Secondary School in each district has also been adopted.

So far as the private management is concerned, the state of affairs is far from being satisfactory. Schools under private management are more often than not victim of financial crisis. They have neither good buildings, nor adequate equipment, furniture and library. The condition of teachers in such schools is not happy. There are certain conspicuous defects prevalent in these institutions proving quite detrimental and pernicious to the growth of Secondary Education in the country; some of them being low scale of salary for teachers, appointment of untrained teachers on a lower salary, dismissal of any teacher through personal jealousy or displeasure, etc. Institutions by different religious denominations or communities are doing a lot of harm instead of benefit to the nation. Institutions immune from communal prejudices resulting in inevitable evil, are few and far between. At the same time there are some private schools which have done appreciable and creditable work in the sphere of Secondary Education. On the whole it may safely be held that most of them are far from being satisfactory.

In addition to this, it is usually found that most of the members of the private Managing Bodies are such as have no interest in education or the problems related there to. The position in rural areas is still more precarious. Some educated or semi-educated persons floundering in the morasses of local politics, regards educational institutions as the symbol of personal prestige and dignity and consequently exploit them in various ways ultimately resulting in inconceivable harm to the cause of education. If under the conditions *i.e.* non-guarantee of teachers' services or dissatisfactions of other kinds, the standard of education is constantly deteriorating. It must not come as a surprise to us. The danger at the hands of teacher politicians is on the increase and the Managing Committees sometimes patronise them inordinately.

It is necessary, however, to take one more point about the management of education into consideration. It has usually been found that the weaknesses in the management of institutions have crept owing mainly to the laxity and inefficiency of the officials of the Government Education Department and specially those belonging to Inspection Department. The corrupt and inefficient management of private institutions is largely attributable to the indifference and inefficiency of the Inspection Department. Examples have been found of the Inspectors of Schools causing irregularities in the management by making unholy alliance with the members of the Managing Committees.

The most important remedy to counteract all these defects is that the government should realize their responsibility towards Secondary Education of the country. If the nationalisation of the entire Secondary Education sounds impracticable at his time though ultimately it has got to be done, the conditions of its management can at least be improved. The U.P. Government had appointed a Committee known as the Raghukula Tilak Committee for the purpose of improving the conditions for private management. The Committee in its Report had recommended that in order to improve the private management it is extremely essential that the Managing Committees must include one representative of teachers and three other members nominated by the Department of Education. But the recommendations of the Report remain merely a pious hope owing to the vehement protest of the private Managing Committees so much so that the modest recommendations made by second Narendra Dev Committee in connection with the improvement of Managements in this state seem to have been shelved. There is no doubt about the fact that the issue of the improvement in the private management can be postponed only at the cost of a great danger to Secondary Education. The problem of management and administration in the sphere of Secondary Education is an important and radical one.

The Standard of Education: It is usually heard today that the general standard of education has shown a downward trend affecting the Secondary Education also. Undoubtedly the policy of the Government has been to expand the quantity of education thus ignoring the quality of it. Other factors responsible for the low standard of education are the low scale of salary of teachers, most of the teachers being untrained, growing discontentment among the teachers towards their profession, abnormally increased number of students in the classes, the serious lack of necessary requirements and equipment, inefficiency of the Managing Bodies as well as improper interference by them in the internal affairs of the institutions, inefficiency as well as negligence of the Education Department to some extent, the wretched financial condition of the institutions, abundance of improper means recreation as Cinema etc. for the students, a growing lack of the sense of responsibility among the teachers and their attitude of negligence towards their duties, unsuitability of the text books and indifference to and unfamiliarity of the guardians of students and the general public with them multifarious educational problems.

The expansion of education is, no doubt, essential to improve the present backward educational condition of the country; but we shall have to take the standard of education into account along with its expansion and ultimately give preference to 'Quality' and not 'Quantity' as had been the case so far during the post independence period at least so in Uttar Pradesh. The problem requires urgent solution before it may reach the danger-point. It is only then that we shall be able to produce such young persons as might prove ideal future citizens of the country in all respects and establish their superiority before the young men of other countries.

Mode of Examination: The problem of the mode of examination has been a very crucial and difficult one in the sphere of Secondary Education "Worse than India's community ridden, social and political system is her examination-ridden educational system. In fact, the Matriculation examination dominates the entire work of our Secondary Schools. The prestige of a school depends entirely upon Matriculation results and very little on real educational merits of the institution."[25] In reality, all the qualities of the students and efforts of teachers are being immolated at the altar of the examination. The student devotes all his energies to the single aim of getting through the examination ignoring all other benefits. This encourages the evil and unpsychological tendency to learn by rote and the children engage themselves in unintelligent memorisation and cramming. Whatsoever material they stuff their brains which is ultimately poured out on the answer-books in the examination hall and then they enter the world empty-minded. They are rendered thus quite unsuitable for the practical affairs of the world. The child thus cannot fully develop his personality.[26]

The present system of examination has, however affected the ethical side of the personality of teachers and students. The use of unafair means by the examinees in the examination hall, is a commonplace occurrence today. The negligent student who does not work at all throughout the year may pass the examination through unscrupulous means. Similarly teachers are there who show preferential treatment towards the students they are interested in and sometimes accept bribery in lieu of their immoral and unjustifiable acts. The state of affairs indeed, is grave and highly objectionable in addition to its being ignominious. Hence is the need of replacing the prevalent system of examination by some more scientific method so that the present mode of examination may fully be purged of all the evils that have crept into it. In his respect, the experiment of P.E.P.S.U. Government is worth mentioning. She has adopted a system of examination whereby promotion will be made in the primary schools in the consideration of the age of the child and his classroom work.

These are, in short, the main shortcomings of the Secondary Education. Hence the most urgent need of the hour is to realize the importance of Secondary Education to accomplish the objective of developing the country and enabling her to complete successfully in the race of cultural progress with other civilized nations of the world. We should understand fully well that Secondary Education is our weakest spot. All the efforts to improve university education will end in fiasco without effecting improvement in the Secondary Education. In a sense, we can hold that without its improvement, the progress of the nation as a whole is quite difficult—nay even impossible. Secondary Education holds a very important position in the educational system of any country. In fact, it forms the link joining the two extremities of education—primary and university education. The defects of Secondary Education seldom fail to contaminate primary and university education because in most of the cases, the matriculates are appointed as the teachers in primary schools. If the students drink deep from a polluted fountain head of education, they will vitiate the entire atmosphere of primary education when they undertake the profession of teaching in those institutions, by transferring those very defects to the students they teach and guide. Besides, soon after completing their Secondary education, students seek admission to universities. Thus they drag with them the defects of Secondary Education to the university sphere. Under such conditions, complete eradication of the defects prevalent in Secondary Education is an urgent need of the hour.

University Education (1937-55)

Educational Progress

The period following the year 1937 has witnessed considerable progress in the sphere of University Education. With the expansion of Secondary Education, the number of students in universities also began to swell gradually. Another reason of its progress is the ambition on the part of the persons belonging to all strata of society to receive higher education. Further cause of the increase in the number of students in the universities was that owing to the political and economic circumstances of the country the sentiments of serving the nation and making individual progress in life were considerably stimulated in the young persons. Moreover, during the war-period the trading class of India had earned large profits, hence they made liberal contributions to the promotion of higher education in the country. The Government needed skilful and trained personnel for the various purposes during the war, hence they increased the grant-in-aid in order to advance university education. All these above-mentioned conditions continued to exist even during the post-war period. All these factors have eventually led to an unprecedented growth of university education in India.

After 1947, with the advent of independence of the country, the sphere of university education considerably widened. At the time of the partition of the country there were only 21 universities in the country now rising to 31. After the partition, only 19 universities remained in India, the two of them (Decca and Punjab Universities) having gone in the possession of Pakistan. Since that time, 12 more universities have been established in the country. Most of them have been founded on the basis of linguistic regions. By the end of 1952, there was no important linguistic region where there might not be at least one university.

The progress in university education can be calculated from the following statistics:

In 1948, the number of students receiving education in bigger states of the country was 1,79,173 rising to 2,69,914 in the year 1953. It means that during five years the number of students in universities increased by 50 per cent. The number of students receiving vocational and special education increased still more. In the year 1948, the number was 44,604 which rose to 94,567 in the year 1953. Thus the position at the close of 1953 was as follows:

1. Number of colleges (General Education) ------------------------ 606
2. Number of technical colleges ------------------------------------- 314
3. Number of students receiving general education --------- 3,59,857
4. Number of students receiving technical education -------- 1,14,937

The progress can be reckoned by the increase in the number of Graduates. In 1948, number of graduates in the States of 'A' category was 27 thousand. Out of these there were 18 thousand graduates in Arts and Science. In 1953, these numbers rose to 52,000 and 34,000 respectively. Further increase took place in these numbers during 1954-55.

So far as the expenditure on the universities and colleges imparting general education in the bigger states of the country is concerned, it was 5 crores and 80 lakhs of rupees in 1948. The expenditure reached the mark of 11 crores and 60 lakhs of rupees in 1953 *i.e.* it became more than two-fold. Similarly, expenditure on technical and vocational education became three-fold. The statistics of expenditure on the entire higher education of the country are as follows:

1. Total expenditure	15 crores and 22 lakhs of rupees
2. Expenditure on technical education	5 crores and 94 lakks of rupees

In addition to the above-mentioned expenditure the Government of India sanctioned a sum of Rs. 30,96,556 in 1953-1954 to the University Grants Commission for the purpose of extending grants to the universities. This amount has been expended on non-Scientific and non-Technical education, Prior to the appointment of University Grants Commission, the Government of India had sanctioned a grant-in-aid of Rs. 43,23,175 to the universities. Similarly, a sum of Rs. 55,47,570 had been given to the University Grants Commission for Scientific and Technical education and another sum of Rs. 5,56,985 had already been sanctioned for the same purpose prior to the appointment of the Commission. Besides these grants, the Government of India sanctions every year special grants-in-aid for research, scholarship and development of finer Arts and cultural activities.

New Universities

As has already been mentioned, 12 more universities have been established in post-partition India. The East Punjab University was founded in 1947. This university conducts teaching in Agriculture, Arts, Commerce, Education, Engineering, Law, Medicine, Oriental Learning, Science and Veterinary Science, etc. Its constitution has thoroughly democratised the Senate.

This year 1948 witnessed the establishment of 3 universities: Gauhati (Assam), Jammu and Kashmir and Roorkee Engineering University (U.P.). Out of these the Gauhati University is of Affiliating Residential and Teaching type. It provides education in Agriculture, Arts Commerce, Low, Medicine and Sciences. The Jammu and Kashmir University provides education in Arts, Oriental learning, Science and Training of teachers. One speciality of this University is that education is provided free of charge. It is the first University of its own kind providing free education. The Roorkee University had been incorporated by the U.P. Government by developing the Thompson Engineering College. Thompson College was well-nigh one century old. It is the only Engineering University in India.

The Poona and Baroda Universities were founded in the year 1949. Those colleges of Maharashtra which were formerly affiliated to the Bombay University, were transferred to the jurisdiction of Poona University. The special feature of Baroda University is that special education is given in Finer Arts, Home Science, Indian Classical Music and Social Service. In 1950, two more Universities those of Gujarat and Karnatak were incorporated in the State of Bombay. There are now six universities in the State.

In the year 1951, by dividing Patna University two separate institutions—Patna University and Bihar University have been established. The area under the jurisdiction of Patna University is confined only to the Municipal boundaries of the city, while the Bihar University enjoys jurisdiction over the remaining area in the State. The former institution is only teaching University whereas the latter is of both teaching and affiliating type.

During 1951-52, a pre-existing institution for the education of women at Bombay namely Srimati Nathebai Damodar Thackersay Bhartiya Mahila Vidyalaya (S.N.D.T.) has been raised to the status of a University. In the sphere of women education, this institution holds a prominent position and enjoys an all India repute. Under this institution, training in B.T. is given at Poona, Bombay, Ahmedabad and Baroda and a special course in Nursing has been instituted under it conferring the degree of B.Sc. Moreover, the University has undertaken the work of publishing text-books of higher order in Marathi and Gujarati.

In 1951, the Vishva-Bharati had passed under the jurisdiction of the Government of India. The University had been founded by Dr. Ravindra Nath Tagore in the year 1929. Under the control of the Central Government, this is the fourth University besides three others—Aligarh, Delhi and Banaras universities. Fine Arts, Education, Philosophy, Art and Science are main curricula of this university. A detailed description of it has already been given in preceding pages. On the recommendations of the University Education Commission, the Government of India has amended the constitutions of the Muslim University, Aligarh and the Hindu University, Banaras. Similarly the constitution of the Delhi University had been amended during 1951-52. According to this amendment, the Delhi University has now become teaching and affiliating university. The president who used to be its Chancellor will now be called Visitor. Many of the powers vested in the Chancellor have now been transferred to the Court of the University. Similarly the State Government of Uttar Pradesh has amended the constitutions of the Agra, Allahabad and Lucknow Universities with a view to eliminating internal maladministration and undesirable party politics which is pernicious to the growth of higher education on sound lines. The amendments have been effected in the constitution of Agra and Allahabad universities. The issue of Lucknow university is on the carpet in the Legislative Assembly of the States. A reference to it will be made later on.

In the end, the 31st University had been established on September 3, 1955 at Tirupathi in Andhra State. Its name is Sri Venkateshwara University. It has been nomenclatured after Venkateshwar, one of Hindu Dieties. A benefaction in the form of the building costing 16 lakhs of rupees has been made by Tirumalai Tirupathi Devasthanam institution the yearly income of which is computed to be some forty lakhs of rupees. In addition to it, the institution has contributed a cash donation of six and a half lakhs of rupees and sanctioned an yearly recurrent grant-in-aid of two and a half lakhs of rupees. The State Government also has sanctioned a grant of 3.5 lakhs of rupees for the purpose of establishing the University. The University for the first two years will remain purely residential. Thereafter college of Rayalaseema too will be affiliated to it. The Chancellor of this University will be the Chief Justice of Andhra State.

Thus it is evident, the gradual but steady progress is taking place in the sphere of University education. Every year, new branches in higher learning are being opened, and new departments are being established in Universities. Sufficient improvement has been made in the scope and quality of investigations and research work in the universities. Many of the urgent educational needs of the country and her higher ambitions are being gratified by including newer subjects in the university curricula.

The following table given us an idea of the number and relative position of Universities in India: (See on next page)

After the independence of the country, the question of the medium of instruction in universities became much more controvertible. The controversy gathered momentum with establishment of new universities on the basis of linguistics zones. Many of the universities wished naturally to adopt Indian languages as the medium of instruction. The opinion of Government of India was in favour of a necessary change in the medium of instruction, but the change should be gradual so that teachers and students might be saved from facing unnecessary difficulties and inconvenience. Hence a conference of all the Vice-Chancellors of all the Indian Universities was convened on May 8th, 1948 in order to discuss this vital issue. The conference placed many a valuable suggestions, majority of which have been adopted by the University Education Commission.

Name	*Date of foundation*	*Type*	*Number of students (1947)*	*Percentage of Govt. grant to total income*
1. Calcutta	1857	Affiliating & Teaching	450,003	22.9
2. Bombay	1857	,,	43,090	8.6
3. Madras	1857	,,	28,888	23.4
4. Allahabad	1887	Affiliating & Federal	3,502	52.88
5. Banaras	1916	Affiliating & Teaching	5,083	9.2
6. Mysore	1916	,,	9,350	69.2
7. Patna	1917	,,	5,471	7.2
8. Usmania	1918	Affiliating & Teaching	4,862	91.3
9. Aligarh	1920	,,	4,009	35.7
10 Lucknow	1920	,,	3,893	53.3
11. Delhi	1922	Teaching and Federal	4,311	52.4
12. Nagpur	1923	Affiliating & Teaching	5,734	15.4
13. Andhra	1926	,,	9,445	20.4
14. Agra	1927	Affiliating	9,936	9.96
15. Annamalai	1929	Teaching	1,81	47.62
16. Travancore	1937	Affiliating &Teaching	5,715	78.6
17. Utkal	1943	Affiliating		9.61
18. Saugar	1946	Affiliating & Teaching	1,828	33.39
19. Rajputana	1947	Affiliating	N. A.	48.23
20. East Punjab	1947	Affiliating & Teaching	,,	N. A.
21. Gauhati	1947	,,	,,	,,
22. Poona	1948	,,	,,	,,
23. Roorkee	1948	Teaching	,,	,,
24. Jammu & Kashmir	1948	Affiliating	,,	,,
25. Baroda	1949	Affiliating & Teaching	,,	,,
26. Karnatak	1950	,,	,,	,,
27. Gujarat	1950	Affiliating	,,	,,
28. S.N.D.T. Mahila University	1951	,,	,,	,,
29. Vishva-Bharti	1951	Affiliating & Residential	,,	,,
30. Bihar	1952	Affiliating	,,	,,
31. Sri Venkateshwara (Andhra)	1954	Affiliating & Teaching	,,	,,

With regard to the University Education, the views of certain thinkers and educationists have been that dimension of University Education are growing more rapidly than those either of Primary or Secondary Education. Moreover, education imparted in Universities is generally urban in character and not vocational or technical. After independence people felt strongly that University Education in India should thoroughly be overhauled and reorientated so that it might suit the new requirements and ambitions of the people of India. The Inter-University Board and Central Advisory Board of Education too supported this idea. In January, 1948, an All-India Educational conference was held which recommended that in order to re-examine the entire sphere of higher education, a Commission should be appointed. The Government of India therefore, appointed a Commission under the Chairmanship of Dr. Sarvapalli Radhakrishnan on November 4th 1948. The Commission began its work the very same year and submitted its Report in August, 1949. A mention thereof will be made in the following pages.

It is a very important and significant Report which expresses the definite views of the Commission well-nigh on all the aspects of University Education in India. It has considerably influenced the opinion of the people about University Education. The Government of India by approving of all the recommendations of the Commission have accepted them as the very foundation of improvement and expansion of University Education in the country. The Central Advisory Board of Education reconsidered the recommendations of the Commission at is 20th annual session held in November, 1953, and made recommendations to the effect that the President of the Board (Central Education Minister) should appoint a Commission in order to ensure how far the recommendations of the Commission were being acted upon and to suggest in what ways those recommendations could speedily be implemented.

On 7th February, 1954, the Report of the Commission was discussed at the 21st session of the Central Advisory Board of Education. The Report suggested that immediate steps should be taken in the direction of amendment of constitutions of Indian Universities so that the University Senates, Syndicates and Academic Councils might forthwith be purged of the curse of internal intrigues and the spirit of partisanship. The Commission has further suggested that the question of the appointment of Vice-Chancellors is immensely vital and in this respect all other universities should follow as far as possible the example of Delhi University. Many other valuable recommendations were made by the Commission, *i.e.* improvement in the scale of salary for the teachers, extension of loan-grants to universities for the purpose of building hostels, adoption of Tutorial method in place of lecture method in teaching and provision of more scholarships for the indigent but intelligent students etc. The Board has accepted nearly all those recommendations.

The University Education Commission had a very important recommendation that a parallel Committee to the University Grants Committee of Britain should be appointed. The duty of this Committee would be to advise the Government with regard to the sanction of grant-in-aid to Universities and other institutions of higher education. On the basis of this recommendation, the Government of India established a University Grants Committee. The Committee was raised to the status of a Commission in December, 1953, and a large sum of money was placed at its disposal for the purpose of sanctioning grant-in-aid to the Universities. Reference to it will be made later on. The Government have taken a very significant step in the direction of encouraging investigation in Humanities. In fact, many students having reached higher classes, leave Arts subjects and offer Science subjects generally because they think that Science possesses many possibilities and a large scope for Research. Thus the efficiency of work in Sciences too suffers considerably. Accordingly, the Budget of 1954-55 provides for one hundred scholarships of Rs. 200/- pm each for the students who have passed M.A. examination order to enable them to conduct research work in Humanities. In the current year the work has shown appreciable progress.

With regard to University Education the opinion of many educationists and politicians is that it has increased abnormally and to encourage higher education any further is detrimental to the interests of the country. They opine that by encouraging University Education, the Primary Education and Secondary Education suffer under indifference and negligence. If we closely examine this view, it hardly contains a modicum of truth in it. No doubt, Primary and Secondary Education falls short of our necessities; but it does not prove in any sense that University Education is being pampered fat at the cost of Primary and Secondary Education. In fact, if we compare University Education of our country with that of other countries, we find that the expansion of it is quite inconsistent with the vast requirements of our country. In this respect, the information that has been furnished by the Sargent Report in 1944 is of much importance and value. According to it, if looking to the vast population of India, we reckon the number of students in Indian universities, we find that our country lags far behind other progressive countries of the world. Prior to the World War II, in Germany, the ratio of students in Universities to the total population of the country was 1:690; that of Great Britain 1:837; in the U.S.A. 1:225 and in U.S.S.R. it was 1:300, whereas the ratio in India was 1:2206.

Further the Sargent Report has given in 1944 the statistics about the number of universities. According to the Report, "there are 12 universities for a population of 4.1 crores in England, 13 universities for 85 lakhs of people in Canada, 6 in Australia for 55 lakhs of persons, 1720 institutions in the U.S.A. for a population of 13 crores while, only 18 universities exist in India for a vast population of 40 crores of people."[27]

Similar views have been expressed by the Universities Education Commission; "It should not be inferred that too large a part of those of college age are going to colleges and universities in our country-quite the contrary. The percentage of the population receiving higher education here is lower considerably than in most countries in the West. For example, in 1946-47, there were 20,78,095 resident students in the college and universities of the United States out of a population of less than 1,50,01,000 while here there were 24,17,954 enrolled in our universities, including constituent and affiliating colleges, out of a population of 32,00,00,000 people. That is in the U.S.A. there are more than more than eight times as many students enrolled in higher education than here, out of a population probably less than half of ours.[28]

It is clear from the above account that higher education in India is not more than what is required. India has to put forth herculean efforts in order to attain an equal footing with other progressive countries in the sphere of higher education.

Research Work in Universities

The work of investigation and research in Indian universities had begun in the second decade of 20th century. Satisfactory progress was made in this direction after the Provincial Autonomy, but the World War II again put obstacles in its way. It was only after the independence of the country that research work evinced an ascending trend. Now-a-days, considerable encouragement is being given to research work in the spheres of Physical Sciences, Humanities and Vocational Education.

The condition of original research work in Indian universities is not at all satisfactory. So long as our universities were of affiliating type, some colleges carried on some research. No doubt some of the researches enjoy international repute. Some of the famous names in the field of original research are Sir R.G. Bhandarkar at Poona, Sir Ganga Nath Jha at Allahabad, Professor Kuppuswami Shastri at Madras, Sir Jagdish Chandra Bose and P.C Ray at Calcutta, Professor S.R. Kashyap at Lahore and Sir C.V. Raman at Bangalore. Most of the research was done especially in the field of science. It was only through the intrepid efforts of Sir Ashutosh Mookerjee that research work was sent on a proper footing in 1914 at Calcutta University for the first time. Since then, research work has been conducted in the fields in Science and Arts nearly in all the universities. The learned and erudite professors of Universities have devoted their attention to this direction and have generally guided the research work. A system of degrees of Ph.D., D, Litt., and D.Sc. to be conferred upon the successful research scholars had accordingly been evolved. The Government also diverted their attention towards this side and sanctioned special grant-in-aid and scholarships for the research students in order to promote the work of investigation in the universities. Some students are sent abroad *i.e.* England, U.S.A., Germany, Japan and France for further studies or research work. It shows that some achievements have been made in this sphere.

At the same time, it is, however true, that the progress in field of research is negligible and insignificant in relation to vastness of the country. While we wish increase in the quantitative aspect of research, it is essential at the same time that its quality must also be superior so that it might be placed on an international footing. In

1948, Radhakrishnan Commission had found out that all the Indian Universities had awarded Ph.D. and D.Sc. degrees in six Basic sciences to 260 scholars during the last ten years *i.e.* 26 persons undertook research work every year whereas in England in the year 1935 more than four hundred men were engaged at Cambridge alone in scientific research.[29]

The main reasons of the slow progress in the field of research work are as follows. Firstly, learned teachers and students try to seek Government posts on account of the low scale of salaries in the Universities. Secondly, Universities are ill-equipped for the purpose of conducting research work. The work of investigation can be possible at a place where the laboratories are fully equipped containing all modern scientific instruments and apparatus and where library facilities are available. Thirdly, there is scarcity of learned teachers for the sake of guiding the research scholars in their work. The teachers who guide research work have also to do daily routine of teaching as well. Under such circumstances they are not in a position to spare either time or energy necessary for research work. Besides, these teachers are not usually paid any remuneration in lieu of their hard work; if at all they are paid, the remuneration is insignificantly meagre. Further, our students lack in intellectual capacity and moral qualities so essential for the purpose of conducting research of any kind. Most of the students cannot undertake research work owing to financial difficulties. Lastly, the industrialist do not help the cause of investigation in the county. Nevertheless, it is a matter of gratification that improvement is being made very rapidly in this field and both the industrialists and Government are evincing keen interest in this direction.

The University Education Commission (1949)

Appointment: As has been indicated above, it was deemed proper that a preliminary survey should be made of the economic and teaching conditions in the universities prior to framing any plans for the improvement and expansion of Indian University Education. Hence the Inter-University Board and Central Advisory Board of Education had passed a resolution recommending to the Indian Government to appoint a Commission on the lines of Hunter Commission in consultation with the state governments "to report on Indian University

Education and suggest improvements and extensions that may be desirable to suit present and future requirements of the country." The Government accepted this resolution and in November, 1948, a University Education Commission was appointed under the Chairmanship of Dr. Sarvapalli Radhakrishnan. Other prominent members of the Commission were Dr. Tara Chand, Secretary and Educational Adviser to the Government of India, Sir James F. Duff, the Vice-Chancellor of the University of Durham, Dr. Zakir Hussain, Dr. Arthur E. Morgan (America), Dr Lakshmanaswami Mudaliar, Dr Meghnad Saha and Dr. John Tigert (formerly Commissioner of Education of the United States) etc. On 25th August, 1949, the Commission submitted its Report.

The Terms of Reference of the Commission were all embracing and comprehensive. Keeping the future national and international circumstances in their purview, they were to make recommendations in regard to the aims and objects of Indian Universities, research work, organisation and administration of universities, their financial problems, problems of teachers, curricula, admission medium of instruction, religious education, accommodation for students, problems pertaining to health and discipline among the students etc. As a matter of fact, no problem pertaining to higher education remained which did not receive the attention of the Commission. The Report of this Commission is more perfect, universal and superior to all the Reports of Commissions appointed hitherto for university education and its recommendations are of paramount importance.

Recommendations

The Commission submitted the first part of its Report in eighteen chapters covering seven hundred and forty seven pages. It has taken all the main problems pertaining to University Education into account. The second part of it contains figures, statistics and evidences etc. In the beginning, making brief historical retrospect of University Education in India, the Commission has placed the aims of University Education in the new political and social structure of the country. It has emphasized, referring to the Constitution of India, principles of democracy, justice, freedom, quality, national and international fraternity among other aims of University Education for the reconstruction of India. Then it has made recommendations about the service conditions of teachers and their training, research, professional education, religious education, medium of education, system of examination, problems of students, education of women, finances, central and other universities and rural universities. Below are given the main recommendations of the Commission:

1. *Problems of Teachers:* The problem of teachers is the most important one in the opinion of the Commission. It has put teachers of universities under four categories: Professor, Reader, Lecturer and Instructor. Besides these, recommendation has been made about the appointment for Research Fellows. Promotion of teachers from the lower to higher posts should be made purely on the basis of merits. The ratio between the junior and senior posts should be 2:1. The age of retirement should be at sixty years but professors can be allowed an extension upto sixty fourth year. Besides these recommendations the Commission has fixed the regulations about Provident Fund for teachers, leave and working hours etc. and scale of salaries of the teachers have been revised.[30]

2. *Standard of Education:* The Commission fixed the Intermediate examination as the stage of admission to University education in order to raise the standard of University education and suggested that Intermediate Colleges of superior type should be established in each State or province. Vocational schools should be founded in large numbers to attract the attention of students towards various professions after their academic career for about ten or twelve years. Refresher Courses should be organized for the teachers of High Schools and Colleges. The number of students in the Arts and Science departments of Universities and affiliated colleges should not exceed 3,000 and 1,500 respectively. The tutorial system should be implemented systematically and regularly by organizing it thoroughly well. The libraries and laboratories of Universities should be well equipped with up-to-date paraphernalia on modern lines. Emphasis was laid on the improvement in the method of teaching adopted by teachers of Universities.

3. *Curriculum (Arts and Science):* The Degree of Master should be conferred one year after Honour's Degree and two years after Pass Examination. The Universities and Secondary schools should start the study of Theory and Practice of General Education and

undertake the preparation of curriculum and subject matter to introduce them in Intermediate and Degree classes. The co-relation between general and special education should be worked out for each sphere and attention should be devoted to the development of students personality by ascertaining their interests and aptitudes for various occupations.

4. *Post-graduate Training and Research:* (Arts and Science) Seeing the miserable and wretched state of this field, the Commission lamented the state of affairs, and opined that vast and unlimited opportunities existed in the field of research in India. Hence research scholars should be encouraged by providing all facilities to them.

   Admissions to the M.A. and M Sc. Classes should be made on all-India basis and conditions for the closest touch between the students and teachers be promoted. For the degree of Ph D., students should put at least two years study work. In the case of the candidates for Ph D. degree, a *viva voce* test besides thesis should be held in order to test their general knowledge and their authority on the subject they have worked upon. Admission to Ph.D. too should be made on an all-India basis. Research Fellowships should be granted to capable students during the period of their research work. Students of M.Sc and Ph.D should be granted scholarships and free seats by the Education Ministry. In Science Departments, additional and capable teachers should be appointed who might remain free from the work of teaching and might devote themselves exclusively to guidance in research work. Besides this, recommendations were made for the establishment of five marine biological stations and special stress was laid on the necessity of original research work in Bio-chemistry and Bio-physics etc.

5. *Professional Education:* The Commission has thrown light on the present condition of Agricultural Education in India with a view to comparing it to Agricultural Education in other developed and progressive countries. In the opinion of the Commission, Agricultural Education should be treated by the Government as the State problem and prominent place should be given to it in the curricula of Primary, Secondary and higher education. Agricultural Education, and research policy should advisably be transferred to those persons who were specialists in it and possessed practical

experience in it. In Agricultural colleges, practical education and investigation should specially be stressed. The new Agricultural colleges should be affiliated to the Rural universities to be incorporated newly. The setting and the character of these colleges should essentially be rural. In addition to that, a number of farms for agricultural experiments and laboratories should be established and facilities in higher education should be provided. The existing research centres should be developed and more financial help should be given to them.

With regard to commercial education the Commission has recommended that commerce students should be provided opportunities to do practical work in three or four firms or shops during their academic period. After graduation, some students should specialize in some branch of commerce. The students of M. Com. also should not remain confined only to bookish learning merely; on the other hand, they should acquire practical knowledge.

The Commission has made practical and useful recommendations in the sphere of Science of Education. According to the views of the Commission, improvement should be made in the curriculum and more time should be devoted to school practice. Proper schools should be chosen for the purpose of practice. Majority of teachers in the Training Colleges should be drawn from that class which might possess sufficient practical experience in teaching. The courses of Educational Theory should be flexible and consistent with local conditions. Only those students who possess experience in teaching for a number of years, should be admitted to the degree of M.Ed. Original work of professors and other teachers should be planned on an all India basis.

With regard to Engineering and Technology, the Commission recommended to improve the existing institutions and found more institutions for higher education in the above-mentioned branches of learning. Students should be provided ample facilities to acquire practical knowledge in workshops along with theoretical, bookish knowledge. Proper improvement should be done in the curricula in order to suit needs of time and place. Research centers and those for higher education should also be established. Besides these, the Commission put forth special suggestions about the reorientation and reorganization of Engineering Colleges.

About the Law Colleges, the opinion of the commission is that they should thoroughly be reorganized. The completion of three years degree course is compulsory for admission to Law colleges. Provision for practical education in law should also be made. The appointment of teachers can be both on part-time and whole-time basis. Permission to Law students to offer another curriculum should be granted only under special conditions and only to the most capable students. Opportunities should amply be given available in every law faculty especially in Constitutional Law, International Law, Administrative Law, Jurisprudence, Hindu Law and Mohammedan Law.

As regards the Medical Science, the Commission recommended that the maximum number of admissions to a Medical College should be one hundred. Facilities for training in rural centers should be available. Sufficient encouragement should be given to ancient Indian medical system. The Commission has further recommended the provision of public Health Engineering and Nursing for the post-graduate education in medical science.

Besides education in these professions, the Commission has made recommendations to provide special education in Business Administration, Public Administration and Industrial Business.

6. *Religious Education:* Giving a retrospective survey of religious education in India, the Commission has drawn our attention to the political situation of our country and has placed certain valuable suggestions about religious education not inconsistent with the concept of a secular state.

In every institution, a short period of silent worship or meditation, every morning before the commencement of daily routine should form an integral part of college life so that every person might look within free from distractions of the practical life, because "the individual is a soul and the purpose of education is to awaken the pupil to this fact, enable him to find the spirit within and mould his life and action in the light and power of the inner spirit.[31] The second suggestion in connection with religious education is that in the first year of the Degree course, biographies of such pre-eminent leaders as Gautama, the Buddha, Confucious, Zoroaster, Socrates, Jesus, Shamker, Ramanuja, Madhava, Mohammad, Kabir, Nanak and Gandhi should be taught. In the second year of the Degree course, some selections of a universalist character, from the Scriptures of the world should be studied. In the third year, fundamental problems of the philosophy of religion should be considered.

7. *Medium of Instruction:* The Commission has tried to solve the crucial and controvertible issue of medium of instruction in very fine way. Firstly, a Federal Language should be developed and made sufficiently rich. The Commission has made recommendations to adopt and assimilate the international technical terms by effecting mutation in them according to the need and limitations of place and time.

   As regards the medium of university instruction, the Commission has recommended the adoption of regional languages. Further, if the students like, they can use Federal Language, Hindi (Devnagari Script) also. At the university and Secondary stages, students should be fully conversant with at least three languages. Mother tongue, Federal Language and English. For the development of Federal Language and regional language, the Commission recommended that a Board be appointed consisting of scientists and linguists who should prepare vocabulary of scientific terms and arrange for the preparation of books in different sciences to be rendered into all Indian languages. Further, the State Governments should take steps to introduce the compulsory education in Federal Language (Hindi) in all the classes of Higher Secondary Schools, in Degree Colleges and Universities. English should be studied in High Schools and in the universities in order that we might remain in constant touch with the living stream of ever-growing knowledge.

8. *The System of Examination:* The commission has vehemently denounced the prevalent system of examination in Indian educational sphere.[32] But it made recommendations about its improvement and its complete eradication. "We are convinced that if we are to suggest one single reform in University education, it should be that of the examinations. We advisedly say reform although we know that, in India as elsewhere in the world, dissatisfaction with examination has been so keen that eminent educationalists and important educational organizations have advocated the abolition of examinations. We do not share

that extreme view and feel that examinations rightly designed and intelligently used can be a useful factor in the educational process. If examinations are necessary, a thorough reform of these is still more necessary".[33]

The Commission suggested that if essay-type examinations were to be co-ordinated with objective test, it would be much more useful. The work done by the student in the classroom during the session should also be taken into consideration and one-third marks should be reserved for it. There should be one University Examination at the end of each of three years of Degree course and not on the contrary, only one examination at the end of three years. Self-contained curriculum should be drawn up for each year. The selection of examiners should properly be made and they should be appointed for a period of three years. Students securing 70 per cent or more marks should be placed in 1st division, those securing 55 per cent to 69 per cent in second division and those securing 40 per cent to 54 per cent in third division. *Viva Voce* examinations should be held to test the competence of candidates in General Knowledge specially in the sphere of professional education.

9. *Students, Their Activities and Welfare:* The Commission have made a deep study and thorough analysis of multifarious problems of students and have made certain recommendations thereabout. They have attached much importance to this problem.

The Commission has emphasized the need of judicious selections of students for the admission to universities. Scholarships should be awarded to meritorious but financially handicapped students on the basis of merits to be tested through examination. It has made many valuable suggestions concerning the health of students. These recommendations concern themselves with physical examination of students, provision of dispensaries in colleges and universities, as well as hostels and proper boarding and supply of water, cleanliness of the dwelling place, appointment of the Director of Physical Education, adequate provision of games and sports and compulsory physical education. Training in National Cadet Corps has also been emphasized by it. Further recommendations have been made about the students training social service. In the opinion of the

Commission, the organisation of Students Unions should be for their mental and moral growth and not to nourish political sentiments of a lower order, An Advisory Board of Student Welfare should also be appointed to study various problems of students.

10. *Women's Education:* The Commission has given a very generous and sympathetic consideration to this problem—a fact which is amply evidenced by the recommendations by it in connection with it. The opinion of the Commission is that women should be provided with all the facilities, and proper atmosphere of general discipline and courtesy of life in the colleges of men. Increased opportunities of education should be given to them. With regard to the curriculum for women the Commission has recommended that they should select a curriculum which might be consistent with the needs of womanhood, their tastes and aptitudes. "They shall not try to imitate men, but shall desire as good education as women; as men get as men. Women's and men's education should have many elements in common, but should not in general be identical in all respects as is usually the case today.[34] For this purpose they should be given sufficient facilities for proper guidance and advice. Men should behave women decently in the colleges conducting co-education. In such colleges, attention paid to the requirements of men should be commensurate with those of women. Women teachers should be paid the same scale of salaries as men teachers for equal work. As regards co-education, the Commission held that at the Secondary education stage, there should be separate institutions for girls and co-education may be conducted in Basic schools and Universities.

11. *Other Problems:* Besides these recommendations, the Commission has put forth other useful ones as well i.e. about the organisation and control of University education, finance, Central University, other universities, Rural universities particularly and similar other problems. Concerning the Finance, the Commission has said that the Government should fully shoulder the responsibilities about higher education and spend nearly additional one hundred million rupees on it. Steps should be taken in the direction of amending Income-tax Laws in order to encourage benefactions for educational purposes. The

Commission's opinion about further establishment of new universities is that their establishment should take place by the permission of the Central Government on the basis of the recommendations of the Universities Grants Committee. Taking all the educational needs of the country into consideration, they should properly be distributed in urban and rural regions.

About the Organisation of University Education, the Commission's recommendations are fundamental and original. Its opinion is that university education should be placed in the Concurrent List of the Centre. The Central Government should co-ordinate their finance and special subjects on all-India basis. The Government should immediately appoint the Universities Grants Commission in order to solve the problem of grant-in-aid. No university should exist which might be purely affiliating. The number of the affiliated colleges to a university should be definite and fixed. The aim of all the affiliated colleges should be to develop themselves gradually into the form of a Federal University. The Vice-Chancellor should be a paid and whole-time official. Lastly the Commission felt strongly that India was mainly an agricultural country with her population residing in villages generally; hence a number of Rural universities should be founded here.

Criticism

These are, in short, the main recommendations of the Commission. It is the first epoch-making Report in the history in of Indian education covering the entire field of higher education on modern lines.

The Report has sought to harmonise the Oriental and Occidental cultures. In the sphere of education, many systems prevalent in the West have been adopted, but the soul of education is essentially Indian. Education has been treated and developed as the reflection of entire life. The Report reflects clearly the picture of higher education needed by free India, its aims and the proper means of their achievement. Though the Commission on the one hand has admitted that the country stands in dire necessity of theoretical and practical training in physical sciences, yet it has, on the other hand, given a profound warning against the danger that if scientific and professional education were to be pampered fat at the cost of Humanities, the Devil's regime would spread in the country in which people would think of merely materialistic growth and progress ignoring the higher spiritual values completely. As a matter of fact, it is an eye-opening warning for the entire world which is in accordance with the spiritual traditions of India.

The Commission have expressed their views after making a thorough study and examination of all the aspects of University Education in India. It has brought to light a number of evils rampant in the educational sphere *i.e.* deteriorating standard of teaching, uninteresting and rigid curricula, defective mode of examinations, mean and undesirable partisanship and intrigues vitiating the administration and management of Universities and long neglected rural education, and has expressed their enlightened and definite views on them, suggesting at the same time practical and proper remedies for their elimination. Far be it from us to say that the Commission's recommendations are the outcome of purely emotional real; they are, on the contrary based upon solid, objective and rationalized facts. The issues of method of teaching and investigation have especially been stressed since the country badly needs them. The Commission's recommendation with regard to the internal administration *i.e.* the reconstitution of the Universities Grants Committee and the appointment of paid officials therein, are thoroughly practical and desirable. The idea about Rural Universities is quite an original and revolutionary one.

It is, however, true that the Commission's views about religious education are quite vague and obscure. Similarly no decisive opinion has been given about the medium of instruction too. Proper encouragement has not been given to women's education, Oriental education and fine Arts.

Despite all this, it is undoubtedly true that the Report has sought to place Indian education on an equal footing with the world standard of education by revolutionizing in and making it adaptable to the spirit of time and place. A new era will surely evolve in the history of Indian education serving as a beacon light to the world, if the Commission's recommendations be implemented with earnest feelings and sincere efforts.

The Recommendations of the Central Advisory Board of Education

A special meeting of the Central Advisory Board of Education was held on 22nd and 23rd April, 1950 in order to discuss the recommendations of the University Education Commission. The Board agreed to all the recommendations of the Commission making necessary amendments therein. Recommendations with regard to Post-graduate education and research were accepted and those dealing with Professional education, specially Agriculture, Commerce, Education, Engineering. Technology, Law and Medical Science were accepted only with certain amendments. Besides, recommendations with regard to the medium of instruction, classification of teachers, their salaries and conditions of service, curriculum, objective system of examination, women's education, incorporation of fresh universities and students, welfare activities were also accepted readily by the Board.

As regards the recommendations about religious education, the Board corroborated the views of Commission and accepted the idea of commencing daily routine in the colleges and universities after a short period of silent worship and meditation. In addition to that biographies of great religious prophets and thinkers should be taught in the first year of Degree course and fundamentals of philosophy of religion in the second year. The Board further opined that philosophy of religion could be included in the curriculum of universities. The Commission's recommendations about the Constitution of universities and their control were also accepted by the Board; but that of placing universities in the concurrent list of the Central Government was turned down. Supporting the recommendations of the Commission about university finance, the Board opined that the implementation of this recommendation will largely be determined by the availability of funds for the purpose. Lastly, the Board considered the means to popularise the Federal Language, Hindi.

As a matter of fact, an account of the progress made by the University Education after the publication of the Commission's Report has already been given. The Central Advisory Board of Education discusses the problems of higher education along with other educational issues. In the 1952, Central Government wanted to place a Universities Bill in the parliament which sought to remedy all the defects inherent in it by increasing the Government control upon the University Education. The bill has not been introduced anew in the Parliament owing to the protests of some important and pre-eminent persons.

A mention has been made about the Report and suggestions of the Committee appointed by the Board in November, 1953 under the convenership of Prof. Kabir for the purpose of implementing the Commission's recommendations. Moreover, it has also been mentioned that the Government of India had appointed on the recommendations of the University Education Commission, the Universities Grants Commission under the Chairmanship of the late Dr. Shanti Swarup Bhatnagar in December towards the close of 1953 an account which will be presented at the proper place. Here we give in brief the provisions of the proposed Universities Bill of 1952.

Universities Bill—1952

After the general elections in 1952, the Central Government had thought of introducing the Universities Bill in the Parliament. The entire contents of the Bill have been published upto this time; but copies of it had not been sent to different Provincial Governments and Universities in order to send their opinions about it. It seems, however that the Government have probably relinquished the idea of introducing the Bill in the face of some public opposition.

According to the Bill, so long as Universities do not pass under the control of the Central there is no possibility of establishing coordination among the educational institutions or raising their standard. Hence the Bill has provided for the appointment of a Central Council of University Education. The Council will be empowered to get information about the internal problems of various Universities. Further it will enjoy the privilege of forcing the implementation of its recommendations and behests through the Executive Councils of Universities.

The Council will be authorized to inspect any University and pass orders accordingly. In case its orders and recommendations are treated with indifference by any University, it will recommend to the Government that the degree conferred by such University should not be recognized so that her out-going alumni might not get any Government job. The Bill further states that any institutions providing higher education can be converted into a University.

The Central Government will determine the number, qualifications and the term of appointment of the members of the Central Council of University Education. At least one-third of the total number of the members of the Council should be the Vice Chancellors of different Universities.

According to a particular clause of the Bill, only that University will be entitled to confer Degrees which might convince that the students had completed the curriculum of theoretical and practical study of Arts, Science or any other branch of higher education. The construction of such university should be through Central Act, Provincial Act or State-Act.

Criticism

Though the Bill referred to above has not been introduced in the Parliament so far, yet it has vehemently been criticized by the State Governments and Universities. It is suspected that a good controversy would emerge if the Central Government proceeds with the Bill. Officials of different Universities hold that the Bill will deal a terrible blow to the autonomy of Universities. As a mater of fact, the creations of such an atmosphere as might be quite free from State intervention or political partisanship is of primary importance and necessity for the progress of Universities, Interference of any kind at the hands of the State in matters of the standard of teaching or examination is very pernicious to educational progress. The autonomy of Universities will also be destroyed by the establishment of the Central Council of Education. The Universities had contended that there was no necessity of the Central Council of Education in view of the pre-existence of an Inter University Board. Why should not the powers and responsibilities of the Inter-University Board be increased, they said.

Here it should, however, be admitted that under present circumstances, the Indian Universities need state control to some extent at least. It is possible that with the gradual improvement in their conditions, we might dispense with the control and Universities might be left free to determine their own fate. At present there are very few Universities out of a number of thirty one which might be immune from the evils of partisanship communal prejudices and narrow provincialism or some such other evils. The very aim of University Education is in constant danger of being defeated on account of corruption and fierce spirit of partisanship rampant in most of them. Needless to mention that in most of the Universities, a caucus monopolises the authority and falls an easy prey to corrupt ways owing to the spirit of party-politics flooding the University Senates and Executive Councils. Consequently, the appointment of teachers and examiners recognition granted to test books and admission to the Degree of Doctorate after research work in such Universities are essentially conditioned and determined by communal partialities and a spirit of favouritism. In order to remedy these defects, the State Government of U.P. has recently introduced certain amendments in the constitutions of Agra, Allahabad and Lucknow Universities. How can we expect those of our Universities which are centers of corruption and intrigues, forgetting their noble aims of higher education, the regeneration and reconstruction of the nation on the nobler principles of democracy, equality and liberty? No wonder then that the standard of education in India is deteriorating from day to day to which educationists of the country have drawn attention again and again. This is the reason why the Central Government had attempted to impose a mild control upon the University education by appointing the Central Council with a view to eradicating all the above mentioned evils. The Bill, it is true, all the same, can be rendered more liberal and suitable by relaxing its rigidity. Here it should be remembered that he Bill had been attacked particularly by those Universities which were afraid of being deprived of undue liberty enjoyed hitherto. But any University can be granted the liberty of practising corrupt ways in the name of autonomy only at the cost of incurring a great risk. In this connection, suffice it to say that the need of State control upon the Universities will persist so long as the Universities do not learn to make a proper use of their autonomous powers.

Conclusion

The Indian Universities, we see thus, are on the way to progress. The Commission has opened the passage to the development of University Education by examining thoroughly the defects of university education and making suitable recommendations for their elimination. Indeed, the University Education of any country is the correct and reliable index to the progress of that country. But, according to the views of Rohertson, "Progressive universities are an index to progressive society, stabilized universities to a stabilised society, stagnant or decrepit universities to a stagnant and decrepit society."[35] Therefore it is absolutely essential for an independent and progressive India that her universities may be developed into the real centers of learning. "The prosperity of the country is linked up with the university. A vicious university is like a contaminated fountain which is bound to imperil the health of those who drink from it."[36]

The Universities Grants Commission

The Commission had been appointed in December, 1953, as said before under the Chairmanship of the late Dr. Shanti Swarup Bhatnager. Other notable members of the Commission are : Acharya Narendra Dev, Dr. Lakshmanswami Mudaliar, Sir N.J. Wadia, Sri K.R.K. Menon and Sri K.G. Sayaidain.

The following are, in short, the responsibilities of this Commission:

1. to act as a special Body for co-ordinating educational facilities for the Central Government, raising the standard of education and suggesting ways and means to achieve these objectives;

2. to advise the Central Government about the sanction of grants-in-aid to universities by examining into their financial needs;

3. to dispose of the funds sanctioned for various universities and distribute the same among them;

4. to advise, when asked, about the establishment of a new university and possibilities of the expansion of any pre existing university;

5. to advise the Central Government or any university about any issue on which advise has been sought;

6. to advise the Central or any State Government on the question of the recognition or non-recognition of a degree conferred by any university, for the purpose of employment;
7. to suggest ways to universities for the improvement in university education; and
8. to do any such work as is considered to be necessary for the good of education or to do any such thing as might be helpful in the discharge of the above-mentioned obligations.

The field of the activities of the Universities Grants Commission is very wide. Under the Five-Year Plan, the Government of India has placed some funds at the disposal of the Commission to be sanctioned as grant-in-aid for higher education. It is hoped that in the light of improvement and plans referred to above, the Indian higher education will be rendered suitable for the requirements of the country by emerging in its pure form.

Five-Year Plan and Education

Aims of the Plan

Education has a fundamental importance in the development and progress of any country. "In a democratic setup, the role of education becomes crucial, since democracy can function effectively only if there is an intelligent participation of the masses in the affairs of the country." In order to fulfill this aim, the Government of India has provided for the expansion and reorganization of education at every stage in the First Five-Year Plan. The Planning Commission is of opinion that provision of increased opportunities and facilities for education is of paramount necessity in order to engender the virtues of ideal citizenship in the people and to foster and develop their cultural and creative faculties.

In comparison to the vastness of the population of India, facilities for education in the country are quite negligible. That is, 40 per cent children of the age between six and eleven years, 10 per cent between eleven and seventeen years and only 9 per cent children falling between seventeen and twenty three years of age can avail themselves of educational facilities in the country. How low the percentage in India is in comparison to that in France, the U.S.A., England and U.S.S.R where 80 per cent to 100 per cent children of the school-going age receive education. It can easily be understood that India, the literacy percentage which is only 17.2 to her total population stands in dire necessity of planning and expansion in the sphere of education.

The opinion of the Planning Commission is that during the planning period, greater emphasis is to be laid on Primary Education. The expansion in Primary Education will naturally result in that of the Secondary Education. The University Education does not need expansion so much as consolidation. The Planning Commission has examined into certain educational problems and thrown light on the main educational needs of the country.[37] The main problems considered by the Planning Commission are: the training of teachers, improvement in the conditions of their service, co-ordination of education in different states, proper distribution of educational facilities in urban and rural areas sufficient co-ordination between the Primary and Secondary Education; means to check inordinate wastage of money in education, sufficient expansion of Technical and Professional education, system of education, particularly between the Primary and Secondary Education; means check inordinate wastage of money in education, sufficient expansion of Technical and Professional education, system of education, particularly methods to render University Education less expensive, decreasing the importance of examinations in the system of education and lastly cultural development of the people etc.

Summing up, the needs of the present situation in the opinion of the Planning Commission are:

1. re-orientation of the educational system and integration of its different stages and branches;
2. expansion in various fields, especially in those of basic and social condition and remodelling secondary, technical and vocational education;
3. consolidation of existing secondary and university education and the devising of a system of higher education suited to the needs of the rural areas;
4. expansion of facilities for women's education, especially in the rural areas;

5. training of teachers, especially women teachers and teachers for basic schools; and improvement in their pay-scales and conditions of service; and
6. helping backward states by giving preferential treatment to them in matter of grants.

Resources

The Government of India had appointed the Committee on the Ways and Means of Financing Education Development in India for the expansion of education. According to the opinion of the Committee, the national education, when it comes into full operation, will require an annual expenditure of at least four hundred crores of rupees, In addition to this sum, approximately, two hundred crores of rupees will be required for the training of 27 lakhs of teacher for basic and High Schools and two hundred seventy-two crores of rupees for the purpose of constructing school buildings. But how can the Government of India spare such large sum of money for the purpose of education? Under such condition, comparatively very little sum of money has been allotted to education under the Five-Year Plan.

The Five-Year Plan has made a total provision of Rs. 155.66 crores (39.02 crores for the Centre and Rs. 116.64 crores for the States) for the educational purposes. It means Rs. 30.33 crores will be spent yearly on education. It is also thought that owning to the scarcity of funds, the public, private and local institutions too will donate funds for the development of education. Out of these funds, Rs 870.28 lakhs will be spent on primary education, 830.4 lakhs on secondary education, 1172.1 lakhs on university education, 2145.4 on technical and commercial education, 1510.0 on social education and the rest will be spent on other educational schemes.

The Education-Target of the Five Year Plan

The Commission is of the view that by the end of planning period 1956, the following targets will be achieved:

1. Provision of educational facilities for at least 60 per cent of all children of school-going age within the age 6-11 years. During 1950-51 this percentage was 44.5;

2. To raise the percentage at the secondary education stage, of children within the age group 11-17 years from 11% 1950-51 to 15 per cent within five years;

3. In the field of social education, provision of facilities with regard to universal social education for at least 30 per cent of people within the age group 14-40 years.

No such target has been fixed in the field of University education because it does not need expansion so much as it does consolidation.

Educational Programmes of the Plan

Under the Five-Year Plan, the programme of educational expansion has been divided separately between the Central and State Governments. Mostly all those programmes which are of all India importance, fall under the Central Government while the different State Governments have to look to provincial educational programmes.

A. Programmes of the Central Education Ministry: The Central programme has been classified as below:

1. Setting up complete units of basic education, from the pre-basic school to the post-graduate basic training college, at least one in each state;

2. Establishment of at least a 'Janata college' and a school cum-community centre in each state for the purpose of social education;

3. Provision in each State of the establishment of at least one Multi-purpose school along with vocational schools for the young boys of the age within age group 4-18 years; provision of Research Bureaux for investigating into the problem of Secondary schools and scholarships for financially handicapped students to study in public schools;

4. Production of Audio-visual Aids by establishing a unit at the Central Institute of Education and provision of assistance to the publishers producing simpler audio visual aids;

5. Encouragement given to the production of proper literature for the children of basic education and young persons receiving social education;

6. Development of Indian languages and that of Federal language, production of original books and encouragement to their translations. Dictionaries, encyclopaedia and Reference books should also be produced;

7. Provision of education for physically handicapped children should be made;

8. Advisory centers to advise students about technical education should be established;

9. The Indian Institute of Science, Bangalore, should be developed and provision be made for the establishment of fourteen Engineering institutions and education in special vocational subjects;

10. Financial help for University libraries and scholarships for research work and training should also provided.

B. Programmes of State Governments: Similarly, under the plan, provision for the educational expansion in primary, secondary, university education as well as technical and vocational education in the States has been made. These programmes can briefly be classified as follows:

1. Establishment of new schools in the sphere of primary education, improvement in the pre-existing schools and gradual conversion of general primary schools into basic schools;

2. Establishment of new schools in the field of secondary schools, improvement of older ones; inclusion of Physical Education, Military training, Gardening, Agriculture and Music in the curriculum and protection of model schools;

3. Incorporation of new universities and opening of new colleges and improvement and expansion of pre-existing ones;

4. Provision of library facilities for social education, as well as Physical Education, programmes for young persons, Audio-visual Aids, literacy and establishment of Adult Education Centres;

5. Establishment of new Craft schools in the sphere of technical and vocational education, conversion of Craft schools into Junior Technical High Schools, opening of Junior Multipurpose schools, conversion of common secondary schools into Technical High schools opening of Diploma courses, establishment of Professional schools, including Agriculture Education, raising the vocational and Technical Schools to the status of colleges by expanding them and awarding of scholarships for training in foreign countries; and

6. Provision of higher education for in-service people, development of regional languages and literature, provision of education for physically handicapped persons, introducing the National Cadet Corps in colleges and to effect improvement in special subjects like Oriental education and *Samkhaya Shastra*.

These are some of the proposal programmes of the State Governments.

Criticism

Thus it is evident that the Five Year Plan covers the entire field of education under its programmes, with the operation of Plan, work had been commenced in this direction. Though a period of five years is now at end yet no marked progress has been achieved in the target fixed in the field of education. Hitherto neither have the required primary schools been converted into basic schools nor have the 'Janta colleges' and Multipurpose schools been established in the states as proposed. The target of educating 60 per cent of children of school-going age within the age group 6-14 years is still very far. The same may be said about University and Technical Education.

This must not, however, lead us to the formation of an erroneous idea that no progress could be achieved upto this time. As a matters of fact, the Centre and States had started the implementation of their programmes but the progress of education by the expenditure incurred on it as given in the following table, under the first Five Year Plan:

(Rupees in Crores)

	1950-51 Actual	1951-52 Actual	1952-53 Actual	1953-54 amended	1951-54 Total	1951-56 Grand Total Initial	1951-56 Grand Total Amended
Centre	18.3	17.3	19.2	23.3	59.8	116.4	119.5
States	1.2	2.0	2.9	3.8	8.7	35.0	41.5
Total	19.5	19.3	22.1	27.1	68.5	151.4	161.0

On the basis of the expenditure on education as indicated by the above mentioned statistics, we see that progress of the plan is slow, so much so that in the first three years only 45 per cent of the funds have been absorbed.[38]

The Five-Year Plan is being attacked in the educational sphere. For example, it is said that the plan is not at all revolutionary in character. The aim of the Plan seems to be but fragmentary expansion of education by eliminating the existing defects from its body and maintaining *status quo*. So long as reorientation of the entire educational system is not effected and pre-existing system is allowed to continue, there is every likelihood of the chronic defects gaining nutrition.

The second charge that is levelled against the Plan is that pre-primary education which is of so magnitudinous significance in the preparation of future citizens of the country, has comparatively been treated with indifference by the Planning Commission. Besides, considering the plight of the teachers, the remedy that has been suggested for it by the authors of the Plan is quite inadequate and ill matches the gravity of the situation. No plan of development can be successful without the sympathy and active co-operation of the teachers. From this standpoints the Five-Year Plan is quite incomplete. Further, whatever funds have been provided for the various educational schemes under the Plan, are scanty and inadequate. In view of the vastness of the country and the crucial nature of educational problems, the sum of Rs. 155.66 crores is too scanty to meet the requirements. Another incontrovertible and irrefutable charge brought against the Plan is that planning of the expenditure has not been properly done. The intelligentsia of the country is of the opinion that lakhs of rupees are going waste in the flatulent name of Five-Year Plan! The programmes that have been set up under it are not beneficial as to bring about a fundamental improvement in the conditions of the countrymen. Some plans are no sooner embarked upon than closed resulting in a stupendous wastage of human energy and public money. Hence the need is that the wasting should, as far as possible be checked and the funds which are already quite inadequate and insufficient, should properly and advantageously be utilized. It should, however, be admitted that for the first time in the History of Indian Education has been placed under planning. This is first nation-wide programme of its own kind. Under these conditions, omissions and remissions are but natural to some extent. It is hoped that the errors found in the First Five Year Plan will be eliminated from the future development plans with Indian's growing experience in the matter. An outline of the Second Five-Year Educational Plan had been drawn after a thorough examination and discussion of the shortcomings and defects left in the First Year Plan by the All-India Education Ministers' Conference held in August, 1954 at Delhi. Decidedly, the Second Five Year Plan is expected to be nobler in ambitions.

Other Central Plans

With the establishment of the Interim Government in 1946, the Central Education Department passed for the first time, under the national control. In 1947, it was given the form of Education Ministry. Since then, the Central Government has been trying to solve the manifold educational problems of the country. A mention about these efforts has already been made in the preceding pages. In the first Five-Year Plan, education has not been given much importance to, though some steps in this direction have, no doubt, been taken. Besides these schemes, there are other programmes of the Central directly or indirectly related to education of the country. Out of these programmes, cultural ones are the most conspicuous and important. There are, in short: the protection of historical buildings and monuments, and historical researches under the Archaeological Department, spread of education among the scheduled, backward classes and aborigines, award of scholarships to Indian students for further studies abroad and to foreign students for education in India, preservation of Indian culture and its propagation, establishment of cultural relations with other countries; implementation of the programmes of U.N.E.S.C.O. and expansion of the Technical and Professional education in the country.

On the basis of the recommendations made by All-India Technical Education Council, a development plan had been launched during 1947-48, in the sphere of Technical and Professional education. This Council, on the basis of the recommendations of seven man Committee, had drawn up, in 1953, a programme of expansion of education; accordingly technical education is being spread on each stage of education. The Central Government has established an Indian Institute of Technology at Kharagpur and the Indian Institute of Science at Bangalore has been further expanded on a cost of 175 lakhs of rupees during the year 1954-55.

Among the educational activities of the year 1954, the establishment of Social Welfare Board, under the Presidentship of Mrs. Durgabai Deshmukh is of great importance. The Board purposes to contribute to the expansion of physical and social education in the country with the co-operation and assistance of the State Governments, Universities and other institutions.

So far as the award of scholarship is concerned, the Government's attitude has been very generous and liberal in this respect during the last seven years. The special feature of these scholarships is that they were awarded mainly for the educational regeneration of scheduled castes, backward classes and aboriginal tribes. In the budget of 1953-54 a provision of 62 lakhs of rupees had been made for this purpose. The amount was raised to 75 lakhs in the budget of 1954-55. The sum is, as a matter of fact, quite inadequate, but when we compare it with that of 1947-48 for the same purpose, it is found that progress has been achieved in this direction.

In addition to the scholarships awarded to the students of the country, they have been awarded to the foreign students in India with a view to strengthening cultural ties with other countries of the world. Some of these scholarships are reciprocal and students coming from foreign countries have been awarded scholarships by the Government of India so that similar financial help might be given by foreign countries to the Indian students when they desire to receive further education abroad. Moreover, Indian students are being sent to foreign countries i.e. China, U.S.S.R. France and Germany for the sake of learning the languages of the countries mentioned above.

A Literary Academy has been established under the presidentship of Pt. Jawahar Lal Nehru for the purpose of encouraging cultural activities. In order to inspire and encourage the writers, literary artists, dramatists and other artists *i.e.* painters, musicians, etc. various educational facilities and financial help are being extended to them. An attempt is being made to develop Arts and cultural relations with foreign countries by inviting cultural delegations from foreign countries and sending the same from India to outside countries. In recent past, cultural delegations from U.S.S.R., Afghanistan and China have made a tour of India. Similarly, artists and literacy persons from India have made tours of U.S.S.R., China and other countries. A board had been appointed in December, 1952 under the chairmanship of Dr. Syed Mahmud for the sake of writing the History of India's struggle for freedom.

India is one of the founding members of the U.N.E.S.C.O. The educational and cultural programme drawn up by this world organisation are being implemented in the country. The Government of India has appointed the Indian National Commission for the successful fulfillment of this aim.[39]

The Indian National Commission

The Government of India has been a member of the U.N.E.S.C.O since 1946. According to the Constitution of U.N.E.S.C.O. every nation that is the member of the body is required to set up a National Commission in order to implement its plans. The function of such a Commission is to advise the country concerned in matters of educational, scientific and cultural development on the basis of the outlines of the U.N.E.S.C.O.

The Government of India had set up an Interim Commission for this purpose as early as Mach, 1949; but the Commission has been given a permanent shape in 1953. It has eleven members on it headed by the Central Education Minister.

The first session of the permanent Indian National Commission was held at New Delhi from 9th to 14th January, 1954.

Representatives from a number of countries *i.e.* Afghanistan, Ceylone, Egypt, Indonesia, Persia, Iraq, Japan, Labnan, Nepal, Syria and Turkey had participated in its deliberations. In this Conference many important and valuable resolutions concerning education of Asia and Africa and other cultural problems had been passed.

It can safely be stated about the educational efforts of this Commission that it has started its work very enthusiastically from the very inceptive stage of its functioning. All the information pertaining to education has been furnished to the UNESCO when required to do so. The Government of India are seriously thinking about the establishment of the National Centre for Fundamental Education in near future. For the fulfillment of this aim, the Government of the country intend establishing a training centre at Mysore for the experts in fundamental education under the UNESCO. The Commission further seeks to propagate the principles of U.N.O. and fundamental principles of human rights. Besides, the Education Sub-Commission, an offshoot of the National Commission and appointed under the Chairmanship of Kaka Kalelkar, has embarked on the mission of spreading and propagating the Gandhian principles throughout the world.

Conclusion

Thus it is evident that education is making progress in the country with gradual but steady steps. The Centre and the State Governments have their own separate programmes to carry out. The entire structure of education, Pre-Basic, Junior Basic, Senior Basic, Secondary and University education, is being moulded in order to suit the growing needs of the country. Whatever tendencies are prevailing in the sphere of Indian education augur well for the future reconstruction of the country. This should not, however, lead us to infer that the educational system of the country is immune from shortcomings and faults. Indeed, they are many and of different categories. A reference to them has already been made.

The glaring weak spots in Indian education are: bookish and theoretical aspect of knowledge, predominance of examination and its being defective, the problem of the educational control at the Primary and Secondary stages; absence of co-ordination in education at different levels; scarcity of capable and trained teachers; the ineffectual and unpsychological mode of teaching; unsuitability of the curricula to the life of the students; inelegant and insufficient accommodation (classrooms and hostels); unsuitable text-books and lastly the wretched plight of the teachers. These defects demand urgent remedy. The country today needs a system of education which might develop the physical, mental and moral aspects of a student's personality and make him fit for adding his own contribution to the economic and cultural prosperity of the country. Education should be related to individual life, national life of the people and should promote the *summum bonum* (material and spiritual) of the mankind. In a way, the future of the country is indissolubly interlinked with that of its education. We shall undoubtedly have to act upon these principles in the educational sphere, if we sincerely wish to make democracy function successfully and efficiently and establish a classless society free from the curse of exploitation in our country. So long as the wide gulf between the Primary school teacher and University teacher exists, all our efforts to eradicate class distinctions are doomed to end in fiasco. Our idea of establishing a classless society and engendering in the mind of the future citizens in the sentiments of self-dependence, self-respect and fortitude will remain an empty dream so long as our teachers groan under the miseries of exploitation, indigence and indignity. "Most people are agreed that our present education should be so shaped that the future citizen of India is physically, intellectually and morally a sound individual, able to contribute to the building of a free, democratic and self sufficient India and so equipped as to help India to play an appropriate role in the modern world order. In the ultimate analysis, this aim would lead to certain definite objectives which the new education should seek to achieve."[40]

REFERENCES

1. The figures are of 1951-52. There has been increase in them. The number of universities is now 31.
2. These figures do not include 23.52 Crores of rupees which are spent indirectly.
3. "By education I mean an all-round drawing out of the best in child and man—body, mind and spirit... . Literacy itself is no education. I would, therefore, begin the child's education by teaching it a useful handicraft and enabling it to produce from the moment it begins its training. Thus

every school can be made self-supporting, the condition being that the state takes overt the manufactures of the schools." —*Harijan* ; July, 1937.

4. *Harijan* 30-10-37.
5. Basu, A.N. *Education in Modern India.* p. 124-125.
6. Dr. Sarayu Prasad Chaube—*An Outline of the Principles of Teaching (Hindi)* p. 327. Laxmi Narain & Sons, Agra.
7. *Harijan* 2-10-37.
8. "The Scheme is one of education and not production... . The craft or productive work chosen should be rich in educative possibilities. It should find natural point of correlation with important human activities and interests", *Work:* Page 4: 8th Annual Report of Nai Talim, 1938-45, published by Hindustani Talimi Sangh.
9. Hans Raj Bhatia: *What Basic Education Means*: p. 42 Orient Longmans, Calcutta, 1954.
10. Zakir Hussain Committee Report p. 50.
11. Report of the Committee appointed by Central Advisory Board of Education, 1938-45; pp. 9-10.
12. "While the superiority of Basic over the old system is admitted by every one, results have not always been commensurate with the hopes entertained about the system." *Progress of Education in India.* (1947-52).

    —Ministry of Education, Government of India.
13. Five-Year Plan : *Progress Report.* p. 242, 1953-54. Government of India.
14. Govt. of India: *Progress Report* for 1953-54 (Five Year Plan).
15. Report U.P. Primary and Secondary Reorganisation Committee, 1939 : pp. 129-33.
16. Report (1939), p. 147.
17. Report of the Secondary Education Commission p. 2.
18. Many piecemeal reforms and improvements have been introduced from time to time...but there were not coherently and consciously related to the right aims and objectives and, therefore, their total impact on the system was unimpressive. What is necessary now—and this is what we are anxious to ensure—is to take bold and far-sighted measures to give a new orientation to Secondary education as a whole in which all these individual reforms may find their proper and integrated place." (*Report of Secondary Education Commission.* p. 23).

19. "The whole modern approach to this question is based on the insight that the intellectual and cultural development of different individuals takes place best through a variety of media, that the book or the study of traditional academic subjects is not the only door to the education of the personality and that in the case of many—perhaps a majority of the children, practical work intelligently organised can unlock their latent energies much more successfully than the traditional subjects which address themselves only to the mind or, worse still, the memory." *Ibid*—p. 39.

20. Report of Secondary Education Commission; p. 163.

21. *Sargent Plan* : p. 36.

22. Report of Secondary Commission p. 24.

23. cf "The education given in our schools is isolated from life, the curriculum as formulated and as presented through the traditional methods of teaching does not give the students insight into the every day world in which they are living. When they pass out of school, they feel ill-adjusted and cannot take their place confidently and competently in the community". *Report of the Secondary Education Commission:* p. 22.

24. cf "the average efficiency of the teachers has deteriorated, their economic difficulties and lack of social prestige have tended to crate in them a sense of frustration. Unless something in done quickly to increase their efficiency and give them a feeling of contentment and a sense of their own worth, they will not be able to pull their weight." *Report of the Secondary Education Commission*; p. 23.

25. Mukerjee S.N.: *Education in India, Today and Tomorrow* p. 80.

26. The dead weight of examination has tended to curb the teacher's initiative, to stereotype the curriculum, to promote mechanical and lifeless methods of teaching, to discourage all spirit of experimentation and to place the stress on wrong or unimportant things in education. "*Report of the Secondary Education Commission;* p. 23.

27. *Sargent Plan Report* 1944. pp. 28-29.

28. Universities Education Commission Report, Vol. I p. 346.

29. Report : *University Education Commission*: p. 147.

30. For example, the following scale of salaries has been determined by the Commission for the teachers of Universities:

Professors	Rs. 900-50-1350
Readers	Rs. 600-30-900
Lecturers	Rs. 300-25-600
Instructors or Fellows	Rs. 250
Research Fellows	Rs. 250-25-500

For the teachers of those affiliated colleges which have no post-graduate classes, the following scales have been recommended:

Lecturers	Rs.200-15-320-20-400
Senior Posts	Rs.400-25.600(two in each college)
Principals ...	Rs.600-40-800

For colleges which have post-graduate classes, the scale of salaries should be:

Lecturers	Rs.200-15-320-20-400-25-500
Senior Posts	Rs.500-25-800(two in each college)
Principals	Rs.800-40-1000

31. *University Education Commission:* p. 300.

32. "For nearly half a century, examinations, as they have been functioning, have been recognised as one of the worst features of Indian education. Commissions and committees have expressed their alarm at their pernicious domination over the whole system of education in India. The obvious deficiencies and harmful consequences of this most prevasive evil in Indian education have been analysed and set out clearly by successive University Commissions since 1902 by a government Resolution as far back as 1904, and by a Committee of the Central Advisory Board of Education in recent years." *Report of the University Education: Commission Vol. I.* p. 327.

33. Report of University Education Commission; p. 328.

34. Report, University Education Commission; p. 402.

35. Quoted by Dr. R.K. Singh: *Our Universities;* p. 10.

36. *Ibid;* p. 9:

37. *Planning Commission:* The First Five Year Plan; p. 525.

38. *Progress Report* (1953-54) Five Year Plan.

39. "... the main purpose of setting up the National Commission was, on the one hand, to make UNESCO conscious of the people's needs, and on the other, make the people conscious of UNESCO's functions and purposes."—Report of the proceeding of the First Conference of the Indian National Commission for co-operation with UNESCO. p. 2, (1954).

40. Munshi, K.M.: *On Future of Education in India* p. 24—The Publications Division (1954).

8

Education Freedom and Democracy

Laying the Foundation Stone of the Kashi Vidyapith on Vasant Panchmi Day in 1921, Mahatma Gandhi had observed: "We have to serve the nation; we shall do everything for the country. We shall make India a *Punyabhumi*—a holy land." It was owing to the supreme sacrifice of Gandhiji and numerous freedom-fighters that we did succeed in attaining '*Swaraj*' and are celebrating its Silver Jubilee this year. But could we say that we have attained *Poorna Swaraj* of Gandhiji's conception?

It is true that we have achieved political freedom and India has won a fair name in the international sphere. We have steered clear of both the Power blocs and, with the policy of '*Panchsheel*', India has been able to enlist the co-operation of almost all the countries during the last twenty-five years. We have maintained relations of goodwill and co-operation with the neighbouring countries and this approach has yielded fairly good dividends. India has never tried to cast a selfish eye on others' territories and has sincerely followed a policy of peaceful co-existence all the time.

However, about two years ago, we had to shoulder the burden of about a crore of evacuees from Bangladesh owing to unprecedented genocide in that region. Not satisfied with this inhuman behaviour, Pakistan mounted an armed attack on India. The inspiring leadership of our Prime Minister, Shrimati Indira Gandhi, and the valour and patriotism evinced by the Army, the Navy and the Air Force would always adorn the pages of our history in golden letters. The public of India also showed remarkable courage, patience and unity on this occasion and our prestige soared high among the comity of nations.

Subsequently, by signing the Simla Agreement, India demonstrated to the world that she really aspired for durable peace in this sub-continent and had no ambition of grabbing Pakistan's territory. During the Silver Jubilee celebrations of *'Swaraj'*, we had the privilege of having *'Sonar Bangla'* as our new friendly neighbour. I have not a flicker of doubt that this happy mingling of gold with silver shall prove to be very happy and auspicious in the coming years.

Social and Economic Progress

The social and economic progress achieved during the last quarter of a century cannot be deemed as wholly satisfactory. It is true that the economic growth in several directions during the last four Five-Year Plans has been appreciable. The per capita income has nearly doubled, and we can be legitimately proud of our progress in the spheres of agriculture, industry, transport, communications, power, and iron and steel. Even so, we must frankly admit that there has been hardly any progress in the sphere of education, and our schools and colleges continue to follow almost the same rut. Notwithstanding the recommendations of several Committees and Commissions, the educational pattern has not been re-structured in accordance with the aspirations and requirements of Free India. That is why youngmen are obliged to face unemployment and frustration.

With a view to introducing certain radical changes in our educational system, an All-India National Education Conference was convened last October in Sevagram in which almost all the State Education Ministers, a good number of Vice-Chancellors, eminent educationists and Basic education teachers participated. After three days detailed discussions, the Conference unanimously adopted a 'Consensus' Statement. I do hope the Kashi Vidyapith will study this document in depth, implement its main recommendations, and give a new lead to the country in the domain of educational reform. Any further delay in this matter is bound to land us in numerous difficulties and even erode the very structure of our democracy.

Below the Poverty Line

Though our average income has registered a definite rise, the fact remains that almost half of our population is still living below the poverty line. The social and economic condition of crores of Harijans, Adivasis and other backward classes continues to be deplorable. We have not yet been able to erase the social stigma of untouchability and are obliged to read in the newspapers instances of ill-treatment towards Harijans almost every day. This is, indeed, a matter of great sorrow and shame. The basic national policy of prohibition is also being discarded by one State after another for petty financial gains. As a result, the economic plight of the poorer and depressed sections has been going from bad to worse; the fashion of drinking is gradually penetrating the younger generation as well. Our Prime Minister is deeply concerned about this growing habit of drinking among the people and has recently drawn the attention of the state Governments towards this unhappy situation. Excepting Gujarat, there is no other State in the country which enforces prohibition in a thorough manner. I expect other State Governments also to ponder over this situation and initiate the right steps without further delay.

For the attainment of social and economic freedom, India has rightly accepted the goal of 'democratic socialism'. Its outline is contained in the Directive Principles of the Indian Constitution; the main point is to determine is exact content and substance. As Professor Joad humorously remarks. "Socialism is like a hat which has lost its shape because everybody wears it." On the one hand, the Communist countries, where there is totalitarian control in place of democracy, name their organisation as 'socialism', and on the other, some of the capitalist countries in their anxiety to look progressive also swear by 'socialism'. But India, like other developing countries, will have to fashion her 'socialism' in accordance with her own traditions and urgent needs. If we begin blindly initiating other nations in this respect, India shall fall between two stools and become the laughing stock of the international community.

What is Indian Socialism?

What is the nature of Indian socialism? First, we have to understand in very clear terms that socialism in India is founded on democracy, without any distinction of caste, language or religion. It would not be proper to follow the pattern of British or American Parliamentary democracy in all respects. If necessary, we should not hesitate to introduce certain innovations to suit our own conditions.

For example, we could lay greater stress on the 'Panchayati Raj' and effect radical reforms in the existing system of elections. It is, surely, a matter of great concern that our elections to the Parliament and State Legislatures have been growing more and more expensive, and if certain concrete measures are not taken soon to make them cheap and inexpensive, our democracy would become the play-toy of a few wealthy families. Our Universities must consider these problems with a keen insight to be able to place before the national leaders some specific proposals. Otherwise, we shall get increasingly entangled in this dangerous net and, later, find it very difficult to get out of it.

It should also be made crystal clear that democracy in India must necessarily be based on the principles of truth and non-violence. Even during the freedom struggle, Mahatma Gandhi had underscored the crucial value of pure means for the achievement of noble ends. On one occasion, he declared in unequivocal terms: "I am prepared to sacrifice everything for India, but not truth and non-violence." The winning of Indian *'Swaraj'* without violence and bloodshed is, therefore, regarded as a unique event in world history. It was mainly due to Gandhiji's non-violent movement that Lord Mountbatten could become the first Governor-General of Free India and our country decided, of its own volition, to remain a member of the British Commonwealth. Even now, our diplomatic relations with England and other countries continue to be friendly and cordial.

No Class Conflict

Nevertheless, it is absolutely essential that the functioning of democracy within the country is based on non-violence and co-operation, and all activities involving violence and class conflict must not find support of any kind. During the last few years, an atmosphere of violence in the country has been deepening steadily, and destructive agitations pertaining to language, religion or State boundaries have been on the increase. Unfortunately, even teachers and students are gradually gravitating towards such violent activities. Presently, several Universities are closed owing to such agitations by anti-social elements and a small number of 'professional' students belonging to some political parties. In consequence, thousands and lakhs of students, who desire to prosecute their studies peacefully, are suffering beyond measure. This situation is, doubtless, unjust and reprehensible and must be rectified without further loss of time. Observes Dr. Toynbee:

> The changes that we hope for lie in restructured code of living, in a more humane attitude to life, and in a renewal of compassion and love. Perhaps if man can feel this love for all living beings, he may succeed in surviving the future. Through these advances in the concern of man for all his fellow creatures, we also hope for a return to a more thoughtful approach to man's problems and to a rejection of destructive impulses."[1]

Responsibility of Administration

Our administration too must share the responsibility of encouraging such violent activities. If any individual or group places its grievances in a disciplined and peaceful manner, the authorities often do not pay any proper attention to them. But the moment a few Post Offices and buses are set on fire and the news hits the headlines, the officers suddenly wake up to the serious situation and try to reach a compromise with expedition. This, naturally, creates a very adverse impression on the Government servants; they begin to feel that violence alone pays under the current dispensation. Those who take part in strikes and riots are let off with hardly any punishment, and this soft policy emboldens the employees to participate in such activities time and again.

In the educational institutions too, only a very small percentage of students indulges in indiscipline and violence, but the University authorities get panicky and, instead of taking strict action against the erring youngmen, hurriedly close down the Colleges or Universities. The overwhelming majority of students who desire to prosecute their studies in peace remain silent and watch the developments as helpless spectators. As a result, the whole student community suffers greatly and a good number of educational centres go to pieces. We must consider all these matters with serious earnestness so that our liberty and democracy are not torn to tatters.

Decentralization of Power

With a view to strengthening democratic socialism, it is essential that political power is decentralized in the form of well-organised Panchayats and Co-operatives so that the people have ample opportunities to plan for themselves. Gandhiji was strongly against economic and political centralisation and desired the masses to advance forward in a spirit of self-help and self-confidence. In the absence of such decentralisation, the citizens are reduced to cogs of the monolithic administrative structure and freedom vanishes into thin air. This idea has been very significantly expressed by Professor W.W. Rostow in his recent book entitled *Politics and the Stages of Growth:*

> Democracy must, finally, embrace all the people and reflect the faith that the people know best... . The modernization of a society requires a strong leadership and even a measure of planning at the centre; and it will not succeed unless it engages the energies and the commitment of the citizens themselves.

It is now agreed on all hands that Indian socialism could neither be Communism nor 'laissez faire'; it has to adopt a middle path which would ensure the harmonious development of both the individual as well as the society. Under our socialism, every person should have full scope for his economic, mental and spiritual well-being, but not the freedom to exploit others for selfish purposes. Furthermore, it will not be desirable to impose unreasonable restrictions on the liberty of citizens in the name of social justice. Such a balance is, assuredly, difficult to achieve. But in such basic matters there could be no short-cuts.

Science and Spirituality

It is also obvious that Indian socialism could not aim at mere material affluence. In the process of achieving economic growth, we cannot afford to bypass the human and moral values of life. India must utilise modern science and technology to augment her agricultural and industrial production. But science without spirituality is bound to lead us astray. Thousands of years ago our great Rishis had upheld the ideal of 'तेन त्यक्तेन भुंजीथाः'—enjoying the comforts of life with a sense of renunciation. Even the well-known materialist thinker, Kautilya, had conceded, that the roots of happiness lay in *'Dharma'*—'सुखस्य मूलं धर्मः'। Romain Rolland gave us the quintessence of his wisdom in these words: *"The more I have, the less, I am."* We shall be overlooking this eternal truth at grave peril.

Several years ago, I had the privilege of visiting the Harvard University in America and meting the eminent economist, Professor Schumpeter. We discussed various aspects of Mahatma Gandhi's thought for about an hour. As I was bidding goodbye, the Professor asked: "Will you please convey a message of mine to your countrymen?" "Surely," I replied with a feeling of surprise. Dr. Schumpeter observed: "Please request the Indian people on my behalf not to imitate us." And, after a pause, he continued: "America today is the richest country in the world; but with all its material wealth, it lacks spirituality. India alone could present to the weary world a new way of life, with a happy synthesis of the material and spiritual values. If she too begins to ape America, to whom shall we look for guidance and inspiration? The world, then, shall be faced with the darkness of utter despair."

National institutions like the Kashi Vidyapith should undertake to evolve this synthesis between science and spirituality with a sense of urgency. The motto 'सा विद्या या विमुक्तये' of the sages of India was not merely a poetic conception; it was based on centuries of profound thought and experience. Only that education is real which enables us to lead a life of freedom, self-reliance and self-respect. This would be possible only if the teachers and students engaged themselves in socially useful and productive activities; only then could the nation forge ahead with self-confidence and unflagging determination. During the last twenty-five years, we have been receiving many gifts from foreign countries. Let us now try to present to the world, in a spirit of humility, a new vision of life which had found expression in the following lines of *'Yajurveda:'*

> मित्रस्य मा चक्षुषा सर्वाणि भूतानी समीक्षन्ताम्।
> मित्रास्याहं चक्षुषा सर्वाणि भूतानि समीक्षे
> मित्रस्य चक्षुषा समीक्षा महे।
>
> Let all beings look at me with a spirit of friendship;
> Let me look at all others with the same spirit of friendship;
> Let all of us look at one another with the self-same friendly spirit."[2]

Humayun Kaber

REFERENCES

1. *Surviving the Future*, by Dr. Arnold Toynbee, (Oxford University Press, London), 1971, p. 155.
2. Convocation Address at the Kashi Vidyapith, Varanasi, on 8 February, 1973.

9

Culture and Education

The identity of an individual is nothing but an aggregate of his memories. During the course of life an individual and the society in which an individual lives have his memories and the individual also has his memories in relation to the society. The mutual memories are placed in a broad framework in which the individual and society interact with each other and are related to each other. Likewise the identity of a nation is also the aggregate of its collective memories. The cultural identity of a nation is established on its ethos, thoughts, literature, way of looking at things, general way of life, general wealth of knowledge, scriptures, traditions and the landmarks depicting the human relations which will include prominent leaders of the society whose shadow is cast beyond ages and immortal works of poets and seers which live beyond millennia. The education is an effort to discover and rediscover self which in the general framework of the nations of the world, a particular nation rediscovers its cultural identity and re-establishes itself in the society of the nations through educating itself. This process goes on world-wide and every nation in the world is itself in the process of discovering and re-discovering itself. This process in general is nothing but education. As the world moves forward, the trend and tenor of education get expanded and modified in keeping with the times. The developments in the field of science and technology inform all other related aspects of life and the knowledge in all the fields rediscovers itself to keep in tune with the language of the time. This language is not the language of words, but is a language of mind, some kind of a universal language that does not depend on the words to resonate with. But it is a kind of collection of mental vibrations adopted to the tunes of the time.

Therefore culture and education are very much inter-related issues. One helps the other and both together help maintain the national identity. It is the cultural element which gives depth and dimensions to the national identity. Geographical limits may define political identity of a country at any particular given time but the geographical limits as definitions of nations has been a dynamic concept and subject to onslaughts of the forces of the time. The forces of time have been altering the boundaries of the countries the world over and wherever the cultural identity has been rather fragile the fissiparousness of the State has been more than apparent but fair. The cultural identity and cultural roots have been deep going beyond the roots of history into the roots of mythology. The identity of the Indian nation has withstood all kinds of adverse adjective forces including enslavement by foreign powers. Even a thousand years of external rule has not been able to smother the soul of India which remained protected in its cultural heritage. The spiritual identity of the country has proved to be a very formidable force and steeped in almost immoralities that is where the nation derives its identity from. Long before the concept of nation emerged in the west, India had an identity in Bharat. As far back as seventh century, the Aadi Shankar had fixed the boundaries. He had fixed the general spiritual identity of the country and given it a firm cultural and spiritual identity which had come under shadow, during some time past. The four main "Peetham" set up at Badrinath, Puri, Rameswaram and Dwaraka cover approximately the length and breadth of the country. Apart from these four main "peeth", there is Aadi Shankar temple in Kashmir (Srinagar). Besides, there are a number of religious places where Hindus have been ferreting around traversing across the entire length and breadth of the country. The co-religionists of Hindus have also similarly religious important places scattered around where people take regular pilgrimages. Kashi, Prayag and Gaya are other religious places where Hindus from Kashmir to Kanyakumari and from the farthest north-east to the farthest west pay regular visits for performing religious rites and for doing penance as also in search of spiritual progress. Even though there have been a number of principalities, small princely States dotting the landscape of Bharat, there has always been regular movement of people all over the country without any restriction whatsoever. People have been marrying according to their traditions without any restrictions as to place and the dominion of the local ruler they were situated under. So much so there was even the concept of an all India spiritual service kind of thing. The temple of Rameswaram would always have head priest from Kashi and the temples of Kedarnath and Badrinath would always have the head priest from down south. The Rawalji, the Head Priest of the Sri Badrinath temple is always a Namboodiri who is in the direct line of Aadi Shankar. The rawal head, priest of the Kedarnath temple is also always from the south, deep south of India. Similarly there are traditions scattered all over the country where the head priests are prescribed certain basic qualifications which the individual has to fulfill before qualifying to become the head priest. But the most important of the traditions continue with the leading tradition of having priest in the important northern India temples from south and having priest in the important south Indian temples from north. There could not be a better example of national integration than this one. The level of consciousness to preserve the cultural and spiritual identity of the country can be well appreciated by this tradition which has been continuing for centuries through the law of spirituality established by Aadi Shankar and other great ancestors of the Indian people. The Indian cultural and spiritual identity is further delineated by being host of almost all the major religions. The Holy Prophet Mohammed (PBOH) had visited India. Jesus Christ lived in India and as a legend goes that after resurrection he spent his life in India and lived here for a long time. These are two great propounders of some of the world's biggest religions. Other religious leaders and propounders of faith have also been visiting India regularly. So it is not only the invaders who came to India in search of material wealth. The great people visited India in search of spiritual wealth and even ordinary people from abroad, from other countries visited India in search of this spiritual wealth. India continues to be destination for spiritual seeker even today. Our own greats travelled a large stretch of the world at least in Asia. Aadi Shanker had been to the Kailash Manasarovar situated in Tibet. As the sitar has several ragas and innumerable notes within it and still continues to be one sitar, as a garden has variety of flowers and plants, as a garland with variety of flowers, looks wonderful as it is bound by one thread, similarly the Bharat is also spiritually just one entity comprising of the true diversities. So the cultural integrity of the country is as important to preserve, to protect as it is important to protect the territorial integrity of the country. The territorial integrity always follows the concept of cultural integrity. The cultural integrity is the sense by which a nation knows itself in a manner an individual knows himself through his name, bio-data and other related memories. India could not be destroyed because of its deep cultural roots and a strong cultural identity. It withstood the devastations of time and invasions, attacks and slavery of foreigners. A true faith from its cultural essence even the freedom movement involved the working principles of truth and non-violence which are deeply embedded in India's cultural ethos and a spiritual sense. Though the foreign rule not only impoverished India as it was robbed of his riches by the foreign rulers, there was also imposition of western cultural value on the Indian masses. A lot of good things have been imbibed as well as some of the unsavoury aspect of the western culture have also crept in. Freedom is nothing but assertion of the cultural identity by India. It is the cultural and spiritual identity which is the hallmark of the Indian nation.

It is, therefore, the duty of every Indian national to preserve, protect and enforce India's cultural and spiritual identity. The Constitution of India provides for growth of every individual to his fullest potential. For the understanding and preservation of cultural and spiritual identity, education is a must. It is here that the problem begins. The bulk of the Indian masses continue to be illiterate in spite of the Directive Principle providing for compulsory primary education for all children between the age of 6 and 14 years. With the available data we can say that the State of secular education in the country is not such that we can be proud of. Apart from this there are a variety of systems of education prevailing in the country. There is no uniformity even in the system of general education. Of course the education of the religious kind will be different in case of different religious persuasions. But even in case of general and secular education, the uniformity is hardly there. In fact there seems to be existing a kind of pattern of education which is on the line of the kind of financial powers one holds. Those who are in a position to pay get a different kind of education than those who are not in a position to pay and of course those who are plagued with the problems of day to day living and have difficulty in making both ends meet for them, there is no education. They continue to be burgeoning statistics of illiteracy. There are public schools, there are convent schools, then Government schools, Zilla Parishad schools, Kendriya Vidyalayas, Navodaya Vidyalayas, Corporation schools in big towns and cities apart from Madarsas and Sanskrit Vidyalayas. All sort of systems of schooling are prevalent in the country. This is the kind of unintended diversity that we have even in our systems of education. The diversity here is needless and not borne out of any inherent factors and parameters but mostly because of economic stratification of the country as well as rural urban divide. It is by and large an inequitable system in which a person having monetary capacity is placed at an advantage as well as a person with better geographical location get better facilities. The people living in rural areas by the very nature of things have much less money with them as also the facilities in the rural areas are very poor in comparison to the urban centres where bulk of the public money is invested whether it is creating basic amenities and infrastructure or it is in creating educational institutions, health care and municipal services. We can clearly see that the State has not been in a position to provide many things particularly in the rural areas. Even if whatever provided in the urban areas is not adequate but the difference is too stark. So the question arises like everywhere else 'can there not be any scope for Private enterprise to come and help in the field of education to ameliorate the status of the common man'. It may be mentioned here that the Indian State being as secular State does not have any State religion and does not provide any kind of religious instructions in the educational institutions. So, as far as the question of providing religious and cultural instructions are concerned, it has to be entirely a private effort and the same cannot be perhaps performed by the State. However, the secular education is one of the basic responsibilities of the state and as per the Constitution it owes to the integrity of the country. Is the present input given in the Syllabi of the secular education enough to meet the requirements or something more needs to be done even in the respect of secular education? The need for expansion has also improved. Can the matters relating to the cultural and spiritual integrity of a nation be left un-guarded as it is so as to permit the ravages of time, to dilute and reduce its force coupled with the onslaught of the cultural values from elsewhere to reduce the faith of the country men in their own cultural and spiritual ethos. So the State be a silent spectator in these matters and allow what are called market forces to operate in this area like it is being sought to be done in the economic field or there is a need to be guarded about the course of things? It may be noted that even the strongest kind of cultural and spiritually rich civilisations have been lost to the ravages of time if the same have not been cared for and properly attended to. The nation owes responsibility to its ancestors to preserve and protect what has been bequeathed to them. This bequest cannot be left and should not be left unguarded and unattended. The State is doing lot of effort in the direction in its normal course of things like protection of monuments, and old manuscripts wherever they are in the Government possession but this falls much short of the required need. It is preserving the cultural and spiritual integrity in its historical sense but not in a dynamic sense in which it is required to be taken and carried forward.

There is however a saving clause as far as the cultural, educational and religious aspects of the religious and linguistic minorities are concerned. The religious and linguistic minorities have been given the fundamental right to protect their cultural, religious and linguistic identity. The religious and linguistic minorities in India can hope in their own educational and other institutions for the purpose of protecting the religious, cultural and linguistic identity of their minority groups. The members of the majority communities are however placed very differently as regards the preservation of their cultural, religious and linguistic identity. The State being a secular State is not charged with the responsibility of catering to meeting any religious cultural or linguistic requirement apart from providing the necessary protection to religious and linguistic minorities under the Constitution. It is not the duty of the State to start running institutions imparting instructions for the religious purposes and there is definitely a grey area as regards the cultural and linguistic aspects in general are concerned. In the general secular education, the state does put good amount of input to understand the Indian ethos and protect and preserve them but it can understandably cover only a very limited area and of course in much narrow sense. The legal problem arises in respect of the religious, cultural and linguistic aspects of the majority community and the problems here are rather real than fictional.

A letter to the Editor published in the *Hindu* daily Chennai dated 25 Jan. 2000 may serve as an indicator of how things stand:

"Free the Temples"

"Sir, The current revival of temples in Tamil Nadu has largely been sponsored and paid for by the participating public. But, I understand, the Hindu Religious and Charitable Endowments Board collects annual fees for auditing the activities of every temple under its control. This is surprising. The temple property generates an income, and the board should be a net revenue contributor to the temples. Instead, they end up paying for the board's bureaucracy.

The Chief Minister can set an example to the rest of India by freeing the administration of the temples from the clutches of the State and handing them back to the people of the area where they are located. Every temple has a trustee or a board of trustees elected by the local population, and it should have the power to run the temple rather than be subject to a bureaucracy which officially has scant regard for the belief system of the people.

I recently visited a temple in Chennai, which was in need of repairs to its Kalyana Mandapam, kitchen and toilets. The executive trustee single-handedly revived the temple from utter destruction and it is now throbbing with daily activity. I was willing to pay the cost of the repairs estimated at about Rs. 50,000. But it was suggested that unless I paid a bribe of Rs. 1,000 to Rs. 2,000, it might take a long while to get approval for the repairs from the HR and CE Board. I will indeed be happy to give my donation to a church or a mosque, which does not have to face these Governmental hassles specially meant for Hindu institutions. I am sure the Ministry concerned will deny the existence of any malpractice, and demand proof of improper activities.

This appeal goes beyond the rectification of a specific situation and demands explanation for the raison d'etre of the HR and CE Board when other religious institutions are not subject to Governmental supervision in secular India.

I appeal to the Chief Minister to seriously consider abolishing the board and transferring its staff to various temples so that they become productive employees responsible for specific services and answerable directly to the trusteees."

The majority community which may be said mostly comprises of Hindus may run educational institutions like any body else, but the problem here comes that the State may intervene and take over any institution run by majority community on the grounds of effecting good governance and accountability in that institution. So the fear of nationalisation causes people to think away from putting private enterprise in the field of education though fortunately in the present times of economic liberalisation, there has been liberalisation even in the field of education. Otherwise there has been an instance that a college run by Ramakrishna Mission in Calcutta was taken over by the State of West Bengal and the Ramakrishna Mission had to go to court and had even pleaded that they are a religious minority in a sense and not exactly Hindus to claim the protection given to the religious minorities in the Constitution. The Calcutta High Court had granted stay in the take over case but finally in the 1990s the Supreme Court of India decided in the favour of the State against Ramakrishna Mission holding that Ramakrishna Mission and the adherents of Rama Krishna Mission are very much Hindus and not any other religious minority other than Hindu and therefore the contention that they were a religious minority is not correct and the State was well with in its rights to intervene and take over the college. However, after the Supreme Court judgement the State Government of West Bengal did not choose to act and enforce the take over of the college immediately but the legal position was underlined that members of the majority community can run an educational institution only at their risk and there was every danger of State take over at any point of time and no legal protection stood against such action of the State. The current position is that in many of the States the members of majority community desist from opening educational institutions as they fear its take over. As a side effect of this, there has been proliferation of minority institutions particularly the institutions offering professional education and a great number of them have been the institutions being opened and run under the cover of the Buddhist minorities. A large number of such institutions which are being opened as some thing like Gautam Budha Institute or any other institution supposed to be owned and run by Buddhist minorities are in fact instituted and run by the members of the majority community. They finding the Buddhism as closest to their own religion and there is no shyness in pretending to be a Buddhist if that safeguards their investment in an educational institution. This is a kind of distortion that has crept in since the members of Hindu community do not want to incur the risk of State take over of their educational institutions. Though this fear is not now so much realistic in view of the states own stated principles for allowing free enterprise at least in economic activities but the pressure and fear continues to work on the psyche of members of the majority community.

But apart from the fear of State take over of institutions, the real question is as to where does the majority community get to learn its own cultural, religious matters. Of course the fact that the general, cultural and spiritual identity of India is so broad and vast that some smattering of it would always exist in any kind of educational syllabus that is being devised even in the foreign universities. An element of this has to figure as a result of its great potential for imparting knowledge on human life itself and the understanding of the life and spirit. But this is not sufficient for its protection and preservation. For example, even Sanskrit language is not taught in all schools and even where it is taught, it is only upto certain levels. The people in general are denied the wisdom of Geeta and Vedant and the majority community does not have the recourse to the educational institution catering to their needs of spiritual hunger. While the members of the minority community have the facility and the right to have the academic institutions to meet their requirements. The people belonging to majority community have difficulty in formulating a syllabus in an educational institution which could be a professional educational institution rooted in the great heritage of India because that institution then could be taken over by the state on the ground that it is imparting religious instruction. So either there will be vidyalaya which will teach purely Sanskrit or similar things. Then the State may have no interest in taking over those institutions. But the moment the education is made broad based an academic institution run by a member of the majority community it runs the risk of State take over on the ground that it is also imparting religious instruction. Such is the position of law that in fact State cannot avoid taking action against such an institution. So far, the secular ethos have come to be defined in a way that an educational institution would impart only secular education and it is only a minority institution that has got the right to impart instructions relating to cultural, religious and linguistic identity of the concerned minority. So this problem of giving broad-based education alongwith the cultural moorings and spiritual ethos of the majority community to the members of the majority community is found militating against the Constitutional practices as they have been perceived in the light of the secular practices that have been obtaining in the country. This problem has assumed such practical proportions that there have been controversies regarding people having the right not to sing national anthem in schools. The alternative national anthem, the national song of *Vande Mataram* has been in the centre of controversy in a number of times when people of certain religious persuasions objected to the recitation of the song. These controversies are not of very ancient origin. The national anthem and national song have deep historical significance and are a part of the freedom struggle which all communities living in India have fought together against the British but unfortunately issues have been created out of nothing. Of more recent origin was the issue of Saraswathi Vandana, the recitation of which was objected to, by even the education ministers of certain States in the meet of educational ministers in Delhi in 1998. These needless controversies have been arising as people have taken liberty to divide the cultural and spiritual ethos of this country in the name of religion. So much so even there have even been objection, of late, on breaking coconut fruit at the time of inaugurations. No one knows as to how many more non-controversial aspects of our existence are going to get added in the area of controversies.

In fact these divisions created out of certain mind sets have been casting their ugly shadow on the education policy of India. A lot which is very important and significant to the cultural and spiritual valuing of the country is denied to the children as it is feared that it would be completely sanitised kind of syllabus in which even the religious stories and stories relating to the great leaders are slowly and steadily vanishing. Taking their place are the stories of current light weights or unknown entities fictionally created and planted on the text-books, with the result the children are not able to relate to those stories as those are not the things borne out in their traditions nor do they hear those stories from their elders. The text book of English of Class I that is being taught in the Kendriya Vidyalayas has a lesson relating to one character called Kutchu. Now this is a name which is rarely heard in any of the household. The name has been brought from nowhere and a fiction has been woven around this to teach the English language to the students of Class I of Kendriya Vidyalayas. Now this story or the stories of this type will always fail to capture the imagination of the children and it is really hard on them to expect that they should be able to relate to this particular character and relating to a particular character is necessary to enjoy the lesson as well as to make it an effortless learning. The text books are replete with such senseless lessons which are quite burdensome on the very mellowable psyche of small children. Even elders will find it hard to digest the stories of the kind given in the text books and whose place these stories are taking and whose place the character like kutchu are taking in the text books. These are invariably at the cost of our great ancestors and heroes like Ishwar Chandra Vidya Sagar and similar other great people who are still embedded in the psyche of the common man. Even the story of Rana Pratap is scarcely finding a place in school text books and in many States the lesson has simply been deleted from the text books. The stories of Jeejabai, the mother of Shivaji, the story of Native ruler of Ahamed Nagar Chand Bibi and even Mahatma Gandhi and Khan Abdul Gaffar Khan may not be finding their place in the same unabridged and unadulterated form as they have been finding earlier and have been taught earlier. There is some kind of a reservation being exercised in the mind itself regarding guided kind of conclusions which should come about after reading the lessons. It is a pity that the lessons are not written with a view to make them interesting, educative and inspiring. Instead there is a kind of judgmental approach which tries to take care to fashion, the thinking of the students in a particular way and take on particular lines. However this kind of guided approach does not take care of what exists in the society itself. With the result the situation can get more confounded as the stories that the students learn from the life, learn from the experience sees it in the behaviour and conduct of others develops. His own views unfortunately are unaided by the required information as the same has been denied during the course of education. The healthiest way of teaching the children would be to expose them to inspiring array of leaders, the inspiring heritage and our cultural and spiritual traditions so that they are able to appreciate the richness imbibe it in their personality and engrain in their psyche a healthy reverence for all beings and for all traditions that obtain in our country. Much can be said on this subject as only periphery has been tested in this write up. Most of the aspects that have been touched and developed on by others have not been attempted here. Only those aspects have been taken up which have fallen by the way side, though there have been a number of education commissions and committees and they have submitted very fine reports but the system of education has only suffered from neglect and deterioration over the years. There has been a new educational policy introduced in the 1980s. However it is not very clear as to how it has achieved the intended objectives. Apart from the fact that the number of years required for completing the graduation now stands at 15 by the formula of 10+2+3 instead of earlier 10+2+2 which was one year less. So on the poor of India, there is burden of another year to fend for the children who aspired to be graduate. For persons who find it difficult to send their children to primary school which do not charge anything and are located nearer to their home. How would they sustain for one more year can be anybody's guess to see?

However the major question is that there has to be involvement of private individuals for the betterment of the field of education. In the age of globalisation, when the private individuals are opening professional institutes, the global players are investing on education and when the rich and influential people of this country are sending their wards to foreign universities, it is necessary that the field of education is thrown open for the private enterprise to operate subject to the reasonable regulation that the State may think fit in the interest of the country. The most important aspect to be studied is whether the majority community can run professional institution in which alongwith secular education, the education relating to the spiritual and cultural aspects of this country is also taught to the children and there remains no risk of State take over of such institutions on the plea that such an institution is also imparting religious instructions. There has to be a very conscious effort to define what exactly the religious instruction would mean when dealing with such cases. For example by merely teaching Geeta and Upanishads and meditation, yoga and certain aspects of philosophy and spirituality in professional institutes of academic institutions opened and run by members of majority community should not run the risk of State take over. On the other hand if any academic institution is teaching/imparting such instructions as are disruptive and may cause division in the society, there has to be a consensus on the issues dealing with such matters. These matters are very sensitive and the right of religious and linguistic minorities to run their institutions cannot be and should not be re-opened in any way. The current position on the same is very satisfactory and has been running satisfactorily except the fact that the other aspects of the education have been missing from the traditional madarsas and also Sanskrit Vidyalayas. It is necessary to enrich the content of these educational and academic institutions. This can be done by permitting opening of academic institutions by members of majority communities in which they could prescribe syllabus which would not only teach the modern science and major modern discipline but also impart instructions on our past.

India cannot shy away from its role of providing peace and solace to the world. The path for peace and solace to the world lies in its deep and vast cultural heritage which needs protection, preservation and need to be brought into the open for everybody's education. This job cannot be performed by anybody else except India. India has to shoulder this one responsibility not only for peace within its own boundaries, not only for the peace within the boundaries of the individual human minds but also for global peace. The Sanskrit language is the language for quenching the thirst for knowledge and seekers of knowledge and spirituality have been taking pains to learn this language to get access to the vast reservoir of wisdom. People from all religious beliefs, persuasions all over the world have taken access to the treasure of wisdom that is available in the Sanskrit language by learning the language. Unfortunately for over thousand years the Sanskrit language has not been receiving the importance due to it and the Indian people are denied the access to the knowledge by self denial of the knowledge of this language. This is the most scientific language of all the languages and perhaps one of the richest languages if not the richest language and the situation has become such that people even have developed a fancy to call Sanskrit language a dead language. Therein lies the fears. Tomorrow the same thing may be said about the Indian cultural and spiritual identity. Such a rich language as Sanskrit may become a dead language one day. Then Indian spirituality as it has been known for ages may also become a dead concept. Already in India the practices of Indian spiritual wisdom are confined to microscopic minority and the seekers from all over the world coming over to India are dismayed and frustrated at the State of affairs in the country of the origin of spirituality and peace. India must wake up before it is too late. It should not take poison erupting in different kinds of arguments paraded by the materialistic culture of the world who at one time have coerced and subjugated the Indian nation to accept others superiority and to denounce its own heritage. And now any number of conceptual packages are on the firmament to confuse the full issue so that the Indians are persuaded against pursuing their own cultural and spiritual identity. Bharat could not be destroyed because there was something deep within, that something emanated from its spiritual force. The spirit of Bharat is so strong that it remained hidden as a seed and gave full vent to the will of self assertion. This seed should not be destroyed in the name of market forces or globalisation or liberalisation. On the contrary if liberalisation permits all sort of materialistic concept to play with the lives of the people in India by the same token, it cannot be meant to deny self-existence and self identity. Liberalism does not mean writing oneself off and upsetting every thing else that is align. Liberalism is a concept that is accepted by the ones who exist by themselves and also accept that others also exist and relate with them in a healthy manner. It does not tantamount to denial or it does not require the kind of self-denial that we in India have become adept in practising.

It is the duty of the Indian nation to preserve and protect the cultural, educational and linguistic minorities. The rights given to religious and linguistic minorities to protect their culture, religion and language are sacrosanct and one of the fundamental rights. Due protection to the rights is necessary for the preservation of the soul of India. India lives in a world community. Therefore, Bharat as a nation cannot be treated in isolation and it cannot be said that the cultural and spiritual integrity of India can take care of itself and there is no need for any one to protect and preserve the same. Indeed the spiritual and cultural identity of India happens to be in minority in the global context. No other country is going to protect and preserve the spiritual and cultural integrity of any other country. The concerned country has to do it for itself. Therefore, we cannot afford to be callous and irresponsible in matters of our own cultural and spiritual identity and there comes a paradox. The Indian State professing secularism can do things in the cultural and spiritual field subject to the evil inhibitions that it has been exhibiting thus far to in-deference to the sensitivity of the other major players on the global platform. While Indian sensitivity to other major players in the world is understandable. The sensitivity of these major players to the Indian ethos is something that hardly ever becomes visible. The fact remains that some of the major religions of the world are minorities in India. Christianity perhaps the biggest religion having the maximum adherence in the world as a major religion of the world and so likewise Islam which again has one of the largest followings in the world. Christianity and Islam are spread over a number of countries and there is Pan Islamic dimension to the religion of Islam on the global scale as well as there is pan-Christian dimension to the Christendom in the world. As against this, there is no country in the world which may be having any close affinity with the cultural and spiritual ethos of India except Nepal and incidentally Nepal is the only Hindu State in the whole world. There is no other Hindu State on the globe. Nepal is a small northern neighbour of India and shares cultural and spiritual identities with India, in many ways. India itself has kept aloof its State apparatus from the things religious or spiritual and confined itself to mostly secular activities. So the problem arises that the Indian spiritual and cultural identity being in absolute minority on the global scale and currently facing the onslaught of aggressive western culture may really suffer damage if due care is not taken. Of course the roots of Indian spiritual identity are too deep even if they are destroyed for a moment they have an inherent force to bounce back for they are seated in the truth and truth can never be destroyed. It can perhaps go in somewhat oblivion for sometime if not taken proper care of but in the bargain though there will be a terrible cost to be paid by the entire humanity for to that extent the human civilisation will be pushed back by as many ages as these values relating to truth are cast in the oblivion. It is, therefore, the duty of the Indian State to be very conscious about the preservation and protection of its cultural and spiritual identity. Unfortunately the concept of religion which exists in the west and which is in the sense of a sect has been borrowed in its entirety on the conceptual plain of India too. The Indian term *'Dharma'* is entirely different concept altogether, which is very wide, and all encompassing. The western religious ethos are in complete variance with the Indian religious ethos in a much as the Indian ethos do not permit of any rigidity, regimentation or central authority in respect of religion. There are great people who have said great things at different point of times. There are scriptures, there are innumerable ways and there are concepts relating to truth, God, re-incarnation, birth, death, pleasure, pain, delusion etc. but the world said even by the highest considered person are not considered to be last word from the matter. As against this, the western religion and many of the other religions are mostly organised. The Christianity has a proper structure. There is a highest seat of religion and there are also pronouncements, which are to be respected by all the adherents of that religion. People can be admitted into a religion and people can also be ex-communicated. This is the system prevailing in most of the religions of the world but the Hinduism is totally different kind of thing. Here there is no proper authority. There are no structures to regiment the religion. While people are free to join the religion and also to leave but there are authorities who can expel anybody from the religion. No body can be expelled from the Hindu religion even for the worst kind of offence. Even if he denounces the entire religion and denounces every thing that it stands for still there is no authority which can expel that individual from the fold of the religion, that is the kind of liberalism and level of tolerance that is inbuilt and inherent in the Hindu religion better known as *Sanathan dharma* which gives its right connotations. It does not have any one prescribed highest book. Any one can read any book, any thoughts, which appear to them. It does believe in one God but people can pray and worship the kind of deity of their persuasion and there are any numbers of them. In fact a person can start worshipping himself and it is admitted within the fold of possibility that individual is in fact the incarnation of God and has the full potential to blossom into becoming one. So Hinduism is the religion of world peace for there is no place for violence or intolerance of any kind of words, mind and deeds in this religion. It is necessary to preserve its ethos. In fact it is by not preserving the ethos that the play of violence has helped in many ways for the true practice of this religion does not stand against any other religion, as all religious concepts are very much admissible within the Hindu kind of thought. Sri Ramakrishna Paramahamsji Maharaj has proved that

God can be reached any way by following any path. He is the only one in the recorded history of spiritual beings who has achieved Godhood through the roots of Hinduism by following the Islamic ways and also by practising Christianity. He reached Godhood by doing *tantric sadhana* and also through the path of *'Nirgun* and *Sagun'*. Having done *sadhana* through all the major ways and taking all the major paths described in the *Sanathan dharam* as also the Islam and Christianity, he has firmly established that all religions lead to the same destination. The liberal ethos and many paths in fact infinitely many paths given in the *Sanatan dharma* are there to cater to variety of needs of various kinds of people who are at different levels of development. One prescription cannot do for the entire humanity as different people have different mental inclinations and attitudes and carry a certain baggage of memories, *sanskar* with them and they have to follow different routes, different ways of neutralising these memories, these baggages and once again travel without any encumbrance in the world. Under the present circumstances the members belonging to the Hindu majority community may establish their own academic institutions which apart from imparting the modern education may also impart education in Indian cultural and spiritual ethos with a lurking fear of the State taking over such institutions as the same transgresses on the professed policy of the State that the religious instructions cannot be imported in the academic institutions in general except the ones belonging to the minority community which are protected under the Constitution. Having denied the facility to the majority community to preserve and protect their cultural and spiritual ethos the State itself also cannot and does not do the same as by its very nature of being a secular State and therefore the Indian cultural and spiritual ethos fall between the two schools finding no pattern to look after its health. The only people who fray out the cultural and spiritual prescriptions are the people at large who may from different organisations and associations and profess may kind of thoughts which may not necessarily be very healthy and on the lines of *Sanatan dharma*. They sit and complain that there are certain organisations which are preaching which they ought not to preach. Many of the actions of different individuals and organisations may actually militate against the spirit of *Sanatan dharma* and may also cause unrest, but the Indian in general are also denied the education in their cultural and spiritual ethos and in their heritage because neither the State can do anything major in this regard nor the members of the community can do it on their own by integrating the modern education with the spiritual aspects of existence because of the State policies in this respect and consequently so many distortions come into play which plague the Indian society.

The cultural and educational scene in India is quite amusing and interesting. The school education has a number of models as already been enumerated elsewhere. While this should have been uniform, the variety has been allowed to prevail and this variety unfortunately reinforces the economic stratification leading to some kind of permanent disabilities throughout the career. The students coming out from the Municipal school find it difficult to compete with the children coming out of public schools or convent schools. Since the primacy of English language has come about in the matters of public and private employment it is really hard on the children from the Zilla Parishad schools, Palika schools and Government schools to compete with the children who are put at an advantageous position by the virtue of their schooling. The cultural scene on the other hand is quite impressive. While the school education scene which should have been informed by uniform school education is given to variety of models playing the school education field, the cultural scene is witnessing some kind of a smothering uniformity. Some 2-3 decades back if one could travel across the country particularly in the rural areas, one could meet the flower of the local cultural variety in the music, folk songs, celebrations and traditions. This variety was found to be found and witnessed at almost every 30-40 miles where new dialect enriched the local cultural scence. Now if one is to travel across the country we find that it is the same music, it is the same filmy tunes that are being lent to the traditional kirtans and bhajans even in the places of worship whether we go to Kanyakumari or to Chennai or to any other place in the North or South of the country, whether in urban areas or rural areas the richeness and variety of the tunes that could be enjoyed are no longer to be witnessed. Only words are different but it is by and large the tunes of filmy songs that have taken over every where. The local music, the local tunes, the local songs, the traditional cultural variety that enriched the Indian ethos are being uniformly smothered by the filmy and western cultures. We find the same every where. All languages are now adopting the pop music and unfortunately this is coming about by suppressing the original authentic music, authentic tunes that belonged to that language, region and tradition. There is nothing wrong in new varieties being added that only enriches the cultural scene but to develop some kind of an inferiority complex regarding one's own traditions and discard them in favour of newer fashions which as experience holds out does not last very long will ultimately leave the nation clueless about its own identity and moorings. It is the question of the collective memory which the nation has about itself. The memory of Bharat cannot be found in the western music, in the pop music, in the western cultural traditions or in the western values in as much as the identity of the western nations cannot be discovered in what is oriental. The enriching from the western values should not amount to liquidation of our own values and identity. The memory of a nation is not created in one day. It is a running tradition which has been coming across the ages across the generations and withstanding the onslaughts of time. The denial of one's own ancestry can be a very costly gimmick. Memory is not a fashion, memories cannot be changed after fashions. The cosmetics should not be allowed to influence what is essentially entrenching. Let everything come and play around and last its own cycle like the waves on the ocean but the depth of the ocean itself has to remain the basic essence of what makes an ocean has to be there. We cannot suffer from self-amnesia from the though of entertaining forgetfulness about oneself, about ourselves. We may find many attractive things in other thought systems and thought systems have been influencing each other whenever civilisation have been interacting. There have been influences rubbed on each other like there are effects made on people when they meet others when they go around.

10

The Future of Education in India

The future of our education is receiving increasing attention at the hands of educational authorities, the State and the general public. A number of commissions and committees have been appointed within the last few years and their reports are now before the public.

A general dissatisfaction with the present state of affairs and a demand for change, the exact nature of which is, however, not clearly envisaged, has been voiced from many quarters. Such dissatisfaction has expressed itself sometimes in a wholesale condemnation of the education imparted in the past and of the products of such a system of education.

Little do such critics realize that, despite some defects, such education had produced great men in every walk of life, to whose initiative, intellectual and moral greatness, patriotism and love of the country we owe our present status as a free and independent nation, looking forward with hope, not unmixed with anxiety, to play our role as harbingers of peace, concord and goodwill in the international stage.

It is not sufficiently well realized that the fundamentals in regard to any type of proper education are the same in all ages, at all times, the world over. But conditions vary from time to time and it is necessary to consider to what extent and in what manner the accessory factors in an educational system should vary, so that the education imparted, while keeping in view the never changing fundamentals, may be adapted to suit the needs of the times and meet the challenge of the changing world. The stress on these accessory factors in education may vary from time to time.

During the last decades of the 19th century and in the early years of the 20th, the education that was imparted was suited to the times. Today, most people look to science and technology as the essential needs in any system of education, little realizing that they are but the varying factors which have got to be adjusted from time to time with the changes in the development of scientific activities and thought.

Techniques of study may alter and new techniques need to be learnt but the more important and deeper things do not alter. To the educated man, the pursuit of knowledge begins because of the sense of wonder; and while new inventions add to the store of our knowledge in an increasing measure, the spirit behind all education remains the same. When, therefore, people speak of modern education, they forget that modernity is a question not of date but of outlook. It is with this background that one must look at the future of education in India.

It should be the aim of all education to teach us, not merely how to use the power that knowledge may give, but how to use it well; and it should be the endeavour of all teachers to build up in every man and woman a solid core of spiritual life which will withstand the inroads of our mechanical world and the insidious assaults of superficial knowledge.

Too often the criticism is levelled that education is not purposive, does not lead the bulk of the people to gainful employment and produces more problems than it seeks to solve. If the true purpose of education were understood better and appreciated, such criticism will not be levelled so easily.

Bernard Shaw, in his own inimitable manner, has stated that everybody seems to know the x, y, z of everything, while nobody knows the a, b, c of anything. All of us, therefore, would do well to attempt to approach the great problem of the future of education in our country with a sense of becoming modesty and a desire to learn rather than to teach. It has been aptly stated that "knowledge is proud that it knows so much and wisdom is humble that it knows no more."

And now about the practical aspects of the question. Let us first of all realize that there are two essential considerations that ought to be borne in mind. If education is to give proper training to the younger generation, it must be built on sound foundations and quality should never be sacrificed for quantity.

There is a mistaken impression that the goal is literacy and that, if somehow the child could learn the three R's, it can be left safely to proceed with the further stages of education. It is in the earliest periods of juvenile life that character can be moulded, that sound impulses can be created, and that the intellect, the emotions and the spirit can be guided along right lines.

This may seem a far cry at present when education is not available to a considerable section of the people. One can well understand the pressure put on politicians and administrators and one can also realize how, unable to withstand that pressure, a type of education may be accepted as a compromise which, however, may not satisfy even the minimum requirements of a sound educational system. But it would be fatal to the whole spirit of the right type of education, if because of the need for such compromise, the basic and essential principles of sound education were to be ignored.

Even worse would it be if it were to be jettisoned as unnecessary or impractical in our anxiety and haste to give some type of education which, while it may be proved arithmetically satisfactory in quantity, will be far from satisfactory in quality.

The next stage of education, generally spoken of as secondary education, is the most important stage, for it is this stage of education which really forms the background for a democratic set-up in any country. It is here that the immature youth is gradually to be tained to value the rights of citizenship and to realize the duties and obligations thereof. The training of the future citizen to become a useful unit and to succeed to a life of gainful employment and service is the ideal that should be kept in view in the whole course of secondary education.

Under the Indian Constitution, one of the rights guaranteed is education for all up to the age of 14 and opportunities for further education for those who have the aptitude, the inclination and the determination to pursue further studies. It will be obvious that when the whole population has to go through a process of education, the type of education must vary with the aptitudes of the pupils at this age-period; hence the necessity for diversified courses of instruction, as much in the interests of the individuals concerned as in the interests of national progress and prosperity. It is here that unfortunately little or no progress has yet been made.

The impact of science on modern society has naturally led to the consideration of a large number of projects for the betterment of the condition of the masses. The Five Year Plan has envisaged many projects in several fields of activity; agricultural, industrial, economic, commercial and otherwise. We are expecting to spend some hundreds of crores of rupees on these many projects.

Yet the success of all these projects depends upon the extent to which the country is in a position to supply trained personnel of all grades in the different categories of employment for any industry, agricultural or commercial undertaking. And it is here that one has to emphasize the need for immediately creating opportunities for the youth of the country to take to such technical education as can give them a gainful employment and a purposeful life for the general improvement of the condition of the industries.

It has recently been stated by a well-known foreign technician that, owing to lack of technical skill in the South East. Asian countries in regard to the care and repair of motor vehicles, 70 per cent of the vehicles are dumped as scrap before half their period of useful existence is over. It was likewise stated that, if only in this one particular industry proper technical personnel at various level could be trained in one particular city alone, the increase in the life of the motor car would result in saving several crores of rupees. It has, therefore, been urged strongly by various Commissions that, in the secondary stage of education, the educational facilities available should be multifaceted and, at the end of that course, further opportunities should be provided for pursuing the studies further to gain the practical skills necessary for the various processes concerned in an industrial organization.

It is not infrequently stated by some who unfortunately have not a through appreciation of all aspects of education that the responsibility of the State is with reference to the Directives in the Constitution, and that, so far as higher education is concerned, it may well be left to the individuals and to the society to cater for those who have the necessary aptitudes. Nothing can be more obvious than the fact that, if education is to serve its purpose and proper education is to be imparted, not only should the foundations be well and truly laid but that an edifice should be constructed thereon. The whole purpose of the plan would be frustrated if the pyramid is not constructed up to the top.

It is hardly necessary to state that the first and most important need for all education is the supply of well qualified trained teachers with the love of the profession and a flair for teaching. No set syllabus, no detailed rules and regulations, no sort of inspection and no bureaucratic methods of extending education could possibly be of any use unless and until the most important and the vital element concerned with education, the teaching profession, is properly recruited. The teacher, therefore, should be the most important and the most respected element in society unlike what obtains in the present unfortunate state of affairs.

We often speak of ancient India in glorious terms. Those who know something of ancient India realize the great place that the teacher held not only in the minds and hearts of his pupils but in the society from which the pupils were drawn. In no other country in the world has the teacher in the past commanded the respect, the admiration and the willing obeisance of the young and the old, irrespective of his material position. It may be a far cry from those days to think of the same position being available to the teaching profession at present but one must and should emphasize the fact that the teacher is not a servant to be dictated to by bureaucratic authority but is a person whose honorable co-operation and keeness should be stimulated by right methods of approach.

There are other and more potent reasons why higher education should be as much the concern of the State as of the general public. The great discoveries of science and technology and the methods of implementing those discoveries for practical purposes imply a high degree of training and technical skill. It is not only in science and technology that higher education is needed. These are varying and variable factors. The right type of education implies that there are well educated savants in society who can interpret not merely the laws of nature but the higher laws of the universe in the right manner and with the proper methods.

It is most unfortunate that today, the study of the humanities and particularly that of the classics should be considered by a large majority of the people as not fruitful and purposive methods of education. The glamour of the so-called modern knowledge has given a set-back to these studies; and yet, if the fundamentals of education are to be properly appreciated and the part that they have to play in the upbringing of the young mind were correctly assessed, there would be less and less talk of the futility or the purposelessness of studies in the humanities and in the classics.

This brings us to the subject of university education, a subject which at present has provoked a considerable amount of criticism in this country. One of the most unfortunate trends in regard to university education is that this education has become but a mere plank, a stepping stone, to some sort of appointment in the public services. Nothing has done greater damage to the spirit of university education than the unfortunate insistence on the part of Governments and Public Service Commissions on the possession of a university degree for the smallest of appointments open in the public services of the country.

Standards of higher education have certainly been the topic of discussion in many places. It is a matter for serious consideration whether the automatic recognition of all university degrees tends to improve standards and whether the insistence upon the so-called first classes has not led to an abnormal increase in the number of such first classes in the universities. The need for a change in the outlook and the methods of recruitment for the public services is one of the immediate problems if higher education is to be freed from the tyrannical control of methods of public service recruitment.

Speaking on higher education, one cannot but refer to professional education and the future of such professional education in this country. Whether it be in regard to higher education in the humanities and the sciences or in regard to professional education, it is now well recognized the world over that there are and should be certain international standards adopted, if a reasonable amount of attainment is to be demanded or expected from the alumni of an institution.

The world has shrunk very much within the last quarter of a century; time and distance have been annihilated; the discoveries of one region become the common place of all regions within a very short time. Whether in the field of medicine or engineering or technology, whether in the field of the humanities or in applied sciences, one must confess that what one has to deal with is not the limited outlook of a particular country but the broad and widened outlook of the international sphere of intellectual attainment and activity. Looking at our standards in higher or professional education, one must confess to a feeling of grave pessimism whether, with the present methods that have been adopted, proper standards can at any time be maintained. Examinations are but poor methods of equating standards. What is far more important is to have a correct appreciation of the personnel who are responsible for teaching, the facilities that are available, the standard of entrance of the candidates themselves to the higher pursuits of knowledge, and the many other factors which can not be detailed in any specific manner but which have such a large sway over the whole field of education and the maintenance of standards.

There can be no greater damage to the progress and prosperity of the nation than a belief that at present one can dispense with those invaluable aids for the acquisition of higher knowledge and for the proper attainment of those high standards which are inevitably associated with the mastery of international literature which can only be attained through the medium of certain foreign languages. Patriotism does not demand that one should eschew what is most essential to gain knowledge and to improve in the intellectual sphere. In ages past, people crowded to various international universities and adopted the language of those universities without any hesitation, because that was the only method of acquiring sound knowledge and imbibing wisdom.

The standards of higher education are in grave peril because of certain commercialized tendencies in educational matters which have crept in. Institutions have sprung up which are subject to no control, some of them awarding diplomas and degrees of a very questionable nature. Unfortunately, some of these qualifications have been recognized by Governments, on what grounds it is difficult to surmise. It would not be uncharitable to suggest that considerations other than academic prevailed in some cases and therein lies the greatest danger for the attainment of a proper standard in regions where such standards are absolutely necessary. Unless, therefore, the future of education is safeguarded by discarding all these unfortunate elements from having a sway on education, unless such trends as are unacademic are controlled, no proper standards can be maintained, nor will there be any increase in the amount of the wealth of knowledge that will flow from such maintenance. This is one of the urgent problems of the day.

In every sphere of professional study, medicine, engineering, technology, commerce, institutions which have no right to call themselves as training institutions have sprung up in different parts of the country and, although there are laws passed against the conferring of bogus degrees and diplomas, the present trend has unfortunately not been curbed and such institutions have sprung up like hydra-headed monsters to the great peril of a sound system of education.

One of the big problems facing all countries in the world is the problem of the control of State in matters pertaining to education. The old adage that he who controls the purse must also control the activities concerned with the distribution of that purse is only partly true. The State as such cannot be indifferent to matters pertaining to education; it cannot stand by and see a wrong type of education being imparted to the youth and wrong attitudes being imbibed by them, attitudes which may be detrimental to the peace and prosperity of the nation. At the same time, as the superior authority the State must not usurp the function to decide on all details in regard to educational matters.

By a wise exercise of authority by a reasoned attitude in regard to these matters on the part of the State, by a proper recognition by the academic authorities of the part that the State has to play and a better appreciation of the responsibilities that devolve upon such authorities, there can be brought into successful working a convention that will make each part of the joint endeavour contribute its useful and natural share of responsibility and control, so that the future of education may be free from the tossing in the billows and hollows of political parties and be placed on a safe pedestal to develop on harmonious lines. It is also necessary for the State to realize that, in educational matters as in most other matters of a lasting nature, best is the cheapest, not cheapest the best.

The future of education in this country should be a matter of grave import for all concerned. Never has education had to face the challenge of the times so much as at present. Never have there been such a large number of persons who fancy that they can advise on matters concerning education, whatever their competence may be. Never has there been a graver danger than at present that a nascent democracy, ill adjusted as yet to realize the respective spheres of influence, may well, in a moment of sudden fervour, toss the frail boat of educational endeavour into the troubled seas of political warfare. It is because of these innate dangers that all those who know something of education and who are concerned with the great problems of education should make a realistic approach to these problems and offer sound advice. If such advice were accepted, India has a great future, for her children are second to none in the world in their capacity to learn and to profit. Given the right type of education and the right encouragement, they are bound to play their part worthily and well.

Dr. A.L. Mudaliar

11

Some Perspectives of Educational Planning in India

It gives me very great pleasure to inaugurate the seminar on "Educational Planning: Its Legal and Constitutional Implications in India." Problems that planners have got to face in all socio-economic fields are not capable of simple solution. They remind one of the wisdom of the old saying that truth has many facets. Ultimately truth is one but wise men describe it in different words. And so, when you deal with problems of planning—whether it is related to education or any other socio-economic problem—you feel impressed by the problem that what you regard to be the true solution may ultimately not be the whole of the true solution. This is justification for seminars of this distinguished character where participants, each one having a status of his own in the academic world, come together and bring into the common thought pool their own approaches and ideals. No prophet is required to anticipate that the consensus which will evolve at the end of these discussions will be of considerable assistance to the educational world.

The concept of democratic planning is an integrating, progressive, dynamic concept and is not based on any belief in dogmas or any absolutes. It purports to adopt a kind of pragmatic approach. It faces problems and tries to evolve solutions to those problems on a rational basis. Reason inspires all efforts of planners and all planning cheerfully submits to the test of experience. Trial and error is the watchword of planners irrespective of whether planning relates to education or any other soico-economic field. Planning in this sense is not inflexible; it is flexible. Provisional character of the conclusions is always writ large on every concenus that is evolved as a result of the discussion on planning. There is one postulate in which all planning believes and that is, that it has before its eye some kind of dedication to a goal. To be effective and purposeful planning must be goal or ideal oriented. When you think of educational planning in relation to its legal and constitutional implications this seminar will have to determine first of all the goals and ideals which education in modern India is intended to serve.

In an inquiry about the goals and ideals of education in modern India discussion about the syllabus and curriculum may be relevant but thinking has to rise beyond that level to the social purposes that they tend to subserve. Planning to be effective has no doubt to be comprehensive,. But perfect planning reduced to an ideal consensus on paper would amount to no more than an exercise in futility if the implimentation of planning is left in the hands of persons who are either indifferent to the ideals of education or worse still if they are cynical. And so planning must not only evolve its ideals and methodology imparting those ideals but should also think about how to bring into existence environments that will give educational planners the human material. No plan, however perfect, can yield any worthwhile results unless its implementation is entrusted to hands that are dedicated and to minds that have vision. And that will immediately take the planners to the problem of finding out how you can create responsiveness both in the teachers and the students. If the teachers are sullen, angry, frustrated, indifferent and the students are busy in the pursuit of affluence and are intent upon starting agitations on the most frivolous excuses even the best of plans will go awry. And so within the scope of the discussion of this seminar will fall the question of evolving the ideals and goals of educational planning, the methods and means which should be adopted to achieve those aims and ideals, and the creation of environment which will bring into existence and encourage effective teaching on the part of teachers who are dedicated to the work of education and have a wision of the purpose which education has to serve. That broadly stated would be the nature of the work that the educational planning in India has got to take into account.

When you think of educational planning, one note of caution is necessary to strike. It is customary in this country that education is regarded a problem on which every Tom, Dick and Harry is supposed to be able to express an opinion. It is forgotten that like all other special branches of knowledge education is very special subject and I would beseech that all persons interested in the future of education should refrain from entering into any controversy in the matter of education unless they have the know-how on the subject.

You will recall that since India became free it has become customary for all kinds of people—cultured, uncultured, educated, uneducated, political, non-political—to say that everything is wrong with our education. I do not subscribe to that view. I do feel that education served a very important purpose even in British days. I do not know whether those who introduced education in India in those days intended that it should serve the purpose which ultimately it in fact did serve. But nevertheless the fact remains that education that we received before our independence did serve to create in our minds a sense of unity of the country and feeling of fairplay, equity and justice.

I do not suggest that everything is well with that education. The only plea I wish to make in this context is that the problem of evolving formulate for improvement of education and devising the aims and ideals of education and prescribing the methodology in that behalf are to be left to the academic people in this country. Non-academic people should keep themselves away from this problem. It is a problem in which they have no right to express opinion. As soon as I say that, I wish to emphasize that in the context of today it is absolutely important that we should revive our ancient set of values. Today politics and political powers have assumed the utmost importance in the conscience of the public. In olden days when we had proper real Indian sense of values if any educated citizen was asked who is more important in the community's estimation whether the persons in political power of a scholar, the answer unambiguously would have been the scholar. It is time that public conscience and the press should realize the significance of scholarship and learning in the evolution of socio-economic life of this country. Martin Luther's warning that "the strength, the glory and the might of the nation depends not on its armaments, not on its political power but on the number of its enlightened cultured citizens" is worthwhile recalling. So, in this context, I would like to emphazise the fact that the world of scholarship must be given the place of precedence in the scheme of national things. The first duty of the education would be to restore scholarship and learning its place of pride in the scheme of national values.

Allied with this problem is the problem of the autonomy of academic opinion. This problem has recently became somewhat, controversial. When we speak of the autonomy of academic opinion, this autonomy has two aspects—one negative and the other positive. The negative aspect of the autonomy of academic opinion lies in the demand that academic opinion should not be allowed to suffer any interference either at the hands of the state governments or the Union Government. We know that education happens to be one of the entries in the state list and so state has competence to deal with the matters of education and the union legislature has competence to deal with matters in relation to coordination of standards of certain parts of education. But the point is not one of legislative competence or sovereignty. The point is one of the wisdom or propriety of a society's use of the legislative power. Legislatures undoubtedly are sovereign and just as they are trying to solve the socio-economic problems by adopting legislative means to meet the challenge of poverty, they are entitled to present solutions to educational problems as well. But in doing so, it would be prudent on their part if they did not think of interfering with the exercise of academic opinion in matters which are primarily educational. That is one negative aspect of the autonomy of academic opinion. When we speak of this autonomy let it be clearly understood that academic opinion does not resent interference only from the state legislatures; it equally resents interference from the union legislature as well. Whether the legislature is the union legislature or the state legislature or whether the executive is the union executive or the state executive the demand of academic opinion for independence and autonomy is aimed against both. Academic opinion merely says we are qualified, we are determined to solve our problems in the best ways we think proper; please leave us in peace to solve our problems.

The second aspect, again negative, of autonomy is that academic opinion in teaching institutions must be protected from interference from non-academic executive organs of the teaching bodies. In all universities the executive council or the syndicate, by whatever name they are called, are predominantly constituted of non-academic opinion. I would appeal to these executive, non-academic governing bodies of educational institutions to be prudent like the legislature and the executive and not to interfere with the freedom of academic opinion. When we make a claim for the autonomy of academic opinion in matters relating to education we are not asking for any privilege as such. We believe that for the proper functioning of academic bodies independence and autonomy, are conditions precedent. Unless you have given to the academic people complete autonomy and independence to experiment in the way they like in matters of education they will not be able to discharge their functions satisfactorily. I would, therefore, appeal to the academic opinion in this country first to demand autonomy, then to deserve autonomy and lastly to exercise their autonomy in the interest of the progress of education. Let it not be forgotten that autonomy in the academic opinion is not a fight for a political right as such; it is a fight for liberty to serve the cause of education. And it is only if teachers are dedicated to the cause of education and have a vision of the ideals which education has to serve that the claim for autonomy would be justified. That is why negative and positive aspects of the autonomy show that the demand for autonomy has to be conceded in the interest of education itself.

Once we agree that the academic opinion alone should be allowed to discuss these problems, we come face to face with the problems of educational planning. It seems to me that what happens in the next five years is going to decide the future of democracy in this country. Let us remember well that the future of democracy in India is tied with the fate of education. Education and educational planning are in a sense at crossroads at this hour of India's destiny. Unless policy-makers in the field of education are able to evolve an inspiring ideal which education is intended to serve, all planning will be futile. Planning does not require regimentation but does involve some regulation. It does not involve uniformity but requires some kind of unity. The unity which planning requires is based on two considerations. The unity which planning in educational matters wants to establish derives its inspiration from the unity of the cultural and national inheritance which we have evolved, which history has developed, and a unity of purpose which inspires us all in pursuing the commonly accepted national goals. It is this two-fold unity which must be the basis of all educational planning. The three words democracy, secularism and socialism would sum up the accepted goals and ideals of Indian democracy.

Now people of my generation and even people of a younger generation who were young enough when India became free are virtually drawing their lives to the end. Some may be in the afternoons of their lives and others may be in the evenings of their lives. There are problems which have eluded the people of my generation and in this sense my generation has failed. Now this challenge has to pass on to younger generation. And it is here that education has to play a very important role. If education is able to impart to the young students studying in the universities of India today, that enthusiasm, that sense of dedication and purpose, that pursuit of the ideals of India, then alone education will serve its purpose. Democracy does not thrive merely because significant provisions are made in the Constitution of India. Democracy will not thrive merely because the Supreme Court and the High Courts, from time to time, pronounce heart-warming judgments in favour of fundamental rights. Democracy can thrive only if every individual citizen deems it his duty to assert his fundamental rights and, what is more important, what is more often forgotten, to submit to the fundamental obligations of Indian citizenship. Harmonious synthesis between the fundamental rights which the citizens are bound to claim and the fundamental obligations the discharge of which alone will lead to progress in this country is the main objective of education in India.

If I were asked as to which was the single concept which would play decisive role in the history of India, I would unhesitatingly say it was secularism. It is on secularism that the future of this multilingual country depends. Now, unless education is able to convey not only to the people who come to universities for education but to the masses at large, the real, comprehensive, creative, positive character of the concept of secularism, all our talk about democratic process, all our talk about welfare ideals, will be futile. Now secularism is a matter not to be talked about on platforms. It is a matter which you and I should begin to preach in our lives.

And the third ideal, of course, is socialism which involves bringing about an equalitarian society according to the democratic way and is sometimes called the ideal of a welfare state. Basing ourselves on the fact that democracy, secularism and socialism are the universally accepted ideals of this Indian democracy, it is not difficult to realize that education will play a decisive role in the achievements of these ideals. That decides the problem of the ideals and goals to which education in India must in the context of today be irrevocably and irretrievably committed.

As soon as educational planners will think of defining the methodology to achieve these ideals, law will inevitably step in. Legal and constitutional implications of educational planning, therefore, will raise their heads. In that context, may I in a very humble way but very earnestly appeal to the judges, lawyers and jurists to consider this problem not as a matter of legal formality, not as a matter of legalistic quibbling, but as a matter of a creative, constructive legal philosophy. If, when educational planners and planners in all socio-economic fields attempt to regulate education, attempt to evolve some methodology to achieve the objects and aims which the education places before itself, any challenge is made to the constitutionality of the measure, the courts will be reluctant to uphold the constitutionality if fundamental rights are violated. But in dealing with the question of the violation of fundamental rights the approach should not be traditional, conservative, legalistic. It should be the approach of those who share the philosophy of the ideals which the country has placed before itself. Naturally, as in matters of law so in matters of education, you will have to face the conflicts between two rival claims. And, as I am never tired of saying, a judge alone realises how difficult, how delicate, sometimes how agonizing it is to prefer one to the other.

Let me illustrate this point by taking some conflicting situations which educational planners will have to face. First problem is of expansion of education versus quality. I have often heard it said by educationists who know more than I do that in order that the quality of higher university education should not be spoiled we must introduce some selective tests for admitting boys and girls to colleges. As mere academic proposition there can be no objection to it. I realize that the level of higher education by its very definition must be higher and must serve certain purposes so that if you water it down and make it less effective, less good, the interest of the country will suffer. Sometimes, I wonder that unless you provide for the young boys and girls struggling to get admission into higher university centres some alternatives, would it be right to stop entries of these boys and girls into colleges on the ground that they do not satisfy the selection tests? I would, therefore, ask this distinguished gathering to consider whether they will not think it right to suggest that while applying selective tests for admission and thereby improving the quality of higher university education demand must be made for the institution of diversified courses and for the starting of vocational centres. You and I who are better placed in life will not be justified in the name of democracy to stop young boys and girls coming from humble families from seeking admission just because as a result partly of their environments, as a result partly of depressed circumstances from which they suffer, they are not able to satisfy the selective tests we impose on them. Give them some alternative source of educating themselves. Give them some alternative source of finding vocation, alternative employment if necessary. Diversify education, start more vocational centres and vocational branches and then you would be justified in insisting upon the selective test. The demand of these young boys and girls who want to learn cannot be totally ignored because it will create an amount of discontent in the economically and socially weaker sections of the community. And discontent in the minds of boys and girls is a source of danger to democracy. That illustrates how when you are face to face with a problem you are in a dilemma and have to find a harmonious solution to it.

Take the other part, equality before the law and protective discrimination. That is the problem the courts, legislatures and executive have been dealing with. Undoubtedly, it must be conceded that in the structure of the Indian community there are a very large number of educationally and socially backward people. And there can be no doubt that unless you give them some special protection and discriminate protectively in their favour so as to give them a chance to come to par with the rest of the community they have no future in this country. Whether you determine the social and educational backwardness of persons by reference to their castes or by other tests is a matter of great significance. Moreover, the problem which sometimes troubles me in this connection is that when you go on giving special protection to the socially and educationally backward communities, unwittingly, unknowingly, unintentionally you create in the minds of these a desire to continue to be educationally and socially backward. I do not blame anyone at all. It is a subtle psychological process so that when we think of evolving some measures of a protectively discriminatory character in order to atone for our sins, we have got to find out the degree to which this protective discrimination could be allowed to create further insoluble problems for our democracy. The sooner the socially and educationally backward communities are able to find themselves able to compete with the rest of the community the better. How does one evolve a formula in order that the socially and educationally backward communities should not perpetually continue to be socially and educationally backward? In trying to be impatient about putting an end to the provisional steps, we may do harm. Here again, you are faced with a problem which is not capable of an easy solution. You cannot apply a formula. No formula can do the trick of solving this complex socio-economic problem at one push. Educational planners have got to think about it again and again because at the root it is an educational and cultural problem.

Let me take yet another instance. What part should education play in the moral improvement of the race? While this generally relates to the field of religion and rests upon religious freedom, educators on the other hand feel that unless you inculcate in the minds of the young students a sense of ethics, the lack of discipline that you see all round will not disappear. Both views are possible, reasonably possible. How do you solve the problem? Would it be open to you in a class of ethics to tell the boys and girls that considered socially from the modern point of view, monogamy is absolutely essential? Would it be hurting the Muslim feelings because the Muslim law allows polygamy? Would it be open for another teacher of a class of ethics to tell the boys and girls that belief in caste is most immoral, most unethical, most uncivilized? Would it trespass on the traditional conservative Hindu notion that caste is a part of his religion? Where will you stop? Where will you draw the line? You have to be brave and courageous in dealing with these situations because after all the traditional sense of values has got to be regulated and, if need be, revolutionized. While trying to change the traditional sense of values, how will you either by legislative or executive means evolve a formula which will obey the legal, constitutional injunctions and yet persist in achieving its object of creating in the minds of young boys and girls of this country a sense of ethos, a sense of civic responsibility for the betterment of the country as a whole? How does religious freedom work in relation to attempts made by education to improve the ethical outlook, the spiritual ideology of the students?

Take yet another problem. What about the Union Government and the State governments? How do they act and react on each other? There has been some controversy. The Union Government desires that education should be made a Concurrent List items whereas the states reject such a claim. So far as I can think of this problem the one solution appears to me would be the same solution which I have respectfully suggested to the lawyers and judges—the solution of not being legalistic or dogmatic about it. It is not a matter of putting one item on list I, list II or list III; it is a matter of evolving some healthy and rational conventions which will guide the destinies of legislative matters in this country. After all education does not want interference either from the state legislatures or the union legislature and so it does not matter really where education is listed. And, in a country like India, which is a federal country, I think, states would naturally resist parting with their powers to deal with education in their own respective fields. Uniformity of education is unreal, and if I may say so, undesirable. Concentrating ourselves on the basic unity of the national and cultural inheritance, and the basic unity involved in the pursuit of commonly accepted ideals, we must allow an amount of diversity, an amount of experimentation. Rigidity which always involves uniformity is completely foreign to the concept of educational planning. These are some of the problems which this distinguished seminar may have to consider. And since the seminar will be primarily concerned with correlating educational reform, educational planning within the four corners of legal and constitutional limitations we come back to where I began. The need of the hour for the judges, lawyers and jurists is to evolve a constructive, progressive, forward-looking philosophy of constitutional law. Constitutional law is a dynamic branch of law. It is not static. It should not be imprisoned within the four corners of a traditional conservative concept. It must be allowed full scope and full liberty to function as a creative force in this country. And so, I personally feel, the justists of today and for the jurists I look for among teachers of law, must in a dedicated manner, consistently evolve a doctrine of constitutional law which can be properly regarded as a progressive constitutional philosophy. Constitutional law is going to play an important role not only in regard to educational planning but in regard to planning in all sectors of socio-economic activities of today. I often like to describe law as a mighty weapon. Law and education both are going to turn out to the flexible instruments of socio-economic change. Law must realize its mighty destiny, its glorious destiny, the part that it has to play in assisting education to find its way to the attainment of the ideals to which I refer. Like education and law the rest of the socio-economic life in this country is on the march and the next five years are going to decide whether this march will bring democracy to fruition or not. Let us not be complacent. Let us realize that we are facing great difficulty in the pursuit of democratic ideals. The problem is urgent and brooks no delay. And if the solution of the problem is unnecessarily delayed, impatience will overtake us. And impatience always makes man angry and anger makes a man blind. Before the blind fury of angry men overtakes the democratic way of life of this country let us plan education well enough so that it does not transgress the constitutional limitations but while doing so the great and avowed ideals of a socialistic pattern of society must not be lost sight of.

P.B. Gajendragadkar